D1374503

THE GREAT DOCK STRIKE 1889

Edited by

TERRY McCARTHY

in association with the Transport and General Workers' Union

Acknowledgements

Thanks to my publishers, David Roberts and Martin Corteel, for their help. Thanks to historians Bill Fishman, Victor Tredwell and Henry Fry. Thanks for the support from Derek Clarke, Betty Fry, John Lloyd, Michael Foot, Gwyneth Dunwoody, Albert Jacobs and from Eleanor and Sarah McCarthy. And especial thanks to Bronwyn Williams and above all Ciara McNulty for her patience.

Picture Credits

The illustrations in this book come from the archives of the National Museum of Labour History with the following exceptions: BBC Hulton Picture Library 69, 71, 171 (below), 185; The Mansell Collection 171 (top), 178; Mary Evans Picture Library 38, 131, 135, 139; Weidenfeld Archive 11, 15, 33, 88, 157.

Published in Great Britain by
George Weidenfeld & Nicolson Limited
91 Clapham High Street
London SW4 7TA

Designed by Gaye Allen

Printed and bound in Great Britain by
Butler & Tanner Ltd, Frome and London

Contents

PART FOUR: THE SETTLEMENT

PART FIVE: THE AFTERMATH

Introduction by Ron Todd

Too few people in the labour movement, let alone the public at large, understand how important the 1889 Dock Strike is to history, or indeed, to society today. So, one simple aim of this collection of contemporary reports is to help put the record straight.

But it goes much wider than that. Rightly we are proud of Tolpuddle's martyrs, of the Chartists, of the years of struggle in the new century that led to the formation of the Labour Party, of the General Strike and the first real Labour Government in 1945. We may have heard a bit about the dockers in 1889, and the match-girls and the gas workers, but the big simple truth of 1889 still has to be brought home.

It was that the unskilled, the poorest, the underdogs, many of them the desperate immigrants to the East End of London from Irish famine, suddenly, one summer, seemed to seize history and get themselves organised. Often the dock strike of 1889 is known as the Dockers' Tanner Strike. Somehow this name both captures the truth – it was around some simple demands that the strike took place. But it also disguises the vital fact that by winning this massive, unexpected and surprising strike a lot more than a tanner was won.

Take the consequences for modern politics. Within five years, union leaders and socialist politicians, who had felt on the margins of mainstream politics, were able to re-group, get themselves together and create the Independent Labour Party, which later led to the formation of today's Labour Party.

Take the impact of trade-unionism. Until 1889, it had largely been based on skilled and socially respectable groups of workers. Despite all sorts of attempts, few people of goodwill thought that the lowest class of workers, the unskilled and casual workers, could really be organised by their own efforts. Trade union and party politics were therefore centred in trying to get the Liberal Party to show humanity and social concern by passing progressive legislation from on high for the betterment of the unfortunate lower working classes.

It occurred in the age of the great social enquiries into poverty, most notably by Charles Booth, whose survey started in 1886, amidst widespread public concern – and perhaps horror – at the condition of the underclass of casual labourers.

We should also recall that memories must have been fresh of the great demonstration against unemployment, known as Bloody Sunday, which saw 100,000 people marching to Trafalgar Square – in the posh West End – on 9 November 1887.

For our own union, the Transport and General Workers' Union, it is beyond question that if it came into being in 1922, its real seeds were sown in 1889. The 'New Unionism' which was brought on to the historical stage in 1889 transformed the shape of subsequent trade union history. It established the idea of general workers' unions, whose fundamental impulse is to look outwards to organising all classes of workers and to representing their broader social and political aims as well.

Specifically, it saw the creation of the Dock, Wharf and Riverside Labourers' Union out of Ben Tillett's Tea Operatives' Union – and in Liverpool, the start of Sexton's National Union of Dock Labourers. These unions and others formed in the aftermath and in sectors previously regarded as unorganisable, went right through to the start of the new century – despite employers' counterattacks and many, many problems, to see the formation of the Transport Workers' Federation in 1910 as the precursor to the TGWU.

It is a lineage, a heritage, an historic opportunity taken and worked through, not in textbooks and paper plans, but through hard organisation and conviction and trust.

It's not even so very distant for some people. I can recall being shown Ben Tillett's sea chest, which he took on his world tours, when his grandson retired from employment with our union when I was the Regional Secretary of the London and South Eastern Region, some years ago.

I would also add that in a period of great strain for our trade union movement in Britain, we should recall that the fundamentally united and outward looking, indeed independent spirit and structure of the British trade union movement was forged in the period after the 1889 strike. Other countries still envy our unity and our breadth. It is arguable that if the 1889 dock strike had failed, our movement today would be a pale shadow of its reality.

Abroad too, 1889 was both a child of other great events and a spur. We remember May Day because of the Haymarket demonstration in Chicago in 1888, with its call for an eight-hour day. Given that money raised in Australia rescued the dock strike, it was only right and proper that the new, popular and independent socialist spirit unleashed by the strike should find its way back to Australia and New Zealand, with visits from British socialists in the following years. And we should recall that the Red Flag – our battle song for socialism – was written at the end of 1889 by James Connell.

At home, the impact was massive. At the simplest possible level, it brought another 200,000 unskilled workers into trade union organisation within a year or so, according to Tom Mann. Given that the TUC's membership before the strike was 568,000, and that when it started in 1868 there were about 100,000 members, it is clear that things could not be the same again.

The intervention and help of Cardinal Manning, the prominent Catholic leader, led to Pope Leo XIII's declaration in 1891 that trade-unionism was a civilised and acceptable part of the new world, and who should be a member of the Royal Commission on Labour appointed in 1891, but Tom Mann, who was a signatory of the Minority Report, objecting to the idea of legal incorporation of trade unions.

Of the events and the characters involved, it seems to me that they defy neat analysis and were truly often larger than life.

Tillett, Mann and Burns, Champion and Thorne, shared the toughness, awkwardness and conviction required to set about organising and trying to win the strike. It is no surprise that they were jostled about by events in turn. On the sidelines, amongst other socialists, was Karl Marx's daughter, Eleanor, who, I believe, was sent by Engels to warn against extending the strike into a general strike. What an amazing fact of history then was the arrival of the solidarity money from Australia, just at that very difficult moment. What a miracle that a strike that was won as much by mass picketing, with trains of scab labour sent back from the mainline stations, saw no overt violence to damage the obvious public sympathy. How different from today, with the *Pall Mall Gazette* arguing the case for the dockworkers with solidly respectable indignation.

However important the leaders and the worthy and the eminent people involved may have been, there was one clear message, or rather it might be better to call it a deep belief, which energised the strike and altered history afterwards. It was that to make any social progress, any political progress, you first of all had to *organise*.

But the story will tell itself. And when we celebrate the centenary of 1889, let us use it to revitalise our movement and its basic message of mass organisation. Let us also continue to delve into our history, and bring its messages alive for current and future generations.

Ron Todd

General Secretary of the Transport and General Workers' Union

1 THE BACKGROUND

Social Conditions

The Sunday orators at Dod Street, Limehouse, addressing unskilled casual labourers – many of them worked in the docks – concerning the misery and poverty of London's East End, would often point to the young people in the crowd as examples. Many of these unfortunates might be scraping a bare living as mud-larks, as described in Mayhew's great survey.

Henry Mayhew, *London Labour and the London Poor* (1851), II, 155

These poor creatures are certainly about the most deplorable in their appearance as any I have met with in the course of my inquiries. They may be seen of all ages from mere childhood to positive decrepitude crawling among the barges at the various wharfs along the river; it cannot be said that they are clad in rags, for they are scarcely half covered by the tattered indescribable things that serve them for clothing; their bodies are grimed with the foul soil of the river and their torn garments stiffened up like boards with dirt of every possible description ...

The mud-larks generally live in some court or alley in the neighbourhood of the river and, as the tide recedes, crowds of boys and little girls, some old men and many old women, may be observed loitering among the various stairs, watching eagerly for the opportunity to commence their labours. When the tide is sufficiently low they scatter themselves along the shore, separating from each other, and soon disappear among the crafts lying about in every direction.

Questioning one, Mayhew found that a nine-year-old who had been fatherless for eight years 'remembered once to have had a pair of shoes but it was a long time since. "It is very cold in winter," he said, "to stand in the mud without shoes," but he did not mind it in summer. He had been three years mud-larking and supposed he should remain a mud-lark for all of his life. What else would he be?' (II, 156)

The sprawling development of London's East End was allowed to occur without any concern at all for its populace. These poor young creatures were an embarrassment to the Victorians who often described such waifs as street arabs, giving a rather romantic air to a problem more conveniently ignored.

Come what may, the kids came first.

Such was the poverty within the inner cities that people would do any possible task to earn or to eke out a living. What poverty there must have been, for any human being to enter the world of the sewer-hunter. Mayhew describes this dangerous trade:

The persons who are in the habit of searching the sewers, call themselves 'shore-men' or 'shore-workers'. They belong in a certain degree to the same class as the 'mud-larks', that is to say, they travel through the mud along the shore in the neighbourhood of ship-building and ship-breaking yards, for the purpose of picking up copper nails, bolts, iron, and old rope. The shoremen, however, do not collect the lumps of coal or wood they meet on their way, but leave them as the proper perquisites of the mud-larks. The sewer-hunters were formerly, and indeed are still, called by the name of 'Toshers', the articles which they pick up in the course of their wanderings along shore being known amongst themselves by the general term 'tosh', a term more particularly applied by them to anything made of copper ... (II. 150).

To enter the sewers and explore them to any considerable distance is considered, even by those acquainted with what is termed 'working the shores', an adventure of no small risk. There are a variety of perils to be encountered in such places. The brick-work in many parts – especially in the old sewers – has become rotten through the continual action of the putrefying matter and moisture and parts have fallen down and choked up the passage with heaps of rubbish; over these obstructions, nevertheless, the sewer-hunters have to scramble 'in the best way they can'. In such parts they are careful not to touch the brick-work overhead for the slightest tap might bring down an avalanche of old bricks and earth, and severely injure them, if not bury them in the rubbish ...

Moreover, far from there being any romance in the tales told of the rats, these vermin are really numerous and formidable in the sewers, and have been known, I am assured, to attack men when alone, and even sometimes when accompanied by others, with such fury that the people have escaped from them with difficulty. They are particularly ferocious and dangerous, if they be driven into some corner whence they cannot escape, when they will immediately fly at anyone that opposes their progress. (II. 151)

And even after the publication of Mayhew's writings in the 1850s to 1870s, nothing was done, though various government reports on poverty had also made those in authority aware of the great distress among the inner-city working class, especially among the young.

The Children's Employment Commission of 1863 highlighted some of the intolerable conditions endured by child labour in its report (41).

William Needham, age 8
Has been here three or four months ... takes half an hour to do one item,

gets a farthing for it, comes in at 7.00 in the morning, stays until 8.00 in the evening. Has breakfast at 8.00, dinner at 1.00 and tea at 5.00. Has an hour for dinner and half an hour for each of the two other meals. Goes home for them just round the corner ... Used to learn to read and write. Cannot write his own name, only short words like ran etc. Never did any sums. 'I know the figures but I cannot reckon them up.' Goes to school on Sundays sometimes. They teach him to read, doesn't know what the book is, it's a little one.

Edward Brown, age 11

Has been here two years. Comes in the morning at 7 or 8.00, goes in the evening at 7.00. Works for his cousin. Never been to school in his life, cannot read, doesn't know who the Queen is, never heard of her. 'Christ was our Saviour, wasn't he? Sea is water, I don't know where it is.'

Charles Booth's social surveys of poverty and work in London caused a storm in liberal circles in late Victorian England. His scientific if somewhat cold approach left the public in no doubt of the true nature of social degradation and near starvation that existed in the East End and other urban areas. His issuing of social survey maps was also important in

A proud urchin displays his boots.

exposing the fact that poverty was not hidden and indeed quite comfortably off people lived in the docklands area, and were obviously aware on a day-to-day basis of the extent of the poverty suffered by their neighbours.

The dock labourers were categorised in Booth's eight-class system as Class C, numbering about 75,000, 8 per cent of the East End population, although the class below this, Class B, was 11.2 per cent of the whole population. Class B he considers to be casual earners, very poor, or semi-criminals. Classes A, B, C, and D added up to a total of 314,000, or 35 per cent of the population.

Charles Booth, *Life and Labour of the People in London,* [1889–1903] First Series: *Poverty* (1889) I. 33

The 8 classes into which I have divided these people are:
A. The lowest class of occasional labourers, loafers, and semi-criminals.
B. Casual earnings – 'very poor.'
C. Intermittent earnings }
D. Small regular earnings } together the 'poor.'
E. Regular standard earnings – above the line of poverty.
F. Higher class labour.
G. Lower middle class.
H. Upper middle class.

Class C **– Intermittent earnings – numbering nearly 75,000, or about 8 per cent. of the population, are more than any others the victims of competition, and on them falls with particular severity the weight of recurrent depressions of trade. In this class are counted most of the labourers in Section 3, together with a large contingent from the poorer artisans, street sellers, and the smaller shops ...**

Section 3 of Labour, which contributes so largely to Class C, consists of men who usually work by the job, or who are in or out of work according to the season or the nature of their employment.(I. 43–44)

Grouping the classes together, A, B, C, and D are the classes in poverty, or even in want, and add up to 314,000, or 35 per cent. of the population; while E, F, G, and H are the classes in comfort, or even in affluence, and add up to 577,000, or 65 per cent. of the population.

Separating East London from Hackney, the same system of grouping gives us for East London 270,000, or 38 per cent. in poverty, against 440,000 or 62 per cent., in comfort; and for Hackney by itself 43,000, or 24 per cent., in poverty, against 140,000, or 76 per cent., in comfort. (I. 62)

Booth went on to describe about thirty families who had kept detailed accounts over a period of five weeks for his survey team.

No. 1. – This is the poorest case on my list, but is typical of a great many others. The man, Michael H——, is a casual dock-labourer aged 38, in poor health, fresh from the infirmary. His wife of 43 is consumptive. A

A street scene in Docklands – a world apart.

son of 18, who earns 8*s* regular wages as carman's boy, and two girls of 8 and 6, complete the family. Their house has four rooms but they let two. Father and son dine from home; the son takes 2*d* a day for this. The neighbouring clergy send soup 2 or 3 times a week, and practically no meat is bought. It figures the first Sunday only: '3 lbs. of meat at 4*d*.' Beyond the dinners out, and the soup at home, the food consists principally of bread, margarine, tea and sugar. Of these the quantities are pretty large. No rice is used nor any oatmeal; there is no sign of any but the most primitive cookery, but there is every sign of unshrinking economy; there are no superfluities, and the prices are the lowest possible – 3½*d* per quartern for bread, 6*d* per lb. for so-called butter, 1*s* 4*d* for tea, and 1*d* for sugar. I suppose the two rooms in which the family live will be those on the ground floor – bedroom (used sometimes as parlour) to the front, kitchen, where they eat and sit, to the back. In the kitchen the son will sleep, his parents and sisters occupying the front room. Neither of these rooms will exceed 10 ft. square; both, I am told (for I have not seen them), are patterns of tidiness and cleanness, which with Class B is

A ragged school, where many dockers were 'educated'.

Food riots common during the Napoleonic Wars haunted the memory of poor families.

not very common. This accommodation costs about 17*s* a month. On firing, &c., the H——s spent 10*s* 4*d* in the 5 weeks – as much as, and more than, many with double the means; but warmth may make up for lack of food, and invalids depend on it for their lives. Allowing as well as I can for the meals out, and the charitable soup, I make the meals provided by Mrs. H——for her family to cost 1*d* per meal per person (counting the two little girls as one person). A penny a meal is very little, but expended chiefly in cheap bread, cheap butter, cheap tea, and cheap sugar, it is perhaps as much as would be taken, providing rather more than $\frac{1}{2}$ lb. of bread, and $\frac{1}{2}$ oz. of butter, besides tea, milk, and sugar. This diet (which, if strictly adhered to, would be unendurable) is somewhat varied, so as to bring in some fish, a little bacon, and a few eggs, besides the charitable soup.

These people are, undoubtedly, 'very poor,' an example of great poverty as it appears when accompanied by respectability and sobriety, and protected from distress by charitable assistance. Imagine the man a drunkard, or the woman a slattern, or take away the boy who earns half the income and put in his place a child of 10 or 12, who earns nothing and must be fed, and it is easy to realize that extremer form of want when distress is felt, or complete pauperism supervenes. From the poor living of the family there is no room to subtract anything; but Class B, none the less, contains numbers who are worse off than this family. (I. 140–141)

The Victorians romantically called these children 'street arabs'. Britain at this time was the richest nation on earth.

As wretched as the employment in the docks were the living and social conditions that prevailed in London's docklands:

John Henry Mackay, *The Anarchists* (1891), 152. Quoted in William J. Fishman, *Streets of East London* (1979)

The East End of London is the hell of poverty. Like an enormous, black, motionless, giant kraken, the poverty of London lies there in lurking silence and encircles with its mighty tentacles the life and wealth of the City and of the West End ...

Even a decade after the strike the American socialist novelist Jack London could write: 'The worst casualties were the children, after they survived their first handicap – being born ... In the West End 18 per cent of children die before five years of age; in the East End 55 per cent of the children die before five years of age ... Slaughter! Herod did not do quite so badly.'

Baby-selling was rife, a casual exchange used as a last resort by a starving mother or to satisfy the immediate needs of a habitual drunkard. Cruelty and insensitivity infected the young. Mackay was shocked by a group of children amusing themselves by the sight of the dying fits of a cat whose eyes they had gouged out, and whom they had hanged by the tail: 'When the bleeding, tortured animal jerked with its feet to get away, they struck at it with the cruel awful pleasure children take in visible pain.' Begging and thieving in some parishes were, not surprisingly, the norm. Jack London posed the dilemma in the case of a young delinquent tried for stealing:

Jack London, *The People of the Abyss* (1903)

Fresh in my mind is the picture of a boy in the dock of an East End police court. His head was barely visible above the railing. He was being proved guilty of stealing two shillings from a woman, which he had spent, not for candy and cakes and a good time, but for food.

'Why didn't you ask the woman for food?' the magistrate demanded, in a hurt sort of tone. 'She would surely have given you something to eat.'

'If I'ad arsked 'er, I'd got locked up for begging' was the boy's reply.

Parliamentary representation as we know it was denied to the dock labourers and their wives. Property qualification still deprived them of the franchise as the following figures show:

Political World Year Book (1889)

- **The constituency of Whitechapel with a population of 71,314 had an electorate of 6,110.**
- **Stepney, population 58,122, electorate 6,925.**
- **Poplar population 74,104, electorate 9,340.**
- **Saint George's in the East, population 49,382, electorate 4,317.**
- **Rotherhithe, population 69,489, electorate 8,455.**
- **Mile-end, population 47,491, electorate 5,804.**
- **Limehouse, population 56,318, electorate 5,954.**

The History of the Docks

Chris Ellmers
The Coming of London's Docks

The history of the docks of London forms a striking illustration of the growth of British trade and commerce. Merchandise was kept afloat in barges, from want of room to discharge it at the legal quays and the plunder was frightful, lightermen, watermen, labourers, ships crews, mates officers and even revenue officers combining in a system of pillage which neither the police nor the terrors of Execution Dock could repress. It is supposed that the earliest of London's docks was made in the time of Charles II, at Rotherhithe. Originally this was a dry dock at Rotherhithe but in 1696 an act was passed making it a wet dock. In 1809 it was opened as the Commercial Docks. It was not, however, until the nineteenth century that the present magnificent series of docks came to be built. The East India Docks were originally constructed for the East India Company and were completed in 1808, the water area being about thirty acres. The enormous West India Docks were commenced in the first year of the century. The warehouses will contain 180,000 tons of merchandise and that there have been at one time on the quays and in the vaults and warehouses colonial produce worth £20,000,000 sterling, comprising 148,363 casks of sugar, 70,875 barrels and 438,648 bags of coffee, 35,158 pipes of rum and Madeira, 14,000 logs of mahogany and 21,000 tons of logwood etc... Another great dock known as the London Docks was commenced in 1802, being capable of receiving '220 mile of square-rigged vessels.' This dock cost something like three million pounds of money. For St Katharine's Docks the fine old church and other remains of the Hospital of St Katharine, with 1,250 houses and tenements inhabited by 11,300 persons had to be pulled down. The docks which comprise 23 acres, 11 being water, cost £1,700,000. About ten years before the construction of these splendid public docks was commenced, Mr John Perry a shipbuilder made the Brunswick Dock at Blackwall for 23 East Indiamen and 50 or 60 smaller ships. On one of the quays he constructed his famous machine for masting and dismasting ships. No fewer than 79,000 sea going vessels of all kinds entered and cleared from the Port of London in 1888 being 216 for every day in the year, including Sundays – These 79,000 vessels had a tonnage of 20,600,000 tons and carried goods of the value of not less than £220 millions sterling.

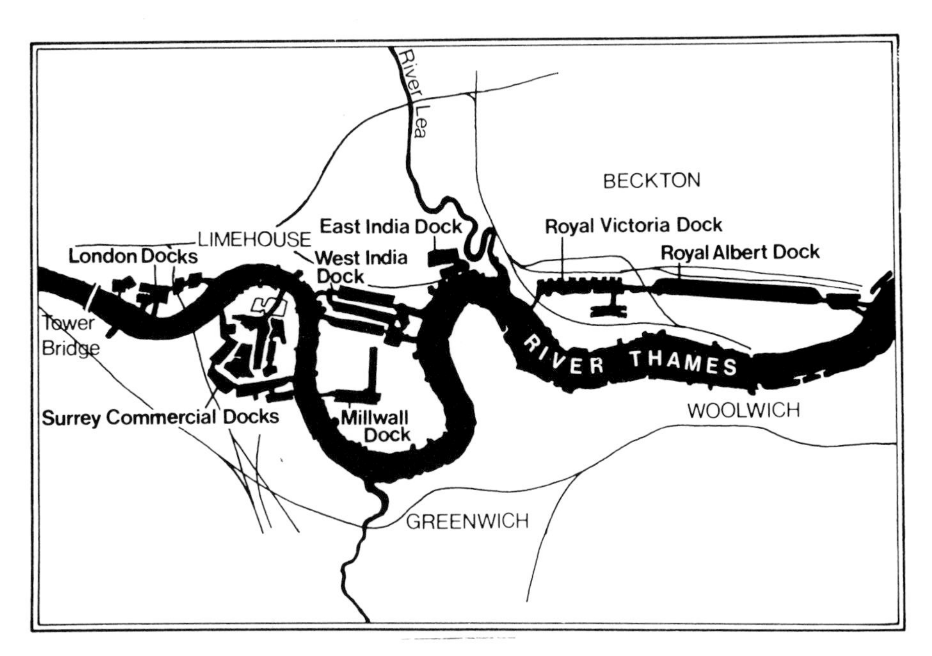

London's Dockland at the time of the Strike.

During the early decades of the nineteenth century the Port of London – and indeed the face of London – was changed dramatically by the construction of a vast series of enclosed wet docks. Starting with the opening of the *West India Docks* (1802), the *London Docks* (1805), the *East India Docks* (1806), the *Commercial Docks* (1807), the first phase of London's dock building activities came to an end with the opening of *St Katharine's Docks* in 1828. By that time, London had been transformed from a river-based port to one with the largest dock system in the world. Of crucial importance was the increase in the trade of the port, which had tripled in value in the course of the eighteenth century, whilst the number of ships more than doubled.

Despite this great increase in trade, however, there had been little improvement in the facilities of the port since Elizabethan times. London was then still a river port dominated by the *Legal Quays*, lying between London Bridge and the Tower, where all goods paying customs duties had to be landed. In addition to the Legal Quays there were *Sufferance Wharves* (established from 1663 under 'sufferance' of the owners of the Legal Quays), on the south bank and in Wapping, where non-dutiable goods, mainly from the coastal trades, could be unloaded.

In 1795 London had only 1,419 feet of quayspace at the Legal Quays and 3,700 feet at the Sufferance Wharves. In this respect London was far behind other English ports in the facilities offered. As London's trade expanded, however, so did the congestion on the river with ships sometimes tied up five and six abreast in the channel. The mooring chains from Deptford to London Bridge were reckoned to take 613 ships, but the number of vessels there was often 900 and sometimes as many as 1,400. These figures excluded the large East Indiamen which off-loaded their cargoes downstream at Blackwall into some of the 3,400 lighters and smaller craft that moved goods around the port. Added to all of these were the large fleets of collier ships and timber ships that served the ever-growing London market.

Amidst the congestion and confusion on London's river, however, there were two large wet docks – the *Howland, or Greenland Dock* at Rotherhithe and the *Brunswick Dock* at Blackwall. Due to the powerful monopoly of the Legal Quays and the vested interests of the City Corporation, neither of these two docks were allowed to act as trading docks (the whaling trade apart, and everyone wanted that kept a respectable distance from London!). As the problems of cargo handling on the riverside quays grew, merchants and traders came increasingly together to act as pressure groups intent on building new trading docks.

The most active group of traders pressing for reforms were the West India Merchants – a group whose activities accounted for some 23 per cent of London's imports by value and who suffered the greatest loss through pilferage and theft. They found an active champion in William Vaughan, a London merchant who recommended that the solution to London's problems lay in the cutting of docks at St Katharine's, Wapping, the Isle of Dogs, and extensions at the Greenland and Brunswick Docks. Within thirty-five years, docks had been established at all of these sites.

This agitation resulted in the setting up of a *House of Commons Committee*, in 1796, 'to inquire into the best mode of providing accommodation for the increased trade and shipping of the port of London'.

Almost immediately the vested interests of the river port – the owners of the Legal Quays and Sufferance Wharves, the City Corporation, lightermen, and the Fellowship Porters (quayside labourers with a monopoly of work at the Legal Quays) – campaigned against all proposals. Two specific dock projects, however, did emerge and were embodied in the *West India Dock Act* (1799) and the *London Dock Act* (1800).

THE WEST INDIA DOCKS

The Act of 1799 allowed for the construction of two dock basins across the northern part of the Isle of Dogs, together with a ship canal to their south to enable craft coming up to the Pool to avoid going around the Isle. To gain the support of the City, the Corporation were to be responsible for building and running the *City Canal* and for the piecing together of the whole dock site. The economic viability of the docks was underwritten by the grant of a 21-year monopoly on all of the West Indian trade, except tobacco. In this respect the Act set a pattern for some other dock schemes, as did its 'free water clause' which was to apply to all subsequent developments. This clause placated another powerful monopoly by allowing lighters free access to the docks for the purpose of taking delivery from, or delivering to, ships directly.

Excavation and building work on the site began early in 1800 and the docks opened for trade in August 1802.

There were two large docks (the northern one for imports and the southern one for exports), a large entrance basin for ships at the Blackwall end, and a smaller basin for lighters at the Limehouse end. When the dock opened there were three large five-storey warehouses on the north quay of the Import Dock and others were built soon afterwards to form a range of warehouses nearly three-quarters of a mile long.

Security measures taken at the docks were remarkable: high walls and a water-filled moat surrounded the docks; a large and well-armed body of militia protected the ships and warehouses from being looted; all ships' crews, except one officer, had to disembark and leave the docks; only the Company's own employees were allowed to work in the docks. The Fellowship Porters were deliberately kept out of the new dock – and all of the later ones. The docks proved to be very successful – ships were discharged in three to four days rather than one month and losses, due to theft, on each hogshead of sugar were reduced from 71 pounds (lbs) to 8.75 pounds (lbs). In 1803, 374 ships were discharged, increasing to a peak of 641 in 1810 and averaging around 500 a year in 1810–20.

Shortly after the docks were opened they gained an immense boost from the *Warehousing Act* of 1803 which established bonded warehouses where imported commodities could be stored free of duties until they were withdrawn for home consumption. Under the Act, goods for re-export were thus exempt of duties and London started developing as an entrepot port on a far larger scale than ever before.

Limehouse Dock boasted its mechanised efficiency.

THE LONDON DOCKS

The second new dock was built at Wapping and christened The London Docks to emphasise its proximity to City trading centres. Once again, the future of the dock was to be secured by a 21-year monopoly, this time on all vessels coming to London laden with tobacco, rice, wine and brandy, except those from the East and West Indies.

Construction work occupied the years 1801 to 1805 and was made difficult by the fact that a large part of the site was built over with houses and workshops and that the war with France was causing inflation. The dock opened in January 1805, but the large range of warehouses on the north quay were not quite finished. These buildings were the best in London, incorporating a sophisticated system of air ducts for ventilating the vaults where wines and spirits were stored.

THE EAST INDIA DOCKS

Although the prestigious East India Company occupied a large number of City warehouses and had strict regulations for unloading their East Indiamen at Blackwall, there were still serious losses of cargoes through thefts. In 1803 they decided to promote the building of docks at Blackwall, three miles from their town warehouses and close to major ship

East India Docks, the hub of the tea trade.

The bustling warehouses where Tillett worked.

repair yards. Once again they were granted a 21-year monopoly – on handling all of the trade with India. China and the East Indies.

The Company purchased the Brunswick Dock at Blackwall from Wells, the ship-builders, as an export dock and cut their import dock in the fields to the north. The dock opened for trade in August 1806. Goods were not stored in warehouses at the docks, but taken to the East India Company's great warehouse at Cutler Street in the City, along the newly built East India Dock Road and Commercial Road (the latter constructed specially to link the West India Docks to the City).

THE SURREY DOCKS SYSTEM

The only docks south of the river had a complex history. In 1801 the *Grand Surrey Canal Company* was formed with the purpose of building a ship canal to Epsom and thence, hopefully, to Portsmouth. Work began in 1803 and finished in 1810 at Peckham! In 1807 the *Commercial Dock Company* was formed and took over the old Greenland Dock with an eye to obtaining a monopoly of the timber trade. The company was disappointed as to obtaining a monopoly and in 1810 it absorbed the *Baltic Dock Company*. This Company had been formed in 1809 and owned extensive timber-floating ponds and yards north of the Commercial Dock. The final element to emerge in the Surrey Docks system was the *East Country Dock Company* which opened a dock, for the Baltic trade, just to the south of the Greenland or Commercial Dock, in 1811.

ST KATHARINE DOCK

When the monopoly of the West India Dock Company came to an end in 1823 there was tremendous opposition from London merchants against a renewal of such privileges for the various dock companies. There was also agitation against the high charges levied at the London Docks, the nearest to the wholesale rackets of the City. In 1824 the *St Katharine Dock Company* was established with the purpose of establishing a dock complex on a compact site between the Tower of London and the London Docks. It was one of the developers' main aims that they would capture a large amount of dock traffic from their proximity to the City.

Thomas Telford was appointed Engineer to the Company and designed a very original dock that made the best possible use of a very cramped site. Between 1826 and 28 some 1,250 houses, 11,300 people, and the monastic foundation of St Katharine were removed from the site, the dock basins cut and vast ranges of warehouses constructed. Due to high cost of the land and the cramped site, the architect, Philip Hardwick, designed warehouses of seven storeys, with vaults, which rose on iron columns sheer from the dockside.

Despite its architectural grandness, St Katharine Dock suffered several drawbacks. The major one was that it took no account of the increasing size of ships, or the likelihood that steamships would be of great importance one day. Secondly, ships unloaded directly onto the quay under the warehouses – there were no transit sheds – which meant that mixed cargoes had to be removed by hand truck, through warehouse to warehouse around the dock.

POSTSCRIPT

By the time that St Katharine's opened, the enclosed docks were only receiving a little more than a quarter of all the trade of the Port of London – they had failed to clear the river of shipping. The docks still received almost the whole of the overseas trade, but the riverside warehouses received the whole of the coastal trades. Furthermore, riverside warehouses were increasingly siphoning off business from the docks by discharging ships overside into lighters, which could come and

Timber ships line up at the Millwall Dock.

go free of charge under the 'free water' clauses. By the early 1850s the docks were in a weak position as against the more centrally located river wharves. The *Customs Consolidation Act* of 1853 hastened this development still further by sanctioning the building of legal quays and bonded warehouses outside of the docks. In addition, Britain's policy of free trade drastically reduced the number of goods needing customs clearance from 1052 in the 1840s to 48 in the 1860s. With their future already jeopardised by the river wharves, and weakened by the coming of the steamships and telegraph, dock companies began to amalgamate and turned their main focus of attention away from the docks mentioned here to larger and more spacious docks for steamships, built further east and served by railways and hydraulic machinery.

The principal docks opened in the Victorian period were: the Royal Victoria (1855), the adjacent Royal Albert (1880), both downstream of the older docks, north of Woolwich Reach; and the Millwall (1868) on the Isle of Dogs, south of the West India and devoted mainly to importing cheap wheat from North America. The other main development, opened in 1886, was over twenty miles downriver, at Tilbury, which since the 1960s has largely superseded the old port of London.

Trade Practices at the Docks

Just at the crucial turning point of the 1889 strike, *The Times* gave a detailed summary of dockers' pay and conditions, taking large sections of the data from Booth's *Life and Labour*. Information like this did much to win over sections of the middle class to the justice of the labourers' struggle. The correspondent also wrote in sympathetic terms of the conditions that the strikers lived under and commented quite favourably on the leaders of the men.

The Times, Thursday, 29 August 1889, 8

Sixteen or 20 years ago dock labouring was a regular trade, in which labourers were bred up from father to son. Although the wages were no higher then than now, a man could be sure of fairly regular employment, say 10 months out of 12, at the rate of nine and 10 hours a day; and he was accustomed to earn on an average 20s to 25s. a week. In the old days of sailing ships there were fewer fluctuations in the numbers of labourers employed. The vessels came in and were not in a hurry to be discharged. Whereas 18 years ago a West India-man of 300 or 400 tons was discharged in a week, and that was thought very good work, steamers now come in with 1,500 tons of sugar, and this cargo has to be discharged in seven hours, to insure which the hands are kept working all night.

Nevertheless, for certain kinds of work, as in the carrying of grain and wood, physical strength still retains its value, and each dock company gives permanent employment all the year round, at from 20s. to 30s. a week, to a number of stalwart men, who are called preference men, or often, in the language of the inferior grades, 'Royals'. At some docks – the Millwall, for instance – these men constitute a large proportion of the labourers, at others they are only a sprinkling, and are employed at the same work with the casual labourers, but in the capacity of gangers or foremen. Still, the introduction of machinery, together with the immense increase in the number of applicants, has, generally speaking, made dock labour a casual employment, only fit for the failures of society, or men whom a revolution in their own trade has forced into taking any pre-

Lucky casuals get a day's work, loading a cargo of tea.

carious work they can find. These are men who lay themselves out for it. But there are others who swell the crowd at particular times of the year. With the summer depart from the dock gates the painter, the harvester, and the agricultural labourer. The tailor and the coster are visitors in bad times; and each skilled trade contributes its quota of men temporarily unemployed. And still the number goes on increasing. Mr. [Ben] Tillett estimates the average number of labourers engaged or seeking employment at the docks and wharves at 100,000. Others regard this figure as excessive, and put it down at from 50,000 to 75,000. The President of the Local Government Board has given 55 per cent. as the average number of those who are unemployed. How extraordinary are the fluctuations in the number of men employed is shown by the statement of Colonel Du Plat Taylor that 'it may be some days 3,000, the next day 200; these are extreme cases.' Asked whether the work could not be carried on by permanently employing a larger regular number of hands, Colonel Du Plat Taylor admits that this would be possible. It is this utter uncertainty of employment which renders the casual dock labourer's earnings so scanty; for the rate per hour by which he is paid is not excessively low. He is paid uniformly at the rate of 5d. an hour, with, in some cases, an extra penny an hour for overtime – i.e., work done between 6 p.m. and 6 a.m. At the Tilbury Docks, however, where country rates of pay and the proximity of the lowly-paid but constantly employed cement labourers exert an influence, the rate is only 4d. The average pay earned per week is put down variously at 3s. and 7s. Striking averages is of course difficult where employment is chiefly a matter of luck. Fifty per cent. of the dock labourers – including, perhaps, the permanent men – are agricultural labourers in point of origin. Although the pressure of the foreigner is one of the chief causes of the influx from other trades, there are few foreigners among them, and only about 2 per cent are Jews.

The news that ships are due in any particular dock soon spreads, and the gates of that dock are besieged in the morning. The struggle varies in intensity according to the system pursued in engaging the men. It seems to be worst where the tin ticket system prevails – i.e., the system by which the foreman distributes to each favoured applicant a tin ticket as his title to admission; and here the London and the St. Katharine Docks seem to carry off the palm. 'The first thing,' says a witness just fresh from the struggle, 'is this, that there is a chain put up right across the entrance to the dock, and the contractors are on one side of the chain and the men the other. You can imagine for a moment from 1,500 to 2,000 men crowded together, the front men forced up against the chain: the back men are climbing over the heads of those in front, and the contractor behind the chain is picking out the men, generally his own favourites or somebody recommended by his own favourites. I myself have had eight or ten men upon my shoulders and my head, and I have been hurt several times in a struggle for employment like that.' 'Unless a man is very strong,' says another witness, 'there is a great possibility of his clothes being torn off his back.' Strength is the great qualification of a dock labourer; but in strength he rarely excels. 'A casual labourer,' says Colonel Birt, 'if he has strength and is steady, soon picks up more or less skill as a casual, and he will by degrees work into the higher class. But it is these poor unfortunate fellows, most of whom are without physical strength – the very costume in which they present themselves prevents them doing any work. They are miserably clad, in a most miserable state, and they cannot run; their boots would not permit them. There are men who are reduced to the direst poverty, men with every disposition to work well, but without the strength to do it. There are men who come on to work without having a bit of food in their stomachs, perhaps, since the previous day. They have worked for an hour and have earned 5d.; their hunger will not allow them to continue; they take the 5d. in order that they may get food – perhaps the first food they have had for 24 hours.' The great bulk of these poor labourers will not work after 4 o'clock, and many people complain of them for it; but the real reason of their knocking off is that they have nothing in their stomachs to support their strength. According to Mr. Tillett, whose figures, however, are disputed, the majority of the labourers, 70 per cent. maybe, are married men, and live in one or two rooms – the 'royals', the aristocracy of dockers, occupying, perhaps, two or three. To the casual dock labourer marriage is a means of support rather than a drag. His wife and children are able to contribute to the expenses. The rest of the labourers are frequently to be found in 'doss-houses,' where they pay for a bed at the rate of 2d. a night. 'The reason of these being able to live at all is that there is some kind of communism among them; for they help each other. It is the practice among them to pay for each other's beds, or "dosses", when the man has not had a turn of work.' The docker's means of subsistence, however, are eked out by multitudinous schemes of charity and various other sources impossible to define.

Many of the casuals at the docks enjoyed the hospitality of the common lodging house.

The Contract System. – Although the Millwall Dock is not a typical dock, inasmuch as a large proportion of the hands employed are on the permanent staff, the contract system as applied there is fully described, and it may be taken to be the same as that which prevails elsewhere. There are attached to the dock about 30 official contractors. These are

exclusively men who have been foremen in the service of the dock for many years. The docks are divided into sections, each section having two or more contractors, working in partnership, attached to it. Each section is called by the names of the particular contractors who work it. When a vessel comes in, she is placed alongside one of these sections, and the contractors belonging to it proceed to provide for the discharge and warehousing of her cargo. This operation the contractor is under a standing contract in writing with the company to perform at a fixed rate of 10½d. per ton for unloading and as much again for loading, i.e., re-delivering to rail, van, or lighter. Unloading consists of two operations – (1) work in the ship's hold, and (2) the manipulation of the goods after they are out of the ship – i.e., warehousing, sampling, weighing, marking, making merchantable, and examining for marks contrary to the Merchandise Marks Act. At Millwall the practice is rather exceptional, inasmuch as the company generally allow the work of unloading the ship pure and simple to be done by the shipowners, who for the most part avail themselves of the privilege. But let us suppose that we are not at Millwall, but at another dock. The contractors, when about to unload, proceed to find two gangs of men, one for work in the ship's hold, another for work on the quay. For this purpose the contractor goes to a sub-contractor or ganger, who engages them and also arranges to do the work both in the ship and on the quay at a rate per ton of goods considerably smaller than the rate which is received by the contractor

Hard, dirty work, but it was regular.

for the same work. A witness who had been employed at the Millwall Docks as ganger stated that the average price per ton which he received from the contractor was from 4d. to 5d., which left the contractor a margin of 5½d. or 6½d. per ton, out of which he has to find a clerk and weigher. The contractor is also supposed to walk about and supervise.

Now for the effect of the system upon the dock labourer. The complaint of the men is, first, that they are compelled to bribe, treat, or fawn upon the sub-contractors who have the selection of the workers. Secondly, and this is the gist of the case against the contract system, that an excessive amount of work is got out of them in return for a disproportionately low scale of pay. It is true that the hourly wage paid by the gangers is no lower than formerly. But for this wage the men complain that they are over-driven. It is the ganger's interest to employ as few hands as possible for a given piece of work, and yet to get the work done as quickly as if it were adequately manned. There is more truth in the complaint where the ganger engages his men by time-work than there is where he engages them under the *plus* system – i.e., a *minimum* wage with a bonus if the work is done quickly. But even in the latter case, the custom of excluding the casual labourer from any participation in the bonus, supplies the same temptation to the ganger to 'sweat' the men – he himself having been already subjected to this process by the official contractor.

British Labour Statistics, Department of Employment.

Wages of trades in and around 1889.
Fitters and turners: 38s., 54 hour week.
Bricklayers: 9d. an hour, average week 52½ hours.
Building labourers: 6d. an hour, average week 52½ hours.
Compositors: 36s. for a 54 hour week.
Skilled furniture workers: 9d. an hour, 52 hour week.
Agricultural labourers: 13s. 4d. a week, hours, master's discretion.

The London docks had emerged and grown with Empire. Trade increased and so did the workforce that was driven to the docks through privation. The employers welcomed the arrival of hundreds of men seeking a day's pay, and used this surplus pool of labour to exploit and cheat and impose appalling work practices and conditions. The plight of the men was of no concern to the employers, who scarcely saw them as being human.

Walter Thornbury, *Old and New London* (1873–78), Vol. 2, 119–121 (summarising Mayhew)

[*Mayhew observed three types of dock labourer, the first being those who did the wheel-work.*]
The wheel-work is performed somewhat on the principle of the treadwheel, with the exception that the force is applied inside, instead of outside, the wheel ... From six to eight men enter a wooden cylinder or drum, upon which are nailed battens; and the men, laying hold of ropes, commence treading the wheel round, occasionally singing the while, and

'Lumpers' discharging a timber ship.

Coal 'whippers' at work.

Thames Lightermen.

Pleased to get the work, coal-porters humped 200 lb sacks as long as the load lasted.

stamping time in a manner that is pleasant from its novelty. The wheel is generally about sixteen feet in diameter, and eight to nine feet broad; and the six or eight men treading within it will lift from sixteen to eighteen hundredweight, and often a ton, forty times an hour, an average of twenty-seven feet high. Other men will get out a cargo of 800 to 900 casks of wine, each cask averaging about five hundredweight, and being lifted about eighteen feet, in a day and a half. At trucking, each men is said to go on an average thirty miles a day, and two-thirds of that time he is moving one and a-half hundredweight, at six miles and a-half per hour. ...

... 3,000 men could be found every day in London desperate enough to fight and battle for the privilege of getting two-and-sixpence by it; and even if they fail in 'getting taken on' at the commencement of the day ... they ... then retire to the appointed yard, there to remain hour after hour in the hope that the wind might blow them some stray ship, so that other gangs might be wanted, and the calling foreman seek them there. It is a curious sight to see the men waiting in these yards to be hired at fourpence an hour, for such as the terms given in the after part of the day. ... Rain or sunshine there can always be found plenty to catch the stray shilling or eightpence. ... Some loiter on the bridges close by, and presently, as their practised eye or ear tells them that the calling foreman is in want of another gang, they rush forward in a stream towards the

The 'gangers' engage labour.

gate, though only six or eight at most can be hired out of the hundred or more that are waiting there. Again the same mad fight takes place as in the morning.

Ralph Stern, *Dock Strike 1889*, 23 (quoting Ben Tillett)

In those days the docker worked an average of five to six months in a year. The 'call-on', bad as it is today, is nothing so terrible as it was in 1889. The men were herded together like cattle in a shed, iron-barred from end to end, outside of which a foreman walked up and down like a dealer in a cattle market.
Ben Tillett wrote:—

'The last remnants of strength [were] exerted in an effort to get work for an hour, a half hour, for a few pence. Such strugglings shoutings, cursings, with a grinning brute selecting the chosen of the poor wretches.

'At the "cage", so termed because of the stout iron bars made to protect the "caller-on", men ravening for food fought like madmen for the ticket, a veritable talisman of life. As a brute would throw scraps to hungry wolves to delight in the exhibition of the savage struggle for existence, with beasts tearing each other to pieces, so these creatures would delight in the spectacle, which, while it imbruted the victims of such a tragedy, impeached and cursed society.

'Coats, flesh and even ears, were torn off, men were crushed to death in the struggle, helpless if fallen. The strong literally threw themselves over the heads of their fellows and battled with kick and curse, through the kicking, punching, cursing crowd to the rails of the cage, which held them like rats – mad, human rats – who saw food in the ticket.

'Calls at any period of the day or night kept men for a week at a time of hungry and expectant for the food and the work which never came.

'Night and day watches, the scraping of refuse heaps, the furtive, miserly storing of refuse rice the coolies had thrown away, to keep body and soul together.'

Millicent Rose, *The East End of London* (1951), 52, 53

[Before 1800] The East End's part in all this activity was to provide the lumpers, or stevedores, who carried the cargoes from hold to lighter, and the watermen who worked with the lighters and other small craft; to provision the vessels as they rode at anchor, and to supply them with ropes and other tackle. Ship's bakers, marine store dealers, instrument makers and boatbuilders lived and worked in the streets by the river. Laundresses of Wapping and Shadwell lived by taking in the sailors' washing; there were professional rat-catchers who visited the ships to rid them of vermin. Carpenters and smiths were numerous along the waterfront and their services were often needed, for in the congested river collisions and other accidents happened very frequently, while the vessels which had been forced to berth a little too close inshore were apt to hole themselves at ebb tide by sitting on their anchors.

Along with the many reputable riverside occupations, and often combined with them, were others: lodging-houses that were also brothels,

dolly-shops (unlicensed pawnshops). The riverside abounded with public houses, whose landladies were, as a class, notoriously grasping and dishonest – though there were many honourable exceptions. . . .

The rich vessels moored all along the river provided an incessant temptation to the people of Wapping and Shadwell, and organized pilfering and smuggling were practised upon a gigantic scale. . . .

Booth's description of dock labour was possibly the best that there has ever been, as a social study. It was not simply a description of the wretched jobs that they did, but a social insight into the class division that existed within the trades and even among the dock labourers themselves. The differences between the casual and preferred men were as great as those between the stevedores and the foremen. Booth also notes the differences in the type of workers employed in the docks and their social origins, especially those on the Isle of Dogs and the south side, perhaps explaining the differences that will appear. An interesting insight into the ingrained racism which was so prevalent in Victorian England even amongst Liberals such as Booth was the statement that 'at least the docks are free from . . . foreigners. The foreign element conspicuous by its absence – unless we are to persuade ourselves that the Irish are foreigners. For Paddy enjoys more than his proportional share of dock work.' The survey goes on, 'The cockney-born Irishman . . . is not favourably looked on by the majority of employers.' Booth estimates there were 10,000 casual labourers, exclusive of waterside labourers, as opposed to the 3,000 regular hands employed by the dock company. The evidence put forward by Booth was to be used by *The Times* and other newspapers and journals to expose the exploitation of dock labourers.

He first explains that the stevedores, who load the ships, form a separate elite, already unionised – though the union had actually split into two, the ironically named United and Amalgamated Societies. An even higher elite, not mentioned by him, were the Thames watermen and lightermen, 'who load and navigate the lighters or heavy barges, by the end of which vessels discharge and load their cargoes overside. The lightermen and watermen form a close corporation nearly two centuries old.' (**Smith and Nash, 1889, 23**). The support of both these groups, who did not themselves suffer anything like the miserable and uncertain conditions of the unskilled workers was to be crucial to the outcome of the strike.

Charles Booth, *Life and Labour of the People in London* (1889–1903), 3rd Ed. 1902–3 First Series: Poverty. Vol IV, 16–17

Dock labour in London is, properly speaking, the employment offered by the import trade. In the export trade the shipowners contract directly with a body of skilled men called stevedores, for whose work the dock company are in no way responsible. These men act under master stevedores, and are the only section of dock or waterside workmen who have formed themselves into a trades union.

The import work of the docks consists of five operations. In the first instance the sailing vessel or steamer enters the dock waters in charge

A good day – the ganger calls men for a days labour. The men were called out of the 'pens' with constables standing by.

A bad day – casuals auction themselves for the rough dock trade at low pay.

of the transport gang, and is placed in the proper berth for discharging. In old days there she would have waited until it suited the dock company to pay her some attention. Now, at whatever time of day, and, in the case of steamers, at whatever time of night, the vessel settles into her berth, the ship-gangers with their men swarm on to her deck and into her hold. Then begins the typical dock labour – work that any mortal possessed of will and sinew can undertake. The men run up and down like the inhabitants of an ant-hill burdened with their cocoons, lifting, carrying, balancing on the back, and throwing the goods on the quay. It is true that in the discharging of grain and timber special strength or skill is required. With timber a growth on the back of the neck called a 'hummie,' the result of long friction, is needful to enable a man to balance a plank with any degree of comfort. But timber and grain are in East London practically confined to the Millwall Docks, and it will be seen that more difficulty in the work means a higher class of men, and in the case of timber porters of a body of men who stand outside the competition of low-class labour. Now, leaving the dock quay, we watch the warehousing gang. Here, again, it is heavy, unskilled work. To tip a cask, sack, or bale on to a truck, and run it into a warehouse or down into a vault, or on to the platform of a crane, to be lifted by hydraulic power into an upper chamber, is the rough and ready work of the warehousing gang.

Three East London docks, classed according to regularity or irregularity of employment.

West and East India Docks

Outdoor staff:		
Foremen, &c.	457	
Police	114	Total . 818 regularly employed
Permanent labourers	247	
Irregularly employed:		
Maximum	2355	Average 1311 irregularly employed
Minimum	600	
Preferred for employment or 'Royals'	700	2129

London and St. Katharine Docks

Outdoor staff:		
Foreman, &c.	400	
Police	100	Total 1070 regularly employed
Artisans	150	
Permanent labourers	420	
Irregularly employed:		
Maximum	3700	Average 2200 irregularly employed
Minimum	1100	
Preferred for employment or 'Ticket men'	450	3270

MILLWALL DOCKS

Outdoor staff:		
Contractors' permanent staff of labour . . .	300	
Irregularly employed (gaining livelihood here) .	500	
	800	(18–19)

The methods of employing the lowest class of labour differ in the West and East India and in the London and St. Katharine Docks, though the work undertaken by these companies is practically the same. The West and East India Company have resisted the pressure in favour of piecework and the contract system; and have shown a laudable desire, from the working-man's point of view, to retain a large permanent staff. On the other hand there is no recognized class of 'preference' labourers, but the foreman of each department has on his books a certain number of men called 'Royals,' who are actually preferred for employment on account of superior power, long service, or more regular application for work. These men and others are taken on each morning according to the needs of the day. They are chosen by the company's foreman and are paid 5*d* an hour. As an encouragement to good work, and supposing the task has been accomplished at a certain rate of profit to the company, a 'plus' is divided in definite proportions among the different members of the gang. This 'plus' averages a halfpenny an hour to the ordinary worker. The daily earnings of the irregular hands at the West India Dock varied last year from 2*s* 9*d* to 4*s* 3¼*d*, and averaged about 3*s* 6*d* without 'plus.'

The London and St. Katharine's Company have a smaller permanent staff in proportion to the work done, and depend more on casual labour. A considerable number of men, possessing a preferred right to employment, act as an intermediate class between the permanent staff and the 'casualty' men. This company has also introduced a mixed system of employing their casualty men. The casuals who work directly for the company are paid 5*d* an hour; but half the work of these docks is let out to small contractors, generally their own permanent or preference labourers. (20–21)

At least the docks are free from the reproach of other London industries; they are not overrun with foreigners. The foreign element is conspicuous by its absence – unless we are to persuade ourselves that the Irish are foreigners. For Paddy enjoys more than his proportional share of dock work with its privileges and its miseries. He is to be found especially among the irregular hands, disliking as a rule the 'six to six business' for six days of the week. The cockney-born Irishman, as distinguished from the immigrant, is not favourably looked upon by the majority of employers. (22)

But the universal dislocation of the social life of East London manifests itself in the docks, not only by the absence of all ties between employer, foremen, and men, but in the complete severance of the different grades of labour, and, among the more respectable of the working class, in the isolation of the individual family. The 'permanent' man of the docks ranks in the social scale below the skilled mechanic or artisan. With a wage usually from twenty to twenty-five shillings a week and an average family, he exists above the line of poverty, though in times of domestic trouble he frequently sinks below it. He is perforce respectable, and his life must needs be monotonous. His work requires little skill or intelligence – the one absolute condition is regular and constant attendance all the year through. He has even a vested interest in regularity – the dock company acting as a benefit society in sickness and death – an interest which he forfeits if he is discharged for neglect of work. By the irregular hands the permanent man is looked upon as an inferior foreman and disliked as such, or despised as a drudge. He, in his turn, resents the popular characterization of dock labourers as the 'scum of the earth.'

As a rule the permanent men do not live in the immediate neighbourhood of the docks. They are scattered far and wide, in Forest Gate, Hackney, Upton, and other outlying districts; the regularity of their wage enabling them to live in a small house rented at the same figure as one room in Central London. And if the temptation of cheap food, and employment for the wife and children, induces a permanent man to inhabit St. George's-in-the-East or Limehouse, he will be found in a 'Peabody' or some strictly regulated model dwelling. He will tell you: 'I make a point of not mixing with anyone,' and perhaps he will sorrowfully complain 'when the women gets thick together there's always a row.' It is the direful result of the wholesale desertion of these districts by the better classes that respectability means social isolation, with its enfeebling and disheartening effect. In common with all other working men with a moderate but regular income, the permanent dock labourer is made by his wife. If she be a tidy woman and a good manager, decently versed in the rare arts of cooking and sewing, the family life is independent, even comfortable, and the children may follow in the father's footsteps or rise to better things. If she be a gossip and a bungler – worse still, a drunkard – the family sink to the low level of the East London street; and the children are probably added to the number of those who gain their livelihood by irregular work and by irregular means. (23–24)

Now, we believe, from our general inquiry, that there are 10,000 casual labourers, exclusive of waterside labourers, resident in the Tower Hamlets, employed principally at the docks. The average of irregular hands employed by the three dock companies stands at 3,000* – that is, there is daily work at 3*s* 6*d* a day for 3000 men. At the London and St. Katharine Docks 400 of the irregular hands have an actual preference right to employment. These 'ticket men' will earn from 15*s* to £1 a week. (25)

Rows of back-to-back houses thrown up throughout every major city. Though multi-occupied, a docker would think himself lucky to be housed in such a dwelling.

At the West and East India, and at most of the wharves and warehouses, there are a certain number of men who are usually secure of work if there be any. They are for the most part an honest, hard-working set, who have established themselves by their regular attendance and honesty in the confidence of their employers. These men, together with the more constant of the casuals, are to my mind the real victims of irregular trade: if they be employed by small contractors, unprincipled foremen, or corrupt managers, they are liable to be thrust on one side for others who stand drink, or pay back a percentage of the rightful wage. Physically they suffer from the alternation of heavy work for long hours, and the unfed and uninterested leisure of slack seasons: and the time during which they are 'out o' work' hangs heavily on their hands. (26)

We know that the professional dock labourer (as distinguished from the drift of other trades, and from the casual by inclination) earns from 12*s* to 15*s* a week, supposing his earnings were to be spread evenly throughout the year. But a large wage one week and none the next, or –

as in the case of the wool sales – six months' work and six months' leisure, are not favourable conditions to thrift, temperance, and good management. Payment by the hour, with the uncertainty as to whether a job will last two or twenty-four hours, and the consequently incalculable nature of even the daily income, encourages the wasteful habits of expenditure which are characteristic of this class. The most they can do in their forlorn helplessness is to make the pawnbroker their banker, and the publican their friend. Many of the professional dock labourers live in common lodging-houses of the more reputable kind. If married they must submit to the dreariness of a one-roomed home which, even in its insufficiency, costs them from 3*s* to 4*s* 6*d* out of their scanty earnings. More likely than not the wife spends her day straining, by miserably paid work, to meet the bare necessities of existence. (27)

Dock and Waterside employers are the only masters of importance who neither give nor require characters. A strong man presents himself at the gate. He may be straight from one of Her Majesty's jails, but if he be remarkable for sinew he strikes the quick eye of contractor or foreman. The professional dock labourer is turned away and the newcomer is taken on. For the casual by misfortune is subject to exactly the same economic and social conditions as the casual by profession. Taken on one day, he is overlooked the next. He may stave off starvation, but he cannot rise to permanent employment. To have worked at the docks is sufficient to damn a man for other work. (29)

Socialism in the 1880s

Though there was a revival of socialist activity in the 1880s, it remained a minority interest in Britain, compared with continental Europe. Karl Marx had lived and written in England; but the first volume of his masterpiece, *Das Capital*, published in 1867, was not available in English until 1887, several years after his death and over a decade later than the French translation. Neither Marx nor Engels, as their correspondence shows, expected much from the British working class or, especially, its leaders in terms of bringing about revolutionary change.

The trade union movement, up to the 1880s, was little influenced by socialist thought – the TUC and most of the craft unions accepted Liberalism as their political commitment, and the few union-backed MPs who sat in the labour interest did so as Liberals or rather 'Lib-Labs'. Victorian class values were largely accepted by the working classes themselves, as were the boundaries of skilled, semi-skilled and 'respectable' working classes, whose main shared aim was to stay above the level of the lower working class, the casually employed or more or less unemployed. Nonconformist religion, particularly Methodism, played a much larger part in forming the values of all these classes than any political ideology; and those who felt the need for change largely emphasised reform rather than revolution.

The foundation of Keir Hardie's Independent Labour Party (ILP) still lay in the future (1893), as did the Labour Representation Committee (LRC) of 1900, which became the Labour Party in 1906. But several small political groups already existed, founded and led by middle-class intellectuals. H. M. Hyndman, a wealthy ex-Tory dilettante converted to Marxism by reading *Das Capital* in the French edition (though he was scorned by Marx himself), managed to found the Social Democratic Federation (SDF) in 1884, in association with the poet/artist William Morris, who left before the end of the year to found the Socialist League, an exclusive group of virtually no influence. The SDF was an eclectic organisation from the start, but it included Marxists among others, and attracted some working-class members from the trade unions, especially the engineers and the new unskilled unions, several of whom already held Marxist views and were capable of expounding them in public.

Keir Hardie, founder of the Labour Party and ILP. He unsuccessfully moved a resolution for the 8-hour day at the 1889 TUC Congress.

Hyndman had no time for the established unions and their reformist politics, and his influence tended to be divisive and sectarian – one of several reasons why Engels regarded him and his party as useless. But Hyndman recruited such key figures as Tom Mann, John Burns, Will Thorne and the editor Henry Champion to his cause. Though the SDF had only 600–800 members, its paper, *Justice*, had a small but influential circulation of 1000–3000. Ironically it was the Dockers' Union which in 1900 forced the SDF out of the newly formed LRC by objecting to its proposed clauses on class warfare. The Dockers' Union's motion to delete these was overwhelmingly carried. Hyndman reformed the SDF as the British Socialist Party, which went adrift during World War One, since Hyndman was a staunchly patriotic supporter of the war. The party finally lost its separate identity in the formation of the British Communist Party (CPGB) after the war.

H. M. Hyndman, founder of the Social democratic Federation (1884), and follower of Marx. He viewed the strike as Reformist Editor of Justice.

The Fabian Society was also founded in 1884 and in the long run had more influence over the future Labour Party. The society took its name from the Ancient Roman general Fabius Cunctator ('the Delayer'), who defeated the invading Hannibal by wearing-down tactics rather than by direct attacks. The Fabians hoped to achieve socialist aims by gradualism and by converting policy-makers with rational arguments. Not seeking a wide following, the Fabians, who notably included G. B. Shaw, Annie Besant and Sidney Webb (Beatrice joined later, in 1893), produced influential pamphlets highlighting the poverty and degradation of the inner cities and urging reform.

At least as influential as socialism was the radical liberal ideology increasingly accepted by the more enlightened upper and middle-class Victorians and the professional classes. These types are represented by W. T. Stead, editor of the *Pall Mall Gazette* (best remembered for his direct action to reform the laws on juvenile prostitution and enforce the age of consent); Dr T. J. Barnardo of the children's charity; Spencer Charrington (of the brewery family), MP for Mile End; and William Booth, who founded a mission in Whitechapel (1865) that was the forerunner of the Salvation Army (1878). Their exposure of conditions in the East End was regarded as virtually seditious by the government and the law. Similarly, Charles Booth's social surveys had great influence on Liberal thinking throughout the United Kingdom. Henry Champion, conscious that Marxist/socialist thought was not having a comparable impact, later wrote of the dock strike that 'we won despite our socialism'.

The impetus for change in the East End, and the small but significant victories of the match-girls, the gas workers and the dockers, did not represent the triumph of any one ideology or leader. Its strength came from the mass of impoverished people and their will to change their environment and the way they were perceived by society. A great weight of oppression lay on the poor, particularly in the inner cities, and was especially hard on women. Women workers had a hard struggle not only against oppressive laws but against the male-dominated culture of their own class. Children also suffered, for the newly invented concept of childhood took some time to percolate down to the lower levels, even after 1870, when primary education was technically available for all. A child of thirteen was still a wage-earner, having to contribute his or her share to the family's struggle for survival. Family love was not necessarily lacking, but there was little room for sentimentality. The young in the inner cities had an incredibly hard time, often abandoned, often left at a very tender age to fend for themselves. They did survive and indeed they were to reap the benefits of the new union movement. Perhaps the mood was summed up by the contemporary poem of Morris Machesky:

Enough I will not sew again,
for idle hands to reap,
I never will bow low again,
the broom and watch me sweep,
Hand me a broom,
I'm through with them,
I'll sweep them off the earth
Yes Yes that's what I'll do with them
One whisk is all that they are worth,
They wore my heart and soul away,
My sweat became their jewel
the crumbs I earned they stole away,
and rode me like a mule,
The black woods cannot harm me now
The curses they can keep
The titles don't alarm me now
A broom and watch me sweep.

Letter from Friedrich Engels to August Bebel, London 15 February 1886. *Marx & Engels Correspondence, 1846–1895* (1934), 445

The Social Democratic Federation which, despite all self-advertising reports, is an extremely weak organisation – containing good elements, but led by literary and political adventurers – was brought to the verge of dissolution at the November elections by a stroke of genius on the part of these same leaders. Hyndman the head of the Society, had taken money from the Tories at the time, and with it put up two Social-Democratic candidates in two districts in London. As they had not even got any members in these two constituencies the way they would discredit themselves was to be foreseen (one got 27 and the other one got 32 votes out of 4000–5000 respectively!). Hyndman, however, had no sooner got the Tory money than his head began violently to swell and he immediately set off to Birmingham, to Chamberlain, the present Minister and offered him his 'support' (which does not total 1000 votes in all England) if Chamberlain would guarantee him a seat in Birmingham by the help of the Liberals and would bring in the Eight Hour Bill. Chamberlain is no fool and showed him the door. Despite all attempts to hush it up, a great row about this in the Federation threatened dissolution.

Engels to Bebel 447

'The unemployed who followed [Hyndman and the SDF] in order to hold a fresh meeting in Hyde Park, were mostly the types who do not want to work anyhow, hawkers, loafers, police spies, pickpockets. When the aristocrats at the club window sneered at them they broke the said windows, ditto the shop windows; they looted the wine dealers' shops and immediately set up a consumers' association for the contents in the street, so that in Hyde Park Hyndman and Co. had hastily to pocket their blood-thirsty phrases and go in for pacification. But the thing had now got going. During the procession, during this second little meeting and afterwards, the masses of the Lumpenproletariat; whom Hyndman had taken for the unemployed, streamed through some of the fashionable streets near by, looted jewellers' and other shops, used the loaves and legs of mutton which they had looted, solely to break windows with, and dispersed without meeting any resistance. Only a remnant of them were broken up in Oxford Street by four, say four, policemen.

Otherwise the police were nowhere to be seen and their absence was so marked that *we* were not alone in being compelled to think it intentional. The chiefs of the police seemed to be Conservatives who had no objection to seeing a bit of a row in this period of Liberal Government. However the government at once set up a Commission of Inquiry and it may cost more than one of these gentleman his job.

Letter, Engels to Bebel, 18 March 1886

As to Hyndman, the way he came out of Trafalgar Square and Hyde Park on February the 8th has done infinitely more harm than good, shouting about revolution which in France passes off harmlessly as stale stuff, is utter nonsense here among the totally unimpressed masses and has the effect of scaring away the proletariat, only exciting the demoralised elements. It absolutely cannot be understood here as anything but a summons for looting which accordingly followed and has brought discredit which will last a long time here among the workers too. As to the point that it has drawn public attention to socialism, you people in Germany do not know how utterly blunted the public are with regard to such methods. After a hundred years of freedom of the press and of assembly and the advertising bound up with them, the first alarm of the bourgeois was certainly very funny and brought in about £40,000 in contributions for the unemployed in all about £70,000 but that has hardly been disposed of and nobody will pay more and the remains the same. What has been achieved amongst the bourgeois public is the identification of socialism with looting and even though that does not make the matter worse still it is certainly no gain to us. The four leaders of the demonstration in Hyde Park Hyndman, Champion, Williams and John Burns were afterwards arrested and released on bail and in April tried and acquitted. A fine advertisement for Hyndman but it comes too late. He has succeeded in running his organisation hopelessly and at the very most the two organisations, the Federation and the Socialist League, have not more than 2000 paying members between them nor their papers 5000 readers before them and of these the majority are sympathetic bourgeois persons, literary men. As things are here it is a real mercy that these immature elements do not succeed in penetrating the masses they must first ferment themselves clear then it may turn out alright.

Civil Disorder

Though the principal trade disputes of 1888–89 were on the whole surprisingly peaceful and non-violent, there was a long history of civic turbulence and public disorder, especially in London, and no doubt many involved in these industrial conflicts had played a role in the recent part of that history.

Mayhew and later Booth and such papers as the *Pall Mall Gazette* (1883–89) and the *Enquirer* were making the better-off aware of poverty and suffering. The indifference and intolerance they mostly showed to the poor was met with similar, more active hostility at times on the part of those who were suffering and who found even the skilled and semi-skilled workers generally unsympathetic to their intolerable conditions. So, in the decade before the dock strike, the unemployed marched from Dod Street, Limehouse, into the West End, bent on confrontation.

Civil disobedience and riot, rather than revolution, as in other nations, was the extreme reaction of the British proletariat. The Riot Act, which dated back in various forms to the fourteenth century, was for over 250 years (until its abolition in 1967) a licence to unleash military and police violence against the 'London mob' and their provincial equivalents (e.g. in Manchester). So a magistrate's 'reading the Riot Act' was not only part of the ritual, frequently a prelude to the slaughter of unarmed civilians, but passed into the language to signify a final warning before retaliation. Between 1730 and 1840 only five men were killed by rioters, but more than 450 rioters were killed by troops and nearly a hundred more were hanged for taking part in riots. The Riot Act itself gave the soldiers immunity from prosecution for their actions following the reading, so it was quite literally a licence to kill.

Rioting had occurred for a strange variety of reasons. In 1760 it was because the bodies of hanged criminals were sold to surgeons instead of having a Christian burial. In 1809 in London there were vicious riots over the price of theatre tickets. And in 1874 in Southsea, Portsmouth, it was because the rich closed the city pier to the poor. Political riots were not uncommon – in 1791 the houses and persons of suspected supporters of the French Revolution were attacked by crowds of 'patriotic' royalists.

March of the unemployed from Dodd Street, Limehouse, to Trafalgar Square.

In 1780 the notorious Gordon Riots, depicted by Dickens in *Barnaby Rudge*, were based on anti-Catholic, anti-Irish sentiments. Four jails, including Newgate, were attacked and burned. History does not record whether the inmates thus set free were interrogated about their religion, but presumably Protestants and Roman Catholics alike welcomed their unexpected liberty.

Of approximately 275 episodes of rioting between 1735 and 1800, some two-thirds were occasioned by sudden rises in the price of basic foodstuffs. But the disturbances of the 1880s concerning the Irish question, unemployment and poverty – for the trade depression of the 1870s lingered on into the early and, especially, the mid-1880s – were comparable in seriousness with the Gordon Riots of a century earlier.

Bloody Sunday. The demonstration over unemployment and the Irish Question ends with Lifeguards dispersing the crowd (1887).

Bloody Sunday battlefield, St Martin's Lane.

The marches that started in Dod Street and other parts of London often ended in Trafalgar Square, symbol of free speech and assembly. In February 1886 demonstrators marched up Pall Mall, smashing the windows of the establishment's clubs. They raced up Piccadilly, Regent Street and Oxford Street, attacking Peter Robinson's store and looting Marshall & Snelgrove. H. M. Hyndman, John Burns, Jack Williams and Henry Champion the leaders were arrested but subsequently acquitted.

On 13 November 1887, 'Bloody Sunday', serious rioting in Trafalgar Square, after the police had tried to prevent the crowd from entering it at all, led to six-week prison sentences for John Burns and for R. B. Cunninghame Graham MP, writer, traveller and later a founder of the Scottish Nationalists. But it was becoming clear that aimless violence was no way to achieve social justice, and that hope for the future lay rather in the organisation of the working classes and the withdrawal when necessary of their labour, their only asset and therefore their only real weapon.

The Match-Girls' Strike

The match-girls' strike of 1888 had a psychological and social significance out of all proportion to the comparatively small scale of a dispute at a single large factory, Bryant & May in the East End. It demonstrated to all union men what a few thousand girls – many very young, mostly of Irish descent, initially unorganised and considered unorganisable – could achieve if they had the courage to defy oppressive and unjust employers. Much of the piecework, e.g. box-making, was not even done on the premises but at home. How was it possible to organise such workers?

The catalyst was the Fabian journalist and birth-control propagandist Annie Besant, whose article, 'White Slavery in London', in her paper, the *Link* (23 June 1888), first drew public attention to the disgraceful conditions in which the girls worked.

Bryant & May protested that they were good employers and threatened legal action, which never materialised. The factory, when built in the 1860s, won prizes for design; but demand for the lucifer match led to an extra storey being added on top, destroying the ventilation. The phosphorus fumes were not only unpleasant but dangerous, leading to 'phossy jaw', a form of bone cancer, as well as skin cancer. Though the government inspectors had had reports and phosphorus work was by then banned in Sweden and the USA, it was considered that legislation would be in restraint of free trade. The work was seasonal, like much manufacturing and other work in London – many girls switched between jam-making in summer and match-making or packing in winter. The regime at Bryant & May was strict, with a system of fines, some severe, for minor offences (talking, going to the toilet, dropping matches, or even matches spontaneously catching fire) and for lateness. The girls started at 6.30 am in summer and 8.00 am in winter, and finished at 6.00 pm, with two short meal breaks, and lateness cost half a day's pay. Their pious employers devoted these fines (which were quite illegal and promptly stopped by the factory inspectors) to the conversion of the African heathen.

Being a match-girl rated somewhere practically below prostitution in

A Victorian artist's impression of match-girls. Even the artist couldn't accept the harsh reality, and pretty pictures like this helped preserve the myth.

the social scale. Girls (and boys too) as young as six worked before and after school – though the 1870 Education Act had theoretically made full-time schooling compulsory, exceptions were made in poor areas. Piecework paid between 5*s* and 9*s* a week, and even better-paid work averaged only 11*s*, up to perhaps 13*s*. This price covered not only 'an occasional blow from a foreman' but yellowing of the skin, bald patches and frequently loss of teeth, the result of having no separate eating room and consequently ingesting the phosphorus. (The employers' contribution to health care was to have teeth checked and pulled out, often against the wishes of the 'patient'.) In the more serious cases, the London Hospital at Whitechapel acquired expertise in treating jaw and skin cancer by dealing with the constant stream of victims from the match factories.

However, these horrors impressed the Victorian public less than the moral dangers to which the girls were subject, since feminine sexual immorality, especially as evidenced by illegitimate children or sexually transmitted diseases, aroused an extreme reaction (expressed in the Poor Law's attitude to single mothers or in the only recently repealed Contagious Diseases Act, which had made STDs a criminal offence subject

Before the strike the girls try a 'humble petition' and march, but are met with indifference.

to imprisonment) hard to reconcile with adult and child prostitution rife.

Despite all the pressures on the match-girls as women and as workers, they decided to strike when Theodore Bryant sacked Annie Besant's three main informants. The *Pall Mall Gazette* and other liberal papers appealed for funds, though *The Times* and similar right-wing journals blamed socialist agitators for the dispute. The strike also found support from existing unions, who contributed to the strike fund, and by late July Annie Besant was able to announce that a Match-girls' Union was being formed. Meanwhile, in mid-July, after a stoppage of only three weeks, the employers gave way and made significant concessions, partly enforced by the inspectors. Some three thousand full-time and part-time workers had been involved.

The importance of the struggle, despite the comparatively small gains, was twofold: it was the first strike by unorganised workers to gain national publicity and be victorious, if only to a limited extent, e.g. the victimised girls got their jobs back; and secondly, women – many of them mere girls, indeed – had shown the socialists, the labour movement and the all-too-chauvinistic working men of the East End itself that so-called second-class citizens could set an example of courage and success.

The Bryant and May Match-Girls' Strike shocks the nation and the labour movement with its success. (1888) This is the reality compared with the artist's impression on page 58.

The Gas Workers' Dispute

One cannot overestimate the importance of Will Thorne's Gas Workers' Union. It was the Gas Workers, who were the first to win the eight-hour day early in 1889, and signalled the new era of trade unionism. Gas workers from the East End's giant Beckton works were often laid off in the summer swelling the ranks of casual dock workers. Their experience of successful organisation was a key element in the overall development of the confrontation.

Will Thorne, *My Life's Battles* (1925), 67–73

Sunday morning March 31st, 1889 – a lovely sunny morning – was the birthday of the National Union of Gas Workers and General Labourers of Great Britain and Ireland. Today it is the largest union of its kind in the world.

A big enthusiastic crowd turned up. I led a contingent from Barking to the meeting place, with a band that I paid for out of my own pocket. We had an old van for a platform. Dear old Ben Tillett was with us, with his new-found powers of oratory; Harry Hobart, Dick Mansfield, George Angle, and one or two other good fighters were the speakers, with myself.

The atmosphere was electric when I mounted the platform. 'Fellow wage slaves, I am more than pleased to see such a big crowd of workers and friends from the Beckton Gas Works,' was my greeting to them. The reply was a heartening cheer, and my stage fright disappeared.

'I know that many of you have been working eighteen hours under very hard and difficult circumstances, that many of you must be dead tired; often have I done the eighteen-hour shift. I am under the impression that the resident engineer knew that I had arranged this meeting, and that he deliberately kept you working late. This sort of thing has gone on for a long time; we have protested but time after time we have been sneered at, ignored and have secured no redress. Let me tell you that you will never get any alteration in Sunday work, no alteration in any of your conditions or wages, unless you join together and form a strong trade union. Then you will be able to have a voice and say how long you will work, and how much you will do for a day's work.

'In my opinion, you have a perfect right to discuss all these matters with your employer through your chosen spokesman. Why should any

employer have the power to say you must do this, that, and the other thing? By your labour power you create useful things for the community, you create wealth and dividends, but you have no say, no voice, in any of these matters.

'All this can be altered if you will join together and form a powerful union, not only for gas workers, but one that will embrace all kinds of general labourers. Some of you only work in the gas works in the winter; when the warm weather comes, you are dismissed, to find that work you can get at the docks, in the brickfields, navvying, or anything that comes along.

'It is easy to break one stick, but when fifty sticks are together in one bundle it is a much more difficult job. The way you have been treated at your work for many years is scandalous, brutal, and inhuman. I pledge my word that, if you will stand firm and don't waver, within six months we will claim and win the eight-hour day, a six-day week and the abolition of the present slave-driving methods in vogue not only at the Beckton Gas Works, but all over the country. Now will you do this?'

There was one loud roar of 'We will!' That yell was the last birth pain of the union. I knew that the men meant business. I told them that I was satisfied, that I was only a rough diamond, that I could not talk as fluently as some of my colleagues, but I knew what we wanted and was

Retort gas workers at the Beckton Works.

prepared to fight for it. I warned the men not to give the foremen any chance to complain at them for losing time, and I made an energetic appeal to them to attend to their work in the usual way and give no opportunity for any of them to be victimised.

Dear comrade and great fighter, Ben Tillett spoke to the men after I had finished. His was an eloquent speech, militant and persuasive. I believe he had a slight impediment of speech at the time. He told of his own efforts to organise the dock workers, and the little response the men made. He had, however, formed an organisation known as the Tea Operatives' and General Labourers' Union, that I remained a member of until my own organisation came into being. Tillett described the horrible conditions under which the dockers worked, and was disappointed at the small response they made; but their time was to come in the very near future. He told the men how glad he was to help 'Mr Thorne' to form a sound and genuine union, and the friendship which existed between us.

After the speeches were over, I called for volunteers to form an organising committee, of which George Angle was appointed the secretary; then we started to take down the names of the men who wanted to join up. Eight hundred joined that morning. The entrance fee was 1s., and we had to borrow several pails to hold the coppers and other coins that

A rally at Peckham during the Gas Workers' Strike.

were paid in. Beside Clem Edwards, Ben Tillett, W. Byford – who later became my father-in-law through my second marriage – George Angle, the first branch secretary, Mark Hutchings, Dick Mansfield, the chief delegate, all helped to take down the names.

The meeting over, we had to get down to business. Ben Tillett, Byford and myself formed ourselves into a 'provisional committee' to draft a set of rules and to discuss ways and means of getting enrolled in the union the workers in the other gas works around London. Byford was made treasurer. He was the proprietor of a temperance bar at 144, Barking Road. He had a good knowledge of trade union administration, because for many years he had been secretary of the Yorkshire Glass Bottle Workers' Association.

I was highly elated at our success. The news of the meeting spread like wildfire; in the public-houses, factories, and works in Canning Town, Barking, East and West Ham every one was talking about the union. Soon my first doubts as to whether the union would succeed were dispelled; the men were solid, enthusiastic, and anxious to get all their mates enrolled.

Sunday after Sunday we would start out from 144, Barking Road, our headquarters, to encourage the men at other gas works. As many as twenty brake loads of workers would go out on these Sunday morning crusades. The idea caught on; enthusiasm was at a high pitch, and within two weeks we had over 3000 men in the union.

Never before had men responded like they did. For months London was ablaze. The newspapers throughout the country were giving good reports of our activities. They were curious to know what we wanted and what we were going to do.

The provisional committee decided to call the union the 'National Union of Gas Workers and General Labourers'. We had a big debate on the amount of contributions to be paid. I pleaded for *2d.* per week; others pleaded for more, but *2d.* was the sum finally agreed upon. We took as our motto 'Love, Unity and Fidelity'; our slogan was 'One Man, One Ticket, and every Man with a Ticket'. The ticket was the union card.... The provisional committee had drafted a code of rules, that was to be endorsed by a delegate meeting. At this meeting we found that the general secretary's salary had been fixed at £2. 10*s.* per week. This the delegates altered to £2. 5*s.*

The fighting spirit was strong in the delegates; it was proposed to petition the directors of the different companies in London for an advance of 1*s.* per day in the wages of all their workers. I opposed this; I wanted a reduction in the working hours. 'Shorten the hours and prolong your lives,' was my plea. I declared that the eight-hour day would not alone mean a reduction of four hours a day for the workers then employed, but that it meant a large number of unemployed would be absorbed, and so reduce the inhuman competition that was making men more like beasts than civilised persons. I won the day.

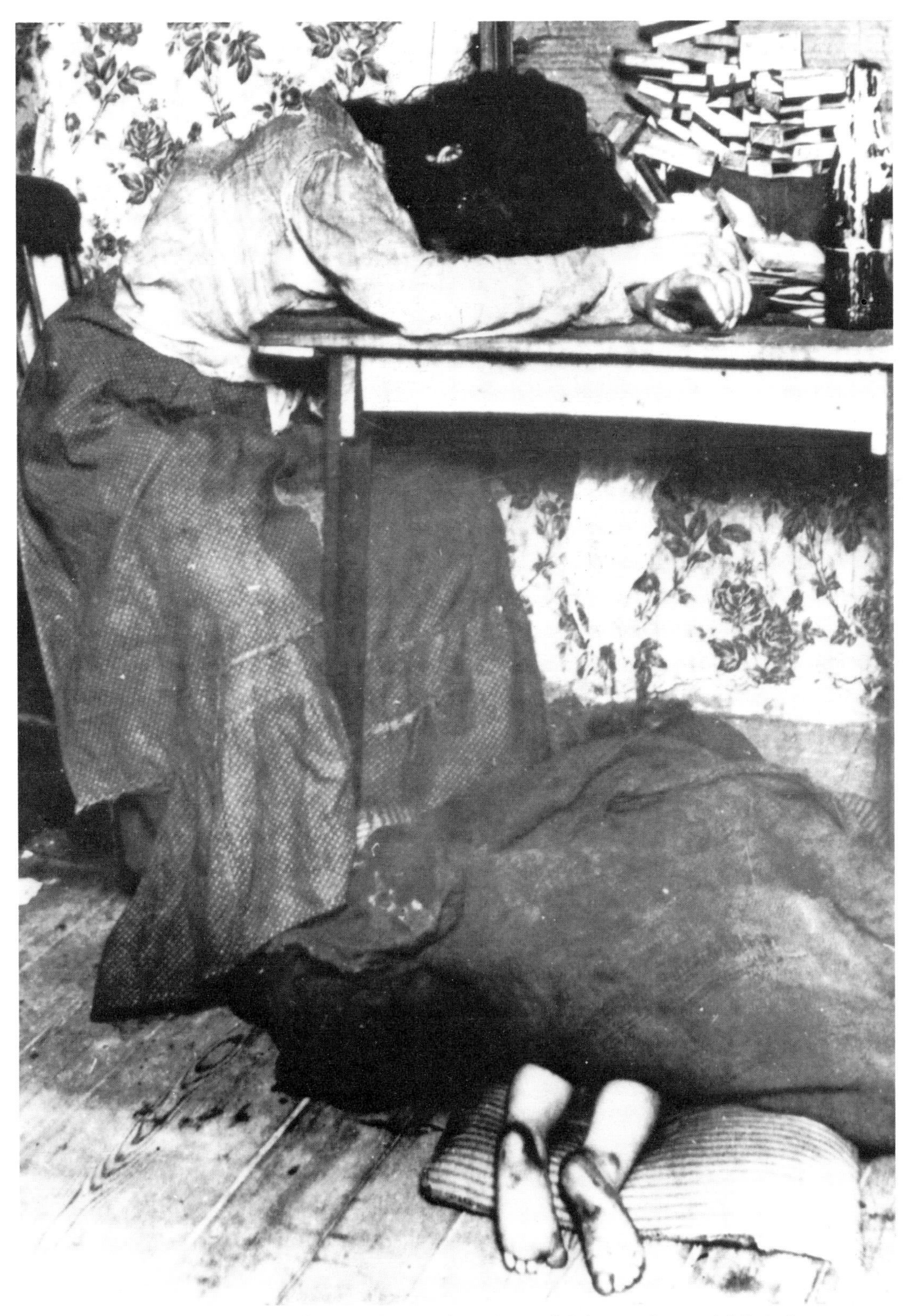

Exhausted after a day's homeworking on the matches. Wages didn't stretch to a child's bed.

A petition was drafted and signed and sent to the companies demanding the Eight-Hour Working Day. We agreed that the men at no one gas works, under the control of any one company, should accept the eight-hour day until it had been agreed that a uniform amount of work should be done in the eight hours by all works. We were quite aware that we would have to do more work per hour under the eight-hour day than we did under the twelve-hour day.

Weeks passed and no reply came from the companies to our demand. The men were getting impatient. A spirit of revolt was growing. Then I received word that the directors of the Gas Light and Coke Company had conceded the eight-hour day, and only the question of making arrangements about the number of retorts to be drawn and charged in each eight hours was left to be dealt with.

We had several discussions with the resident engineer, and finally came to a settlement for the Beckton Gas Works; the men employed at the other works of the Company were satisfied with the terms we had secured, except at the Nine Elms works. The men there sent for me, and after a discussion lasting over two hours with the engineer we got what we wanted.

The formation of our union, and its first victory, put heart into thousands of unskilled, badly paid and unorganised workers.

2 THE STRIKE LEADERS

The real-life social drama that unfolded in August and September 1889 consisted externally of many crowd scenes – particularly the great processions with banners and floats, reminiscent at a long distance of the perambulating performances on carts of the medieval mystery plays at the feast of Corpus Christi.

But five main men played crucial roles: Ben Tillett, John Burns, Tom Mann and Will Thorne as strike and union leaders, Cardinal Manning as 'honest broker' and sage. Brief portraits of these follow. (The sixth, Mr C. M. Norwood, the employers' main leader, will be left in decent obscurity – if not as the Villain, then as the technical Loser.)

Ben Tillett

(Benjamin Tillett, b. 1859, Bristol, d. 1943)

From childhood, when he ran away from home three times, Tillett had a daring and adventurous soul that belied his small, slender frame. He spent some years at sea before settling down in 1880 to work at the London riverside: 'Of slight and delicate physique, but of a restless and energetic temperament with indomitable pluck and a strong vein of amibition, he was just the man to inspire restlessness in others.' (Smith and Nash, 1889, 31)

A dispute concerning a threatened wage cut at the Cutler Street Tea Warehouse where he worked provided his opportunity. Having persuaded the men to organise, he found himself general secretary of a new union, the Tea Operatives' and General Labourers' Union, attempting to operate on a subscription of 2d a week. His first confrontation, at the newly opened and poorly paid Tilbury dock in the autumn of 1888, collapsed after a month, leaving him ill from exposure, the men disheartened and the union in disarray. Yet the success of the Gas workers' Union the next year encouraged him to try again on a larger stage.

He became the fundamental organiser of the 1889 dock strike. An initially diffident but impassioned orator, inclined to stammer when excited, he was closest of all to the ordinary working man, his grievances, sufferings and needs.

Benjamin Tillett, itinerant labourer, self-educated, active socialist and trade unionist, founder of the Dockers' Union and First Secretary.

Beatrice Webb described him as 'a light-haired little man with the face of a religious enthusiast'....

David Wasp and Alan Davis, *The Great Dock Strike 1889* (1974), 72.

His friend Tom Mann said: 'Ben would reach the heart's core of the dockers by his description of the way in which they had to beg for work and the paltry pittance they received, and by his homely illustrations of their life as it was and as it ought to be.'

After the strike Ben took a leading part in organising the Dock, Wharf, Riverside, and General Workers' Union, and in another great dock strike in 1911. He was a prime mover in the eventual foundations of the TGWU in 1921–22. He was one of the founders of the Labour Party, and was MP for Salford from 1917 to 1924 and from 1929 to 1931. He became Chairman of General Council of the Trades Union Congress in 1928 and retired from public life in 1931. He died in 1943, and was one of the key figures in the development of modern trade unionism in this country.

John Burns

(b. 1858, Battersea, London; d. 1943)

Of Scottish parentage, Burns lost his father when young and grew up, with eight other children, in poverty; but his mother ensured that he had a sound basic education. In 1877, while still an engineering apprentice, he was arrested for public speaking on Clapham Common. In 1879 he joined the Amalgamated society of Engineers (ASE) and spent two years in west Africa. On his return he joined the Social Democratic Federation (SDF) and in 1885 he was the youngest delegate at the ASE conference. In the same year he stood for Parliament as a Socialist candidate for West Nottingham.

In 1886, notorious as the 'man with the red flag', he was prosecuted, along with three other SDF members, for sedition and acquitted. But in 1887, in the aftermath of the 'Bloody Sunday' demonstration in Trafalgar Square, he was sentenced to six weeks' imprisonment.

In 1889 he was elected to the London county council (LCC), representing Battersea, and took a leading role in the dock strike. Smith and Nash evoke his 'short and square-set figure, white straw hat, blue engineer's suit and stentorian voice.... Burns's voice is reckoned the most powerful in England and his wealth of picturesque language is derived in no small measure from his extensive reading in his library at home, to which he has devoted his savings.' (36–37) They depict 'This man, with his coal-black beard, his head thrown back, his eyes blazing with determination from beneath his shaggy arched eyebrows,' about to make his first speech to the great crowd outside the employers' HQ, the Dock House in Leadenhall Street. Yet, despite his reputation as an agitator, he played a large part in keeping relations between the strikers and police amicable for most of the strike period.

In 1892 he was chosen as chairman of the TUC and elected MP for Battersea, standing as Independent Labour. Regarded as a leader and

John Burns. A skilled engineer, Burns was known as the Man with the Red Flag, following his arrest after the Bloody Sunday demonstration. Burns was by far the best-known socialist at the time of the Dock Strike. He went on to be a Liberal Cabinet Minister.

hero of the 'new unionism', and described by Sidney and Beatrice Webb as the most glittering personality of the Labour movement, he eventually proved more Independent than Labour, and accepted the Cabinet office of President of the Local Government Board in Sir Henry Campbell-Bannerman's 1906 Liberal government. The first working man to become a minister, he lost credibility as a labour leader. In 1914, promoted to President of the Board of Trade, he resigned in protest against Britain's entry into World War One, and effectively withdrew from public life, taking no part in the pacifist movement either. He did not stand for Parliament in 1918, and maintained a complete public silence, in startling contrast to his earlier eloquence. He devoted the rest of his long life to his vast collection of books on the history of London.

Tom Mann

(*Thomas Mann, b. 1856, Foleshill, Coventry; d. 1941*)

Mann lost his mother at two and was brought up by his father, a clerk at the Victoria colliery. At nine he started work on the colliery farm and at eleven he went down the pit. In 1870 the family moved to Birmingham and he served a seven-year engineering apprenticeship. Eager for self-education, he read books in socialism and joined the ASE. In 1884, after working briefly in the USA, he became friends with Burns in London, joined the SDF and eventually was a full-time lecturer on its behalf. In 1889 he helped to organise the Gas Workers' Union and to run the dock strike, being elected president of the new Dockers' Union at the close of the dispute.

In 1891 he was appointed a member of the Royal Commission on Labour and in 1894–96 he was Secretary of the ILP. From 1901 to 1911 he was organising unions and the beginnings of Labour parties in Australia and New Zealand.

On his return he was at the heat of a brief burst of syndicalist activity in this country and played a prominent part in the great industrial disputes of 1911–12. Having stood unsuccessfully for the secretaryship of the ASE in 1892, he tried again in 1919! The reconstructed and expanded society, retitled the Amalgamated Engineering Union (AEU), elected him this time, though he held the post only until 1921. At this time he was a founder member of the Communist Party of Great Britain (CPGB). Of the key leaders of 1889, he alone retained his Marxist philosophy to the end of his life.

H. Llewellyn Smith and Vaughan Nash, *The Story of the Dockers' Strike* (1889), 34

Ben Tillett did well in summoning Tom Mann, for throughout the weeks that were to come he supplied an element in the councils of the strike leaders in which otherwise they would have been weak. He was the eyes of the strike, always ready to see where there was necessary work to be done, and to set to work to do it. Strong and wiry, and capable of great physical endurance, and withal cool-headed and quietly energetic, he applied himself to the details of organisation, which frequently carry with them the success or failure of a movement, and yet are so often overlooked by those who are great at beating the big drum.

Will Thorne

(*William James Thorne, b. 1857, Hockley, Birmingham; d. 1946*)

Will Thorne was the son of a journeyman bricklayer who was killed in a fight with a horse dealer in 1864. Will, at six, was already working a twelve-hour day for a rope spinner, but declared a one-boy strike when his employer tried to reduce his weekly wage from 2s. 6d to 2s. He took a variety of labouring jobs and was involved in a larger-scale strike before he was fifteen. Following his mother's disastrous remarriage to a drunk

(Above left) Tom Mann, of the Amalgamated Society of Engineers, and a member of the Social Democratic Federation.

(Above right) Will Thorne, the semi-literate Gas Workers' Leader, who won the 8-hour day for his members in 1889.

in 1875 and a period of wandering, he took a job at Saltley gas works, Birmingham, and headed a successful deputation against Sunday working. He married in1879 – both he and his wife were then illiterate and made their marks in the register. In 1882 the family settled in London and he found a job at Beckton gasworks in the East End, just downstream of the Royal docks, near Gallions Reach and Barking Creek.

He had joined the SDF in 1881 and met many radicals and socialists, including H. M. Hyndman, Eleanor Marx (Karl's youngest daughter), Edward Aveling, G. B. Shaw, Tom Mann, Harry Quelch, Charles Bradlaugh, Annie Besant, Wilhelm Liebknecht, Friedrick Engels and Jean Jaurès. Eleanor Marx helped with his reading and writing and he was deeply upset by her suicide in 1898.

Several attempts to found a gas workers' union had failed; but in 1889 a new National Union of Gas Workers and General Labourers won an eight-hour day, with Thorne as General Secretary and without striking. But a further dispute led to an unsuccessful strike in December 1889–February 1890. However, he helped to lead the Leeds gas workers to victory in the bitter strike of summer 1890. The union's open-door policy on membership led to demarcation disputes, notably with Tillett's Dockers' Union; but its success in organising the unskilled in many trades led to greater stability and marked the path of the future.

Annie Besant. A leading Fabian, she took up the cause of women's rights, championed the struggle of the match-girls and was the editor of the magazine Link.

Thorne held his post for forty-five years, until 1934, by which time the union had absorbed two smaller ones and been renamed the National Union of General and Municipal Workers (NUGMW). He also played a leading part in the TUC and local government. He was MP for West Ham South (1906–18) and then Plaistow (1918–45). His staunchly patriotic views in World War One angered the pacifist wing of the Labour movement and may have influenced his gradual rightward move – he accepted a CBE in 1930 and was made Privy Councillor in 1945. He survived three wives and five sons; his fourth wife, two sons and six daughters outlived him.

Cardinal Manning, supporter of trade unions and the dignity of labour, and friend of the poor and oppressed.

Cardinal Manning

(Henry Edward Manning, b. 1808, Hertfordshire; d. 1892)

Educated at Balliol College, Oxford, and later a Fellow of Merton, Manning was made Archdeacon of Colchester in 1840, but resigned in 1851 on his conversion to Roman Catholicism. Becoming a priest in his new communion, he rose in 1865 to Archbishop of Westminster, the Catholic primate of England. In religious and church matters he was conservative – his strong support for the principle of papal infallibility in 1870 was rewarded in 1875 with a cardinal's red hat.

The colour was apt, though, for in social and political affairs he was considered a radical and at times even a dangerous revolutionary! Paradoxically it was his almost medieval views on capital and labour – he regarded money as 'dead' and labour as 'live capital' – that led him to support trade unions (e.g. the Agricultural Labourers' Union), considering them to be analogous to medieval guilds rather than as political organisations.

He himself claimed to be non-political but his support of the right to strike, his appeals for unemployment relief and protests against the Poor Law, his rejection of laissez-faire economic orthodoxy, and his demands for decent housing for the poor would mark him as left of centre even today, let alone in the high Victorian era:

'The homes of the poor in London are often very miserable ... These things cannot go on, these things ought not to go on. The accumulation of wealth in the land, the piling up of wealth like mountains in the possession of classes or individuals, cannot go on if these moral conditions of our people are not healed. No commonwealth can rest on such foundations.'

'On the Dignity and Rights of Labour' (1874) ***The Condition of Labour***

Such views did not endear him to all in Rome or nearer home. But among Roman Catholics his reputation was immense and even outside his own church he was widely respected – his opposition to vivisection and cruelty to animals was a further (again quite modern) testimony of his humanity. Since many of the 1889 strikers were Catholics of Irish origin, his influence and involvement were beyond dispute. He was then eighty-one, so his intervention was among one of the last major public acts of a full life.

He was one of the four subjects chosen for portrayal in Lytton Strachey's *Eminent Victorians* (1918), along with Florence Nightingale, Thomas Arnold and General Gordon.

3 THE STRIKE

The *Lady Armstrong*

Following the successes of the gas workers and the match-girls, meetings took place between stevedores, gas workers, seamen, and the small warehouse and riverside unions. Also taking part were the newly formed but well-established Jewish unions, such as the tailors, the cabinet-makers, bakers etc. whose help and guidance was to be invaluable in the struggle that lay ahead. Mainly Yiddish-speaking, Jews in the East End were more advanced in their social theories and eager to teach not only the politics of socialism and anarchism but the practicalities of literacy and organisation and were pleased to welcome the new recruits to the social institutions set up by the Jewish community in back rooms and halls and at the tops of pubs. One can only conjecture what these Yiddish-speaking Jews from Poland, Russia and Eastern Europe thought of their new comrades in the classes – and indeed, what a mixed bunch they were! Many of them had thick Irish accents. Many of the seamen and dockers were Lascars, a name given to any man or woman who appeared to be of foreign origin or dark skinned. (It is quite strange how many social scientists of the period described Negroes, Asians and South Americans as 'Chinese'.) There were also the migrant workers from Wiltshire who specialized in the timber trades in the Isle of Dogs and Deptford and Millwall, who still wore their traditional garb of no boots, but feet swathed in cloth. There also were all the misfits of downtrodden London, attracted to the East End and the dockside for a day's labour. But this divergent group all shared one thing in common and that was they were all poor, underfed and badly clothed. This any observer could witness, with their tight cheeks, hollow eyes, ragged clothes, the look of hunger, worry and neglect on their faces. And yet amongst this poverty was a certain dignity and an air of defiance. The air had been electric in London's East End since the match-girls' strike. With the success of the Beckton gas workers in March 1889, the word among the unorganised dockers was 'When, When?' Though there was much expectation and agitation amongst the rank and file the leader of the strike, Ben Tillett, on hearing the news of the strike, stated 'I could scarcely believe my ears. It had never occurred to me that they were ready for such a thing' (*East End News*, 1939, article

Henry Hyde Champion, an ex-Artillery Officer and the son of a Major-General. He was editor of the Labour Elector *and Press Officer during the strike.*

by Ben Tillett). Indeed there has been much confusion and controversy as is so often the case as how and when the strike began. Tillett, over forty years later in his autobiography, *Memories and Reflections* (1931), claims that he inspired and inflamed the dockers after he had made a particularly rousing speech at the dock gates on a previous Sunday. This may be more wishful thinking than reality but Tillett had been active in the docks and had formed the Tea Operatives' and General Labourers' Union some two years before, at the Royal Oak Pub in Hackney Road and he had been a leading figure in the unsuccessful Tilbury dock strike the year before.

There was obvious rivalry among the various groupings inside the emerging labour movement. Tillett had not endeared himself either to H. M. Hyndman, the leader of the Social Democratic Federation nor to Henry Champion, socialist agitator and editor of the *Labour Elector*. Tillett had stood against Will Thorne, the leader of the gas workers, for the post of Secretary of the Amalgamated Society of Gas Workers in July 1889.

Tillett was resoundingly beaten by Thorne for the General Secretaryship by 2,296 votes against a mere 69 recorded for Tillett. On the other hand, during the weeks before the strike he got hardly any mention in Champion's *Labour Elector*. This despite the fact that Tillett was also becoming very active on public platforms agitating for a General Dockers' Union.

Meeting outside the West India Dock Gates when the dockers agreed to the resolutions taken and gave a show of hands.

The first documented meeting appears to have been on Monday, 12 August. It was called by Will Harris who worked on the tugs at the Albert Docks and a close personal friend of Will Thomas and Tom McCarthy, the Secretary of the Amalgamated Society of Stevedores. Even though Tillett may not have been keen on taking the initiative, his oratory carried the meeting and it may well have been that Harris, McCarthy and Thorne deliberately played on Tillett's vanity by calling the meeting knowing that Tillett was far from certain that it was the right moment.

This is Thorne's description of the meeting in his autobiography *My Life's Battles* (1925), 83:

'It was on Saturday August 10, 1889, that I received a telegram from one of my old pals, Will Harris, who worked on one of the tugs at the Albert Docks. He wanted me to meet him at South Dock gates on the following Monday morning and said that an effort was going to be made to organise the dockers and start a Union for them.

I met him on the Sunday morning, and he told me he was particularly anxious to get me to come along, because of the success I had achieved in organising the gas workers in a union and securing the eight-hour day and other improvements for them. I arranged to meet him at 7.30 the next morning. When I arrived at the South Dock gates, who should I meet but my dear old friend Tom McCarthy, a stevedore. He was one of my best pals, and one of the greatest fighters in the Labour Movement at the time, although he has never received the full measure of recognition that he deserved. The time of the 'call-on' was eight o'clock. Tom got a chair from a coffee-shop close by. The chair was our platform, and it was placed near where the men gathered and waited for the 'call-on'.

Tom mounted the chair and started the meeting; he rubbed into the men the facts of the terrible conditions they worked under. He was in a position to do this, as he was a stevedore and had an intimate knowledge of the dockers' work. He was a fine platform speaker and his Irish ancestry gave him a much-needed vein of humour. I followed Tom with a speech in which I pointed out to the men what organisation had done for the gas workers. I backed up Tom's appeal to them to form a union and then refuse to go to work. Finally the proposition was put to a vote of the meeting, and every man voted to stay out. That was the beginning of the great dock strike in 1889, that for many months filled the news columns of every paper in the country, aye, of the civilised world ...

It has been commonly held that the strike was a spontaneous act rising out of a dispute concerning the *Lady Armstrong*, lying in the South Dock basin of the West India Docks. After her cargo was discharged, there was a regular dispute over the bonus or 'plus' money to be paid to the workforce. There was of course such a dispute and the men did leave the dock disgruntled and prepared to take action against their employer but as Smith and Nash comment:

The Story of the Dockers' Strike (1889), 32–33

The nature of the dispute – about the division of the 'plus' on a certain cargo – is of little importance, for it was avowedly only the pretext for a revolt against all the grievances which had long rankled in the minds of dock labourers. The men wanted to come out at once, and their leader only managed to restrain them until he had formulated their demands in writing and sent them to the dock authorities. The demands were as follows: No man be taken on for less than four hours at a stretch, contract and piecework to be abolished, and wages to be raised to 6d. an hour and 8d. over-time.

The letter was written on Tuesday, 13 August, and an answer requested by twelve o'clock next day but events had overtaken this. The demands put forward by the men were almost the same that Tillett had requested a week earlier (7 August) to the dock authorities, a letter which had been ignored by the employers. Tillett, in fact, still showed some nervousness as to the outcome of the dispute. It was with great difficulty that he persuaded the men to go to work on Tuesday but by Wednesday, 14 August, no one at all was at work on the South West India dock and all the signs were that the dock strike would soon spread to the whole of the dock complex. Tillett felt that he needed allies and he sent off a telegram to Tom Mann, enlisting his help in the dispute. Mann recalls his autobiography:

Tom Mann's Memoirs (1923), 61

I was at the office of the *Labour Elector* in Paternoster Row, on 14th August in that year, when about midday I received a wire from Ben Tillett asking me to make my way to the South West India dock. I went

at once. There was no difficulty in finding the men, for Ben was with them and they were about to hold a meeting. I was soon put in possession of the main facts. The men had been discharging a sailing ship named the *Lady Armstrong*. They were working for fivepence an hour and 'plus', this meaning that in a vague fashion, very ill defined, there was a recognized time for discharging certain goods, and if the men did the work in less time they received a surplus of a half-penny or penny per hour. The men argued they had kept a correct tally, but the dock superintendent refused to admit the claim. The dockers were told that their demand for more pay would have to be dealt with by the chief authority. The London and India Docks Joint Committee. The men refused to return to work.

Serious discussion must have taken place prior to the *Lady Armstrong* difficulty, because almost immediately it was proposed that now they were out, they should insist in the future on an established minimum of sixpence per hour for ordinary time and eight pence an hour for overtime. When I arrived they had already decided to claim at least as much as this, and to call upon their fellow dockers to help them. No need here to go into detail beyond that of giving a correct idea of the definiteness of aim, and the effect of their achievement. For myself, I kept at that strike until it was over; and for long after I remained in touch with the dockers and the movement of which they were a part.

Memories and Reflections (1931) 121

Tillett recalls:

Tom Mann came down about midday just as I was about to hold a meeting. Harry Orbell joined up. Tom McCarthy was already by my side . . .

A joint manifesto was then drawn up with the stevedores' unions on the following lines:

18 August

DOCK LABOURERS' STRIKE
AMALGAMATED AND UNITED SOCIETIES OF STEVEDORES

To the Trade Unionists and People of London

FRIENDS AND FELLOW-WORKMEN

The dock labourers are on strike and asking for an advance of wages – the wages they now receive being 5d. per hour day time and 6d. per hour overtime. They now ask 6d. per hour daytime and 8d. per hour overtime. The work is the most precarious nature, three hours being the average amount per day obtained by the 'docker.' We, the Union Stevedores of London, knowing the condition of the dock labourers, have determined to support their movement by every lawful means in our power. We have, therefore, refused to work because of the dock company employing scabs and blacklegs, who are now taking the places of the

Harry Orbell was given the task of organising Tilbury.

dock labourers on strike. We do this, not to inconvenience the brokers, shipowners, or master stevedores, as our quarrel is not with them, but we feel our duty is to support our poorer brothers. We are promised the help of the Seamen's and Firemen's Union, and we now appeal with confidence to members of all trade unions for joint action with us, and especially those whose work is in connection with shipping – sea-going engineers and fitters, boiler makers, ships' carpenters, painters and decorators, shipwrights, iron ship builders, caulkers, etc., etc., and also the coal heavers, ballast men, lightermen and their watchmen. We also appeal to the public at large for contributions and support on behalf of the dock labourers, which may be sent to Ben Tillett, Great Assembly Hall, Mile End Road; and in doing this we feel sure that our efforts will be appreciated – not as disturbers nor peacebreakers, but as a demand from men determined to sway not one inch from the attitude they have taken up, to succour the poor and uplift the down-trodden. – On behalf of the Almagamated and United Stevedores,
Thos. McCarthy,
T. M. Williams, *Secs.*

This was no mean achievement. The Stevedores' Union came into being in November 1871; the driving force for its conception was that of Patrick Hennessey, an Irish trade unionist. A tailor by trade Hennessey was also a prominent member of the Land and Labour League. After subsequent meetings the title given to the Union was that of the Labour Protection League. In 1872 the Stevedores could boast of a membership of about 3000 with five branches. After a successful strike in 1872 5000 members at the time of the 1889 strike. Unfortunately because of factional difficulties inside the Stevedores Union the Union split into two separate categories in 1887 to become the United Stevedores and the Amalgamated Stevedores Union.

Smith and Nash *The Story of the Dockers' Strike* (1889), 22–23

Passing to the export trade, we at once strike a vein of higher class and better organised labour. The stevedores are a body of skilled men, many of Irish extraction, engaged by master-stevedores, who provide the necessary gear, and contract direct with the shipowners and agents. The stevedores earn about thirty-six shillings a week and have two strong trades unions, the 'Amalgamated' and the 'United' Societies which, between them, included before the strike from a third to a half of the whole number of Stevedores in the port.

Indeed the stevedores had a very strong Irish connection and in fact Roman Catholicism was very strong among their ranks. It was this coupled with the fact that they wanted to keep their own identity and to some degree their own conditions and pay free from competition from other labour which led them in no small part to be reluctant to change and give help to the unorganised dock labourers, although many of these

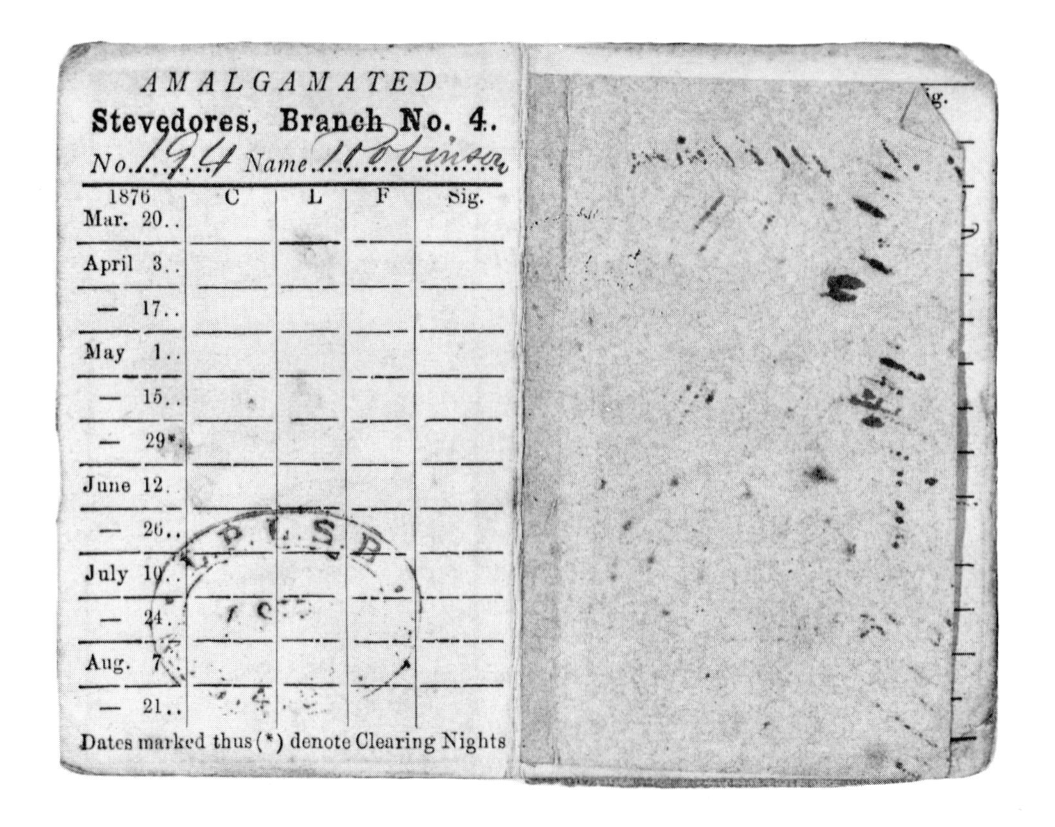

AMALGAMATED
Stevedores, Branch No. 4.
No. 194 Name J. Robinson

1876	C	L	F	Sig.
Mar. 20..				
April 3..				
— 17..				
May 1..				
— 15..				
— 29*.				
June 12.				
— 26..				
July 10..				
— 24..				
Aug. 7..				
— 21..				

Dates marked thus (*) denote Clearing Nights

An early Amalgamated Stevedores' Union card.

too were of Irish Catholic descent. So it is with some courage that Tom McCarthy, the Secretary of the Amalgamated Stevedores actually threw in his lot with Tillett before even asking his executive their views on the situaton. It was no understatement when Tillett commented:

Memories and Reflections (1931), 122

'It was no small triumph to secure from the Unions of Stevedores a proclamation of this description. It is dated four days after the beginning of the strike. That fact alone indicates how strenuous and protracted had been the effort necessary to get the Union Executives to throw in their lot with us.'

Ironically, when the strike first began, the strike was led by a man, not of the Dockers Union but of the Stevedores. So quickly did the Dockers Union come into being, such was the shortage of funds etc that there was no time or money to get a banner struck but a banner they had to have. This was supplied by Tom McCarthy, who took, without leave, the banner of the Stevedores.

No doubt McCarthy knew what chances he was taking. This move obviously worked well, as many of the stevedores still at work were totally confused as to whether or not the Union was involved and this gave heart to the unskilled who before any proclamation was made would not have indeed believed their own eyes when they saw that the Stevedores in fact were taking up their challenge, a fact which must have encouraged many of the faint hearts to join in the dispute.

The strikers and their leaders soon became conscious of the importance of marches and public opinion. Not only did they derive a quick source of revenue to support the strike from the bystanders but their actions, and their very presence, not only encouraged their own supporters but gave publicity to the strike itself. That is, they learnt at a very early stage that public relations and their attitudes whilst on the marches were to play a crucial part in winning over public opinion. They also knew that the memories still remained in the minds of many people of the riots of the 1870s and early 1880s. Anti-Irish feeling was still prevalent in the capital following the Fenian bombings, when 'No Irish need apply' was a common sign outside many factories and works.

They were aware that they had to win public support. Luckily for the strikers, Mr Norwood and the other leaders of the dock companies were not available as they were on vacation or at business meetings outside London when the dock strike broke and the strikers were able, because of their behaviour and manner of demonstrations, which was most orderly, to win over the majority of the press. Even the sectarian ***Justice***, the paper of the Social Democratic Federation, had to remark **(31 August)** in a front page leader.

'No one will accuse *Justice* of having any prejudice in favour of Liberals or the Liberal press. We have never failed for years past to point out that

until the workers acted without the slightest reference to the convenience of Liberals and radicals and without the least regard to the criticisms of their newspapers they will gain nothing. We are in duty bound therefore to say now in regard to the Great Dock Strike that the whole Liberal and radical press of the metropolis has taken the side of the workers. The contrast between their conduct and that of the Tory organs is indeed the best possible evidence of the way in which our opinions have worked their way through the ranks of advanced politicians of all shades of Liberalism. It is not too much to say that the line taken by the *Daily News*, *Star*, the *Pall Mall Gazette*, *Reynolds's* and *Weekly Dispatch* etc. etc. gives hope of a peaceful organisation of our existent society. The Tory party can maintain, as Lord Randolph Churchill's speeches clearly showed its present attitude of reaction on social questions, but for the moment the radicals had the word. It is for Social Democrats to force them to speak out and act vigorously.

South London Press, Saturday, 17 August 1889

Large bodies of police were held in reserve at the various stations, to be ready in the event of rioting, but the demonstrations were orderly and quietly carried out.

Smith and Nash, *The Story of the Dockers' Strike* (1889), 92

After the first couple of days of the strike, the dock workers and their leaders could look back with some pride on what they had achieved. The mass of the dockers were now out on strike with them, up to 20,000 men. They had also been joined by the seamen and firemen, the lightermen and watermen. The watermen and lightermen, though from an ancient guild class of workers, soon accepted the case of the unskilled dockers and were very solid in their support and help. The seamen and firemen, too, were to prove invaluable allies during the dispute.

When the men came out they had nothing to fall back upon. The Tea Operatives' and General Labourers' Union comprised only about 800 members, and its funds at the time of the strike were almost nil. The stevedores were somewhat better off; there were nearly 3,000 members of one or other of the two trade societies, and they had funds at their command amounting to some £3,000. This, however, was but a drop in the bucket; and as the world did not wake up all at once to what was going forward, and no explicit directions were given as to the receipt of contributions, no adequate attempt to feed the strikers and their families was possible in the outset. During the first week or more of the strike the men, for the most part, had to rely on their old allies – patience, and the pawnbroker.

The matter was also further confused by two rival societies being in charge of the funds for the strike.

Urgent necessities made the strike leaders concentrate on the distribution of food. The rowdy element amongst the dockers began to exert

The dockers placed the words 'Socialist Commonwealth' on a contemporary photograph. Would their boat come in?

themselves for distribution of the funds which were now being raised throughout the City of London and by contributions from trade unionists, sympathisers and the radical and left. By Wednesday 21 August bread and cheese was being distributed to the dockers and their families.

(94)

A considerable party amongst the strikers objected to the bread and cheese. The collecting boxes were known to have come back plenteously loaded from the city, and an equitable distribution of the proceeds commended itself to them as the satisfactory course. They accepted the bread and cheese, however, under protest; and on Saturday evening, the 24th, a crowd, some two thousand strong gathered outside Wroot's [coffee tavern] and began to clamour for their money. The leaders were busy elsewhere; the policeman who kept the door yielded to the pressure of the crowd, there was a clatter of broken glass, and a tumultuous inrush of the mob was only checked by the firmness of half-a-dozen men, customers of the house, who planted themselves in the doorway and kept the crowd at bay. But for their firmness the strike might have begun with riot and plunder, and ended in the dock at the Old Bailey. On

Monday the crowd gathered again, and, better counsels prevailing, they accepted the shilling food tickets, which from that time onwards were to be the recognised method of relief. Arrangements were made with tradesmen in the locality for accepting these tickets when properly stamped, and they had strict instructions to give no change.

There was at first no strict inspection of those who actually came in to get relief, as there were no union cards yet issued. People were taken at their face value, tickets were given first-come-first-served, and often after

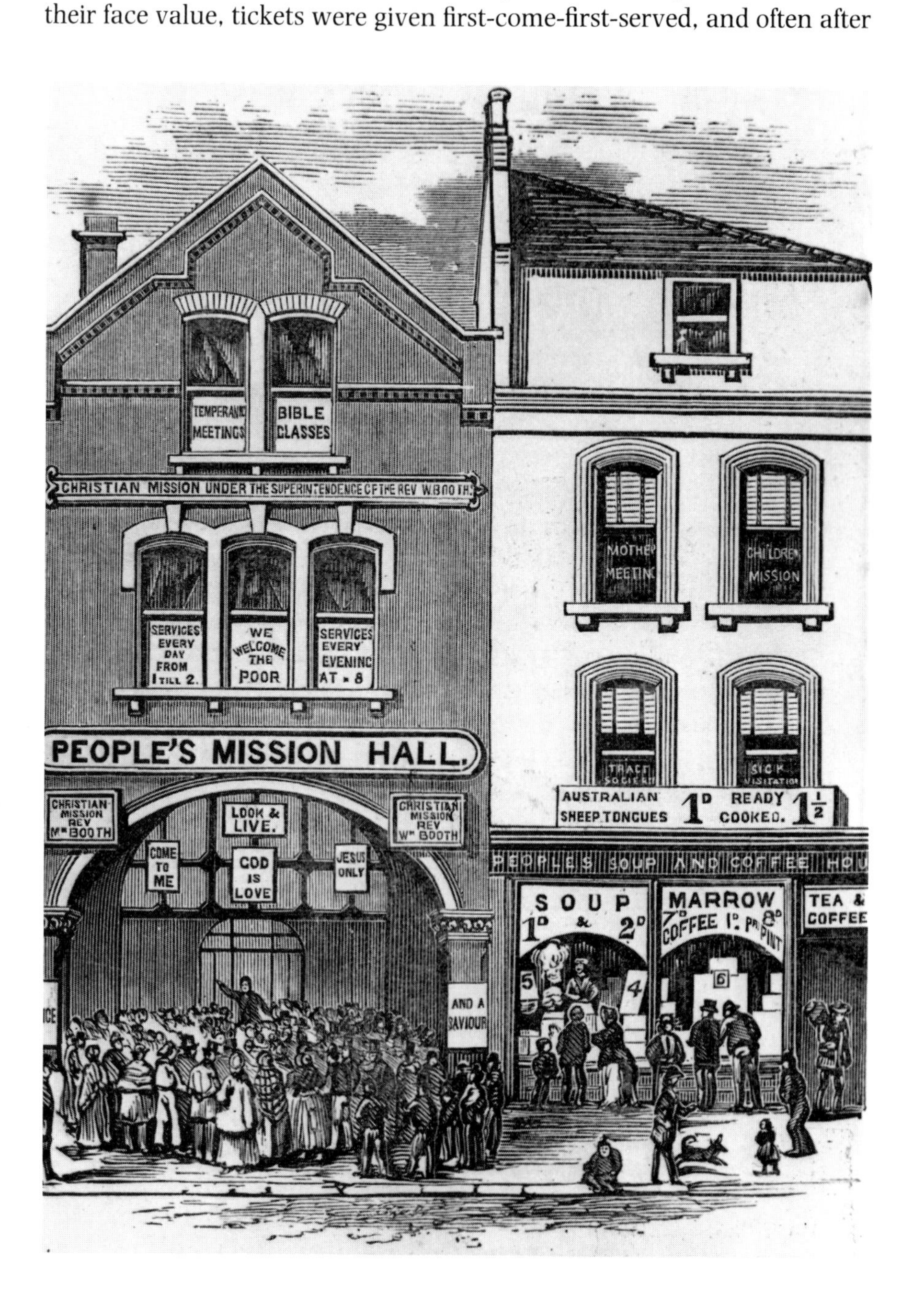

The Salvation Army headquarters, 188 Whitechapel Road, a centre of strike relief, food and funds.

hours of queuing dockers and their families had to leave empty-handed. Wroot's coffee house was obviously too small for the task and accordingly after Wednesday 28 August Wroot's was abandoned, although it remained an important picketing headquarters and pay office throughout the strike.

(94–95)

On the last day at Wroot's, Tom Mann took the relief work in hand ... There was a crowd of nearly 4,000 men waiting outside. Mann pledged them his word that every man should get his ticket if he would take his turn and bide his time; then, planting himself in the doorway, his back jammed against one side of the frame, his foot up against the other, he allowed the men to creep in, one at a time, under his leg. Hour after hour went by, while Tom Mann, stripped to the waist, stuck to his post, forcing the men down as they came up, to him, chatting, persuading, remonstrating, whenever the swaying mass of dockers got out of control, until at last the street was cleared.

Mann was helped in this task by Burns's wife, Tillett's wife and by Eleanor Marx, who had been a close associate of Will Thorne's and who also acted as a clerk to the strike headquarters. (She was also not quite accurately, known as Mrs E. Ward Aveling.) From the first total confusion and disorganisation, relief began to become more professional and as day after day went by and the strikers and their family were being fed, if somewhat meagrely, there were no major outbursts, disputes, riots or fights. The strike leaders knew that the very survival of these people depended on their raising sufficient funds for food. The success of the strike depended upon fund-raising. The great marches that the dockers undertook through the City of London and through the East End and West End brought in hundreds of pounds in donations. These marches were stage-managed, often in fancy dress, although this was of course in tatters of rags as there was no spare clothing at all, and accompanied by the dockers' children bearing the slogans 'Please feed us'. On one occasion a cart was drawn with someone depicting a Neptune and Britannia and they made great use of the idea that they were peaceful and that this was in the spirit of Britannia.

Mann's version [*Memoirs*, 1923, 62] is that it was the *first* day that tickets were distributed, and that he took off his sweat-soaked shirt *after* the crowd had dispersed to find that 'my back had a good deal of skin off,' not surprisingly. It is very important that these demonstrations remained peaceful because public opinion was slowly being won over. The press remarked how peaceful and orderly these demonstrations were.

Curiously enough the balance sheet of the strike fund shows that the general public through collections and by letter donated over £11,700 whereas the Engineers contributed £670, the Compositors £301, the Amalgamated Society of Railway Servants £104 etc. The bulk of the strikers' money was to come from Australia and from the general public.

Tussy (Eleanor Marx), daughter of Karl Marx. She taught Will Thorne to read and write and acted as unpaid secretary to many of the new unions.

Evening News & Post, 17 August 1889

The banners were a striking feature of the procession. First came a white canvas, on which in plain letters was set forth the demands of the men, then the banner of the Stevedores' Protection Association and lastly that of the Original Grand Order of Abstinent Sons of Temperance, bearing the words 'In thee God is our trust' and 'The Greatest of These is Charity'.

As the days passed, more and more people joined the great processions that would march westward to the City. On each side of those there world be cheering amongst the crowd, the wives and sweethearts of the men on strike – amongst them, many of the match-girls who had first lit the flame.

The Wade's Arms

David Wasp and Alan Davis *The Great Dock Strike 1889* (1974), 80

Right from the start the Wade's Arms, a pub in Jeremiah Street, Poplar was the centre of the strike. The landlady, Mrs Hickey, was like a mother to the strikers. She would be there any time of day or night, cooking soups and stews for the weary leaders as they trudged back into the headquarters after long marches and meetings. Often they came back in the middle of the night, tired out and with the prospect of only an hour's sleep before them. But they were always welcome and refreshments were rustled up on the spot. Tom Mann described this remarkable woman's work with great affection: 'The hostess, her son, and her daughters had, indeed, a heavy task. We practically took possession of the house, not for an hour or two, but for all day and every day during the five weeks the strike lasted. But Mrs Hickey treated these fellows as though she had been a mother to the lot. She literally kept a shillelah handy, with which she frequently, in a half-serious way, would threaten any young fellow who was too noisy.' [*Memoirs*, 1923, 66]

The strike committee had designated Harry Orbell to be sent to Tilbury to look after events there. James Toomey, a close friend of Ben Tillett's, and Tom McCarthy were set the task of ensuring that the stevedores kept firm and also liaising with the other trades upon the river. It was also decided, such were the numbers of people seeking assistance, that at least another seven offices should be set up alongside the original headquarters. On average, 4000 food tickets worth a shilling each were issued daily at first – later rising to 25,000, and double that on Saturdays. With the success of the strike, the leaders' problems increased, as more and more men came out in sympathy or just broke off from work – the numbers being fed increased daily by the thousand. Although the strikers gained maximum publicity and funds were pouring in at a level higher than any other dispute in British labour history, still there didn't seem to be enough money to feed the empty bellies which confronted the organisers every day. **(89–91)**

Despite all this publicity the problem of money became acute. As the

The Strike Committee at the Wade's Arms.

number of men on strike rose, so did the problem of feeding them. Many other organisations helped in this. The Rev. the Hon. James Adderley of Christchurch Mission, Poplar, opened a soup kitchen to give free meals; the Salvation Army Food Depot in the East India Dock Road supplied supper, bed and breakfast for $1\frac{1}{2}$d. a night; at Austin House 5000 breakfasts were served daily in sittings of 400. By the end of the month [August], however, many dockers and their families were starving. An article by David Schloss in the *Fortnightly Review* says that:

'Women wandered for hour after hour with weak and weary foosteps in search of help and in some cases fainted away in the streets here help was found: others stood in gaunt-eyed, silent, miserable groups watching the densely-packed mass of men at the doors of the relief office, in utter despair of fighting their way through to the tables at which tickets were being given out. I have known a big-limbed docker, tall enough for a guardsman, to drop down into that seething crowd in the back room at Wroote's, overcome by want of food and by the foul air and be carried out all but inanimate.'

Schloss also lists the articles pawned by a crane-driver with a wife and five children, who would normally be earning 26s a week:

'19 August. Man's Sunday Suit 3s. 6d
20 August. Daughter's New Boots 1s. 3d
Handkerchief and Jacket 1s. 6d
22 August. Man's Tools 2s
24 August. 24 Yards of Calico for children's dress 2s. 6d
26 August, Daughter's Sunday Jacket and Frock 2s. 6d
Daughter's Sunday dress 6s
28 August. Wife's Shawl 6s 6d
and Flannel (for children's underclothes) 1s. 6d
31 August. Man's Flannel shirt 2s
3 September. Man's Trousers and Vest 6s

Then entries cease and nothing remained to pawn but the bedding and this I found in many instances to have been pledged, the people sleeping upon coarse sacking.'

While the men starved, arguments were going on with the Dock Companies, but Mr Norwood was still unwilling to grant the men 6d an hour. By now the strike had been going on for a fortnight. Meal tickets were to be issued at the rate of 25,000 a day. Funds were running low.

Burne Street Shelter. The Salvation Army supplied these coffin beds for the thousands of East End homeless.

The Times
Wednesday, 21
August 1889

Yesterday the strike extended to all the docks. Men out of almost every branch of work came out and joined the movement on behalf of the labourers, early in the morning and then again formed in procession in front of the West India Dock and with banners of various descriptions and brass bands marched around the docks and wharfs and through a number of streets. The procession was between one and two miles in length. The men walking seven deep. There was no disorder ....

In the evening an open air mass meeting was held in the neighbourhood of the docks at which Mr John Burns LCC presided. In addressing the meeting he said the labourers had already achieved a victory, for they had brought out men to support them from almost every department. The Masters had said that if they conceded an extra penny per hour, asked by the labourers, it would increase their expenses by about £100,000 a year and that if they were to meet these demands, that they would have to so far increase their dock charges, as to run the risk of sending freights somewhere else. His answer was to that, was that the old dock companies received a profit of £218,000 a year and if they paid out another £100,000 a year in wages, they would still have a profit of £118,000 to share, which he thought was a very good sum. The men had been told that by their strike they might drive some of the freight to Antwerp. He did not fear that, for it did not pay ship owners first to ship to Antwerp and then to reship here the produce and imports which must come here (jeers). As to driving the trade from London to other British ports there were but four of any consequence, which might rival them, Liverpool, Glasgow, Grimsby and Hull, but from each of these places they had received telegrams stating that the men so much approved of the London strike that if there was any danger of the London men suffering freights coming there, they should strike for such higher wages, as would make an equivalent, so that one port would be no cheaper than any other. He thought that was another victory. Mr Thomas Mann of the Amalgamated Engineers also addressed the meeting and encouraged the men to pursue the course they had adopted, for their strike was based on simple justice. Mr B. Tillett who acted as Secretary to the men urged them to hold together because he was sure that before long they would secure the object they had in view. Mr Toomey of the Stevedores' Society then gave a report on the day's picketing. The delegates from Millwall and Victoria Docks and also from the Albert Docks have returned with the news that they had got every man out. The delegate from the Tilbury docks had also just arrived with the news that they had brought out a 1000 men from Tilbury Docks and some of them were going to march to London to join in the Movement. The Companies were trying to get coolie labour but the coolies refused to work under the circumstances. The statement was received with loud cheers by the men. The proceedings shortly afterwards ended. Several vessels were detained in the docks, being made unable to load for coal and if some arrangement is not soon arrived at the situation will it appears become serious'.

The Times, Thursday, 22 August 1889

THE DOCK LABOURERS' STRIKE

The strike at the various docks yesterday assumed still larger proportions and the struggle is kept up night and day by relays of men watching the gates, lest strangers should be got in to do their work. The masters have placarded the whole district with posters offering permanent employment to a thousand men at 20 shillings a week, and it is stated on the part of the dock companies that, although the strike has so much extended, yet by the employment of other men the serious interference with business at the docks which was felt at the outset had been much lessened. In the course of the morning, a number of meetings were held by the men on strike.

At midday a procession was formed to perambulate the City. The procession, in which it was computed more than 20,000 men took part, got into line near the Custom House Docks, and accompanied by four brass bands and a large number of banners and flags, marched through Aldgate to the City, cheering and being cheered along the route. When they got to the companies' Dock House in Leadenhall Street, the men roared and growled violently. In the procession were various groups in wagons illustrating the work many of the men had to do. After a very long march the procession turned off down Fenchurch Street back along Aldgate, down the Commercial Road to the West India Docks, where late in the afternoon a great mass meeting was held, and varied accounts were given of the progress of the strike and the work done during the day. Mr Burns, L.C.C., again presided, and said that if Tuesday was an important day that was much more so, for they had had large meetings everywhere, and by desperate efforts they had got larger additions to their numbers than on any previous day. They had made nearly a clean sweep of the docks, and there were very few blacklegs left in now. He was glad to tell them that they were receiving sympathy on every hand, because their cause was just. The Amalgamated Society of Engineers had sent them £25 towards their strike fund; and the Amalgamated Society of Painters had sent them £50. Besides that, the merchants and people along the route the procession took had helped them by their money, which showed that public feeling was strong in their favour. There was, however, one point he wished to allude to once for all, and that was that today they had had imported into that district no less than 2,000 extra police. The authorities had drafted some of his old friends of the A, E, B, K, and L Divisions. Their services, however, had not been wanted yet. He was quite sure the thousands of men there assembled did not intend to give the police any trouble, and so far as he was concerned it should be a regular holiday and beanfeast for them. (Cheers.) Mr B. Tillett, the organizing secretary of the Labourers' Union, who was received with cheers, explained the result of the day's work in support of the strike. A delegate had been sent to Tilbury to rally the men there, and he himself and another delegate went to the Surrey Commercial Docks where, after a very earnest appeal, they succeeded in bringing out no less than 3,500

The children learning early what life was really about, yet the Victorians still referred to these people as loafers.

men from those docks alone. (Cheers.) At the Millwall Dock they held two meetings, and were successful with the men there also. (Cheers.) By the magnificent procession, two miles long, of that day, he thought they had shown the dock directors and companies what the working men could do when they rose in their might with the conviction of a just cause. The directors were endeavouring to make the people believe that what the labourers were now doing would drive the trade from the Port of London; but they need not fear that result. The directors, in their own interests, would give in rather than run that risk. . . .

The companies, however, have taken up a firm attitude, and believe that the strike will not be of long duration.

But by August 24 the *East London Advertiser* was able to announce that between 20,000 and 30,000 men were now on strike. The paper also commented: 'that the logic and laws of political economy breakdown when confronted with the extremeties of circumstances'. The paper went on:

. . . not only are these men who came out before the world starving but these dependent upon them who hide away in cellar and attics would be

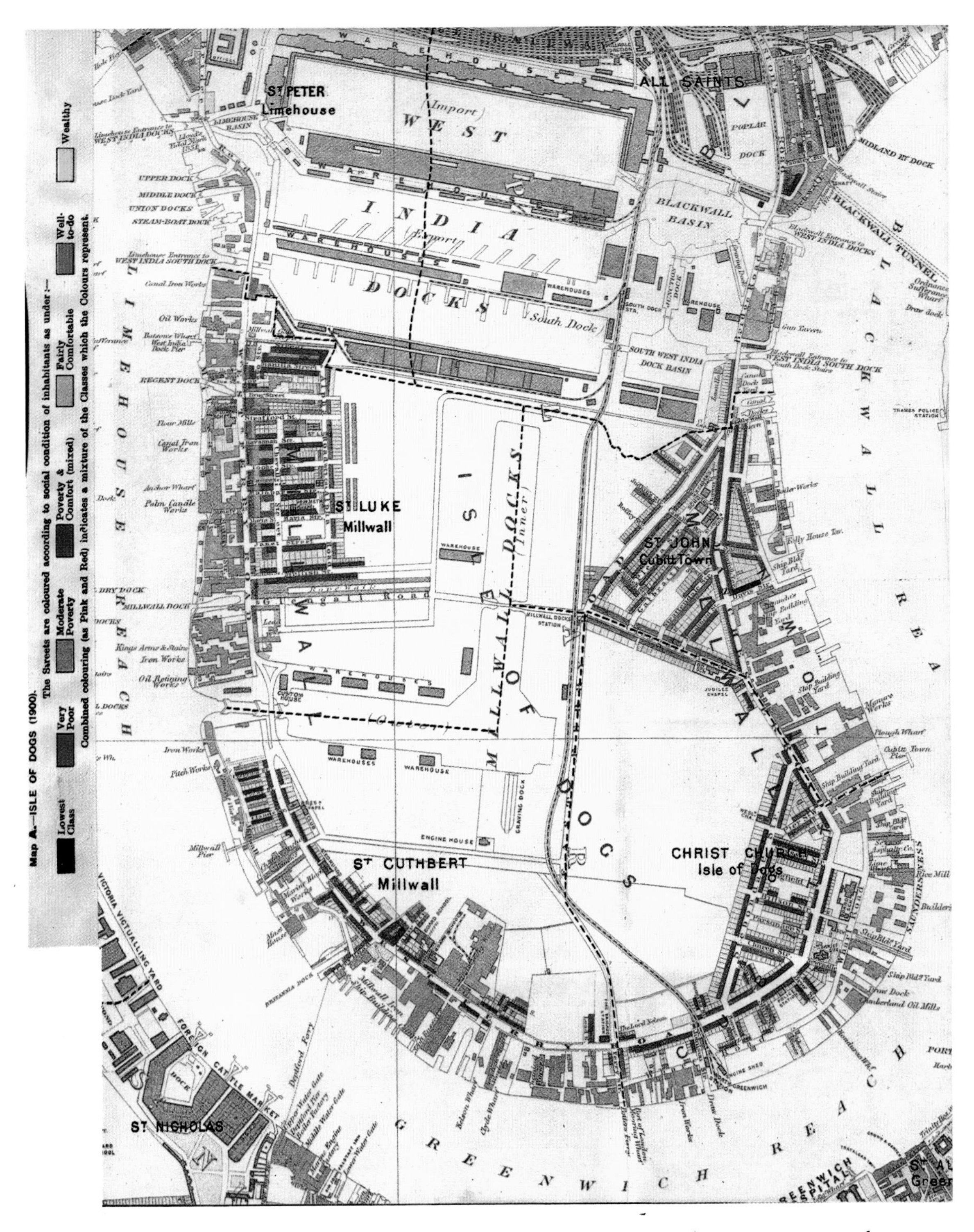

(Above and overleaf) *Booth's Poverty Survey maps first published in 1890. It's important to note the mixture of social classes. These maps once and for all destroyed the myth that the middle and wealthy classes were unaware of the plight of the poor.*

Map H.—INNER EAST LONDON (1900).

The Streets are coloured according to social condition of inhabitants as under:—

Lowest Class | Very Poor | Moderate Poverty | Poverty & Comfort (mixed) | Fairly Comfortable | Well-to-do | Wealthy

Combined colouring (as Pink and Red) indicates a mixture of the Classes which the Colours represent.

William Booth's answer to the deprivation and misery amongst the poor in East London was mass emigration. In the 1880s and 1890s more than a million people chose to leave Britain's shores. After 1889 Australia was considered to be the place for labour men and women to emigrate to.

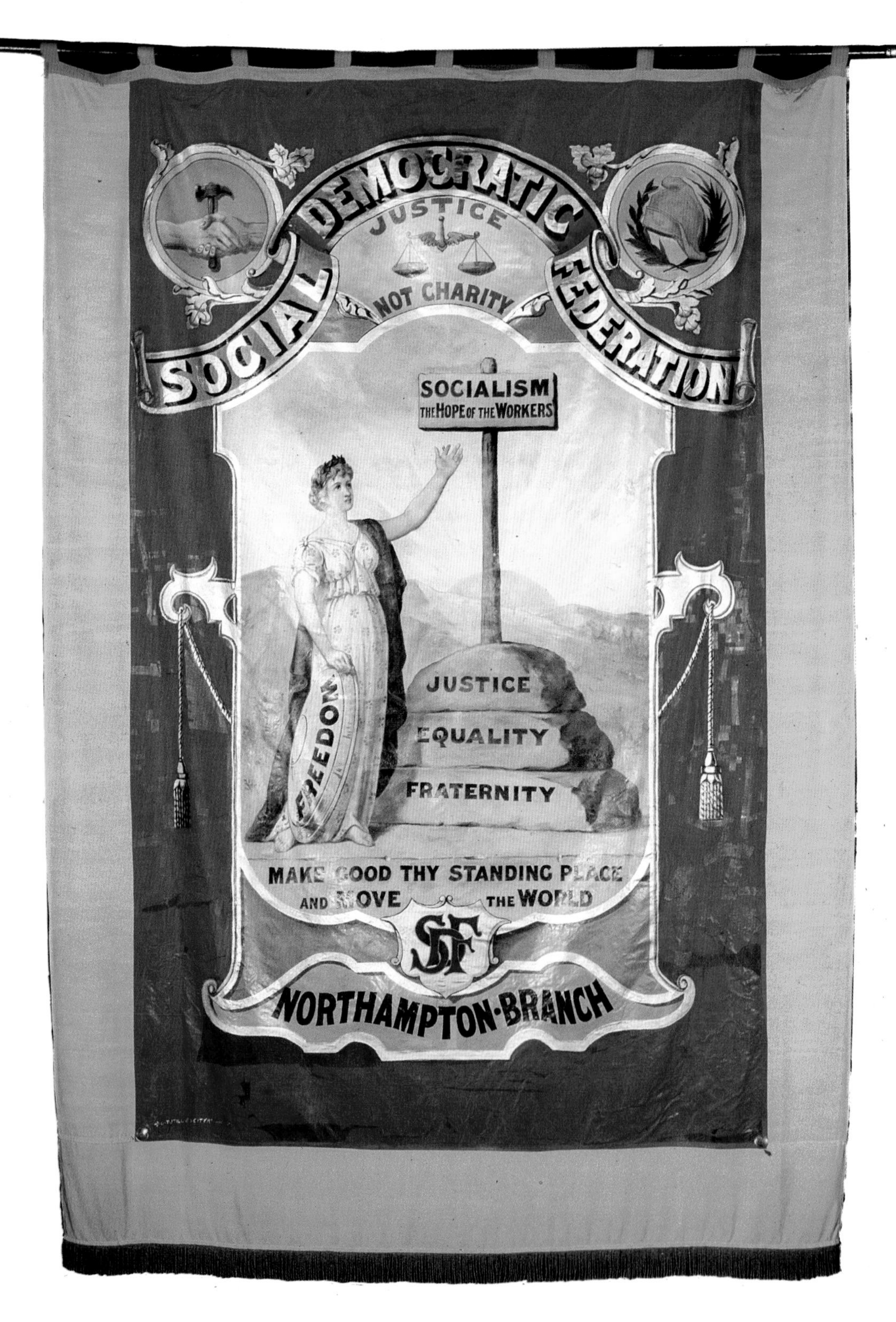

Banner of Hyndman's Social Democratic Federation – one of the many Socialist banners banned by the dockers from their demonstrations.

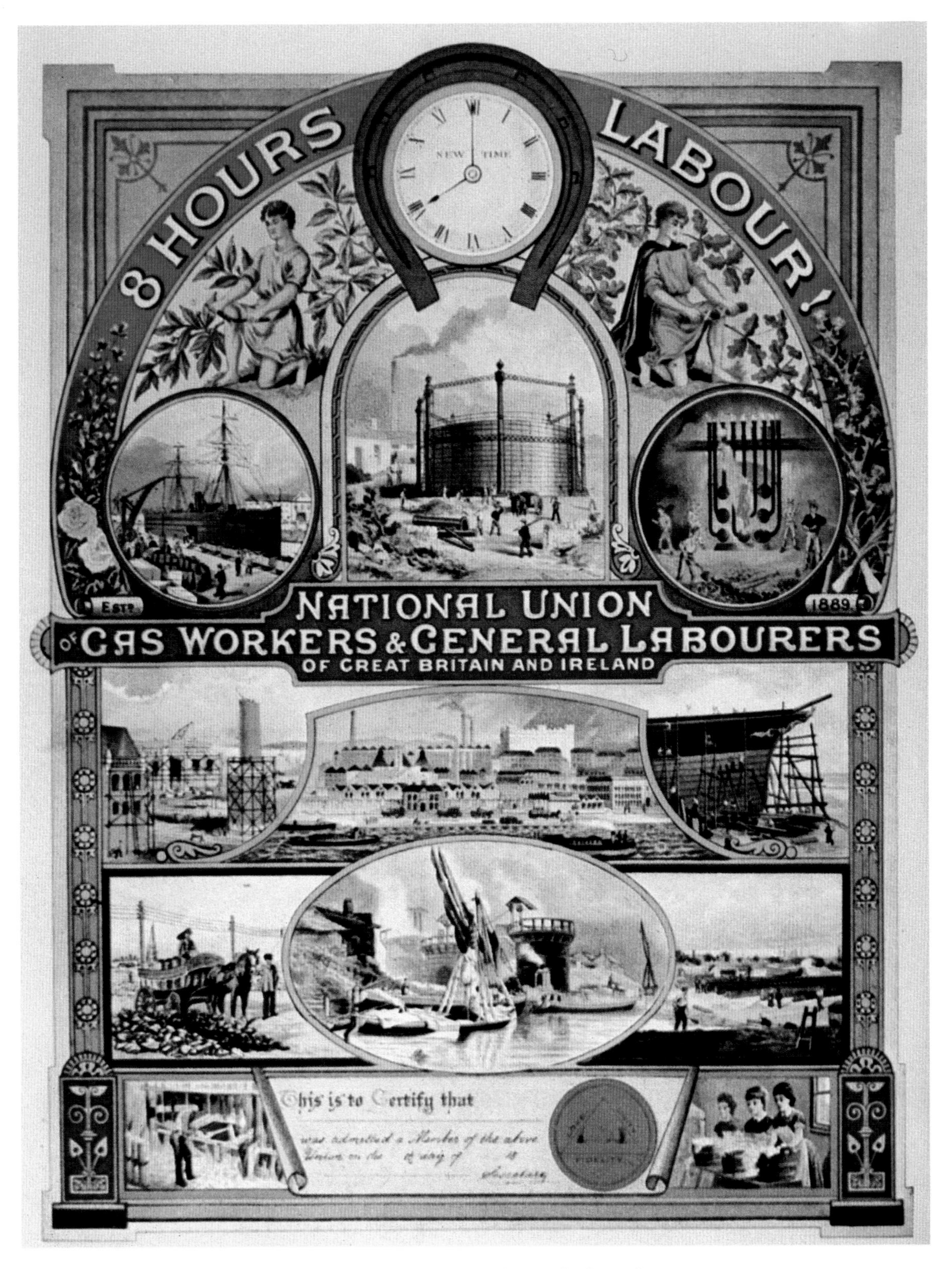

Emblem of the gas workers commemorating the winning of the eight-hour day, 1889.

Portrait of Ben Tillett taken from the first banner of the Dockers' Union commemorating the 1889 Strike.

An East End family enjoying the fresh air of the Kent hop fields at the time of the Great Strike. 'Hopping' gave the East-Ender a working holiday away from the grime of inner city life.

The Amalgamated Society of Watermen & Lightermen. The Greenwich branch banner pays tribute to Cardinal Manning for the support he gave the dockers during the 1889 Strike.

The banner of The Workers' Union – formed in 1890 by Tom Mann following the Dock Strike. It merged with the T&G in 1929.

'Labour Clears The Way' poster. The Great Dock Strike was instrumental in launching the new union movement without which Keir Hardie could not have formed the LRC (Labour Party) in 1900.

glad of the food daily thrown to the kennels of noblemen. Looking on that seething mass in which were so many a powerful frame, strong arms, broad chests and muscular legs it was impossible not to admire the self control of those who could in ten minutes have sacked every shop within a mile and satisfied the craving of nature. Contrast this crowd with the French mob which cried hoarse with passion 'Give us bread'. Not so the English docker, independent still in his direst straits 'Give me work' he says and in this case a rider is added and 'pay me fairly'. That is the grit of the whole matter, a fair wage.

The article however did complain of Social Democrats, Anarchists, Revolutionaries, Republicans and others who were trying to use the strike for their own aims and the article noted that:

The shipping company as well as the dock companies state that the efforts to produce labour to take the place of those who are on strike are considerably retarded by the organised intimidation to which the new hands are subjected. The dock companies have advertised for about a 1000 steady, responsible and able-bodied men for permanent employment, hours between 8.00am to 4.00pm, wages 20 shillings a week. Numerous applications have been received in response to this advertisement at the office of the Committee.

One of the first things that the dock company director did was to contact Mr William Collison, who described himself as the Apostle of Free Labour.

Collison was born in June 1865, the son of a policeman. Collison notes in his autobiography that his father served his country wearing the unpopular uniform for twenty-eight years in the H or Whitechapel division of the Metropolitan Police. It is obvious from Collison's recollections that his childhood was a very unhappy one. He had hardly any friends, in view of the nature of his father's job, a scar which he carried throughout his life. He obviously equated lawbreakers and malcontents and others with anybody that was in any way connected with organized labour. Financially supported by Randolph Churchill and other eminent Tories, Collison had built up an organisation of scabs, who were used prior to the 1889 dispute to break up strikes whenever and however they could.

Collison does not go into much detail in his book, about his role in the 1889 Dock Strike because, as far as scabs, blacklegs and others were concerned, it was to be an unmitigated disaster. In a backhanded compliment Collison concedes:

'Hence, the New Unions acquired a disastrous sway over the trade of the River Thames ...' (92)

The Apostle of Free Labour (1913)

In their autobiographies both Tillett and Thorne are cool about John

Strong faces – traditional East End defiance, which would not accept defeat.

Burns. This is due not to Burn's actions but to the fact that at the time of writing Burns had become a Liberal (in fact, a Liberal Cabinet Minister) and sectarianism actually led them to play down Burns's role.

Ben Tillett, *Memories and Reflections* (1931), 115

John Burns was another salient figure at that time. He was enamoured of Revolutionary Socialism, a member of the Amalgamated Society of Engineers and a forceful open-air speaker. He, too, dismissed with flippancy the possibility of forming a Docker's Union. He had a cheerful grin at our efforts. He volunteered his service, however, when the Strike was well under way. He joined our procession at the lower end of Commercial Road, when we marshalled our troops to march on Tower Hill, while I visited the Dock House in Leadenhall Street at a special request from the dock directors, thrown into panic by the swift development of events. In his blue reefer suit and white straw hat, familiar to the cartoonist, John Burns lent us his stentorian voice and picturesque personality. . . .

John Burns did a great deal for the workers, and the workers did much for John, raising him to a lofty pinnacle and making him almost a living statue of himself in a perpetually heroic pose.

Will Thorne, *My Life's Battles* (1925), 85–86

John Burns had not yet entered the fight. He did not come until the strike was complete.

William Collison, *The Apostle of Free Labour* (1913), 90–91

From a Socialist point of view [Burn's] speech is perfect. And the Socialists, from their point of view, were justified in thinking the words might be transformed into deeds.

I remember hearing the late Tom McCarthy say that in recent history there were two men who had an opportunity of making a revolution and did not avail themselves of it. The one was General Boulanger – who, had he ridden on his black horse after the celebrated Review, to the Elysée, would have been dictator of France. The other was John Burns – the only Socialist in England who ever had a mob of forty thousand men marching through the richest city in the world at his command, and who refused to let them loose against law and order.

For this neglected opportunity of bringing about a revolution the Socialists have never forgiven John Burns; but in earning their opprobrium he also earned the thanks of all decent citizens.

Whatever mistakes Burns might have made in his later life, real or imaginary, the fact remained he was a most charismatic and well known figure and was essential to the success of the Dock Strike.

Spontaneous strikes now began to occur along and beyond the waterfront. In one aspect this was good for the dispute in terms of putting pressure on all employers engaged in the riverside trades, but it also meant that more relief funds had to be found to support the extra men and women now in dispute, and the strikers had their first major victory in turning away blackleg labour:

The Times, Friday 23 August 1889, 6

One of the first exciting incidents which took place yesterday morning was the fact of the dock companies securing men from Liverpool. The information was sent on to the strike committee-rooms, and pickets were soon on the alert to ascertain where the men were. Having found 40 at the East India Docks, a great effort was made to induce the men to come out and not to remain in to injure the cause. The men said they had been engaged for a fortnight certain at 5s. per day; but they were told they were wanted for railway metal work, and they were not informed that there was any strike on. There were more men, they said, to be sent on from Liverpool and the district. Eventually they all came out, and six were at once taken to Euston and sent back to try to stop other men from coming to London.

H. H. Champion, *The Great Dock Strike in London, August 1889* (1890), 17

As soon as it became obvious that the Strike was not merely a local dispute, but would be carried on with courage and energy and on a very large scale, numberless trades threw in their lot with the Strikers, abandoned their work, and joined the processions. Men who had been working for years with every appearance of being resigned to their lot suddenly discovered that they too had grievances, and must have an increase of wages or reduction of hours. So rapidly did the discontent spread that the Committee were seriously hampered by the applications to them for advice, encouragement, and assistance by workmen whose precipitate action hindered rather than helped the Dockers' cause. Each day one saw in the processions larger numbers of rudely-improvised banners, setting forth that their bearers belonged to this trade or the other, and had struck work until their demands were conceded. In the general rush and hurry of the movement, it was impossible to ascertain the rights and wrongs of these innumerable disputes; but it is certain that a very large number of East London workmen, who took occasion by the hand and demanded a higher wage, obtained it after stopping work for a few hours, as an indirect result of the Dock Labourers' action.

The Great March

The Times, Saturday, 24 August 1889, 10

Mr BENJAMIN TILLETT, the secretary of the Dock Labourers' Union, presided, and, addressing those within sound of his own voice, said that the procession that morning had been truly a magnificent one, and though they took 50,000 to the City yesterday, they had taken nearly 80,000 that day. Many men who had now come out and who had marched with them had done so simply in the interest of their fellow-men. That fact showed how much working men feel for each other, when they were put to the test. In this movement, one of the largest they had ever seen, they had had no assistance whatever from the political representatives of the people. Their speakers had been men from among themselves. It had been said that those got most help who helped themselves, and if the labouring men could by their own combination show such power as they had done in this movement, they ought to use it and get their own representatives in the House of Commons.

The first split appeared in the employers' ranks as early as 24 August, when John Burns was approached by representatives of certain wharves who wanted to discuss terms of settlement.

South London Press Saturday, 24 August 1889

Three gentlemen came up to Mr Burns and asked permission to speak to him. They explained that they were owners of some of the wharfs outside, of which he had been speaking in the morning, and they asked him if he would see a deputation of wharfingers who had proceeded to the London and St Katharine's offices in Leadenhall Street in order to discuss the situation with certain of the directors.

It was becoming increasingly clear, as far as the media and employers were concerned, that John Burns was 'the man,' and Tillett, who saw him merely as a born showman, paid him the compliment that he was advertising the strike as no one else could. However, as the strike progressed, Burns began to emerge as the organising brain of the dispute.

The coal heavers' float, part of a demonstration through the City of London.

Asleep on the hay boats, ready for the next day's labour.

Tillett – *Memories and Reflections* (1931), 136

[John Burns's] position in the Strike was something of an anomaly. He was not directly connected with our dockers' organisation. He was an engineer. But he had become, through years of agitation and leadership of the unemployed workpeople, a popular, almost a heroic figure. His appearance in the dock at the Old Bailey three years before, to share responsibility for the events of 'Bloody Sunday' with the aristocratic and saturnine Cunninghame Graham, made him the idol of the multitude. He had a voice like a megaphone: undoubtedly a descendant of the Boanerges! He used his great voice to good effect in the early days of the strike, when he marched with other demonstrators round the Docks and, standing on the backs of those who accompanied him, peered over the walls or the gates which barred his entry to the Company's premises, denounced the men who remained at work, and summoned them to join the strike, in a voice of thunder. He had the instincts and the qualities of a born showman, and did wonderful things on Tower Hill and other meeting places. He touched the imagination and imported humour and good temper into the Press Conferences which took place every day, feeding the hungry pressmen with good copy. Burns advertised our Strike as nobody else could have done.

The dock companies now made the accusation that they could obtain men to break the strike but intimidation was frightening away the free labour. Picketing became increasingly important and various means were being employed to detect and alert the strikers to any breach in the wall that they had thrown round the docks.

INTIMIDATION BY PICKETS

The People Sunday, 25 August 1889

On Friday night the strike among the dock labourers had further increased and much anxiety was felt in various quarters. Pickets were on duty in the neighbourhood, and the subjoined placard was posted in every direction and containing the following caution – 'Notice to all men working in holds and on the quays. As men we beg you to clear out at once, or we must inform you that the consequences must be extremely serious – ALFRED CREMER.' As information has been obtained from the scouts at an early hour that some men were sleeping in the docks, and that security men had been brought from Liverpool and had already begun work, some of the pickets succeeded in getting into the docks and communicating with the men. After a good deal of persuasion the pickets brought them out.

The Strike Spreads

Strikes in support of the dock labourers were breaking out daily and sympathisers from all sections of labour took part in the marches and rallies. The Gas Workers were now considering an all-out strike in support of the men. Tillett, at one of the rallies, stated that the dock labourer intended to take his position amongst the ranks of working men, a seemingly odd statement until one considers the low esteem in which casual dock labourers were held. Not just amongst skilled labour but with general workers themselves, they had not enjoyed the status of being referred to as 'working men'.

Evening News & Post, Monday, 26 August 1889

GIRLS JOIN STRIKE

Messrs Frost's girls (ropemakers) struck work this morning. Messrs Westwood and Bailey's carmen also joined the movement. At one-o'clock the employees of Messrs Peek, Frean, and Co, the biscuit makers, also struck.

GAS WORKERS TURN OUT

Early this morning the coal workers in the employ of the South Metropolitan Gas Company at their works, Thames Street, Greenwich came out on strike. A large body of police were sent for at Blackheath Road Police station but there was no disturbance.

TINPLATE WORKERS JOIN

At Bermondsey today the employees at Lloyd's tin plate works, Mill Street, came out on strike to the number of 150.

The Times, Monday, 26 August 1889

Yesterday afternoon the dock labourers and others on strike held a demonstration in Hyde Park. A procession was formed at the West India Dock, and it reached Hyde Park Corner at a quarter past 2 o'clock. Many thousands of men took part in it, and it occupied fully an hour in passing a given point. As the different bodies marched up, the spectacle which was presented was a remarkable one, and the gathering of people was enormous. At the head of the procession a banner was carried bearing the words 'Unity and Victory,' and several others stated that the par-

Other workers join the Strike.

TO PRINTERS' LABOURERS

AND OTHER WORKERS IN THE PRINTING TRADE

We, the Printers' Labourers, are on strike for a wage of **20s. per Week** and 6d. per hour overtime. We appeal to the Machine Minders and other workers to aid us in obtaining our just demands.

Our present wages vary from **12s. to 14s. per week,** and many among us have wives and families to sustain. We work on an average fifty-four hours a week, and

SEVENTY-FIVE HOURS TO EARN £1.

How, and under what conditions do we work? In heated cellars where gaslight replaces daylight; amidst perpetual din; breathing a stifling, filthy atmosphere. We have to keep eye and hand ever on the alert to **KEEP STROKE** with the machines we tend.

Our kind, respectable Christian employers would not put their pet cats and dogs in the styes where they condemn us to pass our best working years. Above are the demands for the toil which destroys our health.

We appeal to all fellow labourers to join us. Do not listen to the specious talk of interested foremen and employers who "**promise to favourably consider your demands.**" They want time to work off urgent orders. If you on strike are selfish enough to go in because a few employers grant concessions, you help to ruin the cause. Will you purchase your gain at the expense of our defeat? Show the same spirit as our comrades in other industries are displaying.

STRIKE!!

STRIKE ALL TOGETHER!!

Stand Together and Win

Printers' Strike Committee,

RED STAR COFFEE HOUSE, CLERKENWELL GREEN.

GEORGE EVANS, *Sec.*
GEORGE WALDEN, *Treas.*

ticular branch or trade it represented had got what was demanded, but were 'out' on principle in support of the other men. The crowds were very orderly, and the men marched steadily into the park to the music of the different bands. There were four platforms, and it was computed that nearly 100,000 persons were present. A vast audience assembled round platform No. 1, on which Mr John Burns stood, but at this, as well as at the other meetings, a large portion of those who stood around the platforms must have been quite unable to hear the speeches. At No. 1 platform Mr. McCARTHY, the secretary of the Amalgamated Stevedores, presided, and in opening the proceedings said the pinch of poverty had driven the members of an hitherto despised class to Hyde Park to show the country that they had sense and power, and intended now to take their grievances into their own hands. During the past few days, in spite of many incentives to disorder, thousands of men had been kept in check, and that proved that they possessed enough brains and intelligence to rule themselves. The word must therefore go forth from that meeting that they would be no longer governed by men who were not of themselves. They earned the bread they ate, and they would have the control of the profit they earned too. The horrors of a dock labourer's life had been exposed by the Sweating Commission, evidence given before whom had showed that these men were in a worse position than the bushmen of Australia, in spite of all the flaunted riches and mock religion of Great Britain. They did not desire to utter threats, for they were conscious of their own power, but he might state that the Gas Workers' Union were considering that day the important question whether they would give notice to the various gas companies to stand out, and put London into darkness unless the demands of the dock labourers were granted. (Loud cheers.) They had been told that if the men persisted in the strike the ships that would, under ordinary circumstances, come to London would be sent elsewhere. That was very unlikely, for through the agency of the organisation known as the Sailors' and Firemen's Union every port in the kingdom should be blocked. (Cheers.) Their watchwords were 'Federation' and 'Unity', and the resolution they would propose that day

A Hyde Park rally – one of many during the strike.

The original banner of the Tea Operatives & General Labourers Association.

was, 'That this mass meeting pledges itself to support to the uttermost the men on strike at the whole of the docks and wharves of the port of London, and calls upon all true friends to aid the labourer in obtaining his just rights.' (Cheers.)

Mr BENJAMIN TILLETT said they were determined to resist until it was acknowledged that the dock men had acted on a right principle. During the week they had had a determined fight with the authorities, and the courage which had been displayed during that time was the courage of starved and hungry men who had fought against the greatest trials which could befall human beings. Those hungry men had stuck together as they should do, and he was proud of them. They wanted enough to live on, and were determined, with the assistance of those who were backing them up, to fight to the bitter end, with the obstinacy of bulldogs. The dock companies were resting content with the idea that the poor docker was cornered, and that no one would give him assistance. The lie had been given to that, for from all quarters came cheering sympathy which encouraged them to continue until victory was won. The shipowners were taking their side, and recognized the fact that by this strike the groundwork had been laid for a federation of labour. Their power would be felt through the length and breadth of the land, and if they had done nothing else they had laid the foundation of something which would benefit their children. Their victory would be a victory of bread and butter. (Cheers.)

Mr. JOHN BURNS, who was loudly cheered, claimed that the meeting was one of sympathizers from all parts of London, who were ready to sacrifice a week's pay if necessary to aid the campaign the dockers had undertaken. The rights of the people must be won in the port of London by hard, determined action. It was 12 days since that a few degraded dock labourers met together and decided to resuscitate the trade union which capitalism had almost crushed out a few months before. They met and decided that fivepence an hour was not enough for a man and his wife and children, and as a result the most remarkable labour movement of modern times had followed. (Cheers.) These men were the embodiment of weakness, and everything poor and insignificant. They were the despair of the social reformer, and the ghost of the milk and water politician, and had been regarded by political economists and by all men as the embodiment of the worst specimens of the degraded labourer of all countries. In 12 days, however, the dock labourer had shown the country that he intended to take his position amongst the ranks of working men.

Will Thorne, *My Life's Battles* (1925), 86–87

Several thousands of the members of my union were thrown out of employment by the strike. None of them was entitled to lock-out pay as the union had not been in existence six months, and one of the rules of the union was: 'No member is eligible for benefit until he has paid twenty-seven weekly contributions.' There was only one union, the Stevedores, that did pay strike pay, but their funds were soon exhausted. The strike in the docks had obviously caused hardship to some workers who were locked out, or thrown out of employment by their employers. Many of them, like the gas workers, had no benefits whatsoever to fall back on, and even the stevedores' funds were soon used up.

Nevertheless, whatever hardship was incurred by the men and women either directly or indirectly involved in the strike, their sympathy never waned.

The strike committee was now being embarrassed by the numbers of sympathetic strikes and had to issue a manifesto asking workers to contact the strike committee before any more disputes took place.

FISH PORTERS WANT TO JOIN

Evening News & Post, Monday, 26 August 1889

It is stated that the fish porters at Billingsgate have been in communication with the leaders of the agitation, with the object of ascertaining whether it is thought advisable that they should come out on strike, to support the demands of the dock labourers. They have received a reply that they had better await instructions from the strike committee before taking any action.

The Times, Tuesday, 27 August 1889, 6

After addressing the meeting on Tower Hill, Mr. Tillett and Mr. Burns proceeded to other rallying points, where men were drawn up in procession, and were making their way to the great rendezvous – the front of the West India Docks. Mr. Burns and the other leaders then took their place at the head of the great procession, which again started on its way. The route this time was varied. Instead of going to the City, the procession marched through Burdett Road and Globe Road to Bow, and then to Victoria Park. The streets were lined with spectators, and the men were heartily cheered. The procession was larger and more imposing than before, for there were many additions to the illustrated displays of the hard work performed at the docks. Cheers were raised whenever fresh bodies of strikers, who had just turned out, came up, or when information was brought that 'another big lot had come out'. In Mile-end, Peek, Frean, and Co.'s men joined, and the men from McDougall's Chemical Works came up. Nearly 400 men turned out from Johnson Brothers, Carmen and Contractors. Great excitement ran along the line when the word was passed that 7,000 men were coming out of the Thames Ironworks at Blackwall. Further efforts were made to get the men out of all the large carrying companies, and strong appeals were made to Pickford's men, and to Carter, Paterson, and Co.'s men, as well as the labourers of the various railway companies. In some instances some expressed themselves willing, and came out.

A great scene took place last night. The Dundee Shipping Company had brought 70 men from Dundee and had landed them at Dundee Dock. The pickets in the afternoon got in and prevailed on 66 to come out. These men afterwards went to one of the chief committee rooms, expecting to get strike pay or be sent home. The committee refused to send them back or allow them anything. The men pleaded very hard, saying that they had been got to come by being told that they were simply wanted to unload the company's own boats. Nothing was said about terms. They thought it very hard that, after they had come out, they should be left without anything. Their case was considered in committee, when it was strongly urged that they must have known that there was a strike on, and that they had no business to come. The committee were firm in their determination. Some of the men not on the committee expressed themselves in strong terms, and said they deserved to be made to walk back, or they could go to Poplar Workhouse. Late last night the men were in the streets. The following important manifesto by the Strike Committee was issued at a late hour last night:—

'MANIFESTO OF UNITED DOCK LABOURERS' STRIKE COMMITTEE.

August 26th.

'FELLOW-COUNTRYMEN, – We, the undersigned, who have resolved to unite our efforts to bring the dock labourers' strike to a successful issue, strongly deprecate the rash action taken by unorganized workmen, not directly connected with the dock work, of coming out on strike without reflecting that by so doing they are increasing the strain upon the strike committee's resources and lessening the chances of success for the dock labourers.

'We insist that any body of men who do this without consulting the committee are hindering the movement and playing into the hands of the enemies of the dock labourers.

'We are appealing to the public for funds, which are being generously subscribed, but not a penny will be paid to men engaged in any trade or occupation who come out on strike without our authority.

'The success of the dock labourers is assured, owing to their splendid determination, their perfect orderliness, the assistance of the Trades

A strike poster appealing for relief funds.

DOCK LABOURERS'

STRIKE!

RELIEF FUND.

Fellow-workmen—An earnest appeal is made to you to help your fellow-workmen, the half-starved, under-paid Dockers, in their great struggle. The men **MUST** win, or so much the worse for all of us. It will be our fault if they do not. Their cause is the most righteous and reasonable in modern times.

GIVE LIBERALLY & SECURE THE VICTORY!

Public Relief Fund Sheets supplied to duly authorised Collectors. All Clubs and Institutions are asked to co-operate. Shops and Factories should appoint their own Collectors.

SUBSCRIPTIONS RECEIVED at the OFFICE OF COMMITTEE, 23, RUTLAND STREET, every Evening at 7.30; 4 on Saturday.

COMMITTEE

John Potter, (Leicester School Board), **Harry Woolley,** (New Co-op. Shoe Works), **Hipwell,** (Vine St. Radical Club), **C. O'Sullivan,** (Irish Nationl Club), **Messrs. L. Brown, Staughton, Warner, Gorrie, Barclay, Richards, &c.**

Unions, and a sympathetic public; but this opportunity may be thrown away by want of discipline and foresight on the part of those whose zeal outruns their discretion.

'Organization must precede strikes or failure is certain.'

The manifesto is signed by Henry Phillips, Alderman, James Toomey, Chairman, and representatives of stevedores', sailors' and firemens', painters' and tea operatives' societies.

Meanwhile, though smaller in comparison, the south-side men were organising demonstrations and eliciting support, using the same tactics as the north-side men in keeping perfect order in their ranks.

AFFAIRS IN SOUTH LONDON

Evening News & Post, Monday, 26 August 1889

A procession consisting of about 1,000 persons with bands and banners has been perambulating New Cross today. Everything passed off very orderly.

At Bermondsey today great efforts are being made to induce the employees of several large firms notably Messrs Peek, Frean, and Co's, the biscuit makers, to come out on strike. At this firm a number of boys left work yesterday, but the majority of the hands remain true to their masters. It is expected however, that in the end they will join the ranks of the strikers. The neighbourhood is in rather an excited state today owing to the presence of a large band of strikers, and the superintendent of police had given instructions for the reserve to be in readiness for any emergency but judging from the past behaviour of the men, it is not thought that the services of the police will be required.

At eight o'clock this morning several hundred men attended a meeting around the drinking fountain opposite St Olave's Grammar School, Tooley Street. Several persons made speeches, including the Rev. Mr Carlisle of Abbey Street Chapel, Bermondsey who urged the men to maintain order in their ranks.

The extraordinary state of affairs prevails at Topping's Skin Wharf, Tooley Street. The majority of the men there have been struck, and today the clerks are performing manual labour, one acting as driver of the steam crane.

Will Thorne *My Life's Battles* (1925), 86

The new Labour Protection League, headed by Harry Quelch, composed of waterside and dock workers on the south side of the river, were with us. The strike was complete. The marine and contiguous traffic of the world's largest port was completely paralysed, and the world waited and wondered what was going to happen next.

Letters began to appear in the press, usually anonymously, complaining of the intimidation and brutality employed by the strikers against blacklegs. However, there were no subsequent prosecutions to bear this out.

Copy of letter dated August 25, 1889.

The Times, Tuesday, 27 August 1889, 6

Sir, – As one of the newly-appointed permanent men who have remained at work in the London Dock during the strike, I beg respectfully to bring under your notice the following facts, which will account for so many men leaving their work. They have done so under the influence of extreme terror, being unable to enter or leave the dock with safety, and have in many instances been robbed and most brutally assaulted. If some means could have been found for getting them in and out of the dock with safety I am confident not a man at this department would have left. They were satisfied with their pay; many of them a few weeks ago would have eagerly accepted permanency on the committee's terms. On Friday evening five of them were so violently assaulted on leaving the dock that they were unable to come to work on Saturday. They were men who had worked for a number of years at the same warehouse, doing responsible work. The papers all speak of the orderly conduct of the strikers, and no doubt their processions through the streets are conducted in a peaceable manner; but let the writers come down to the dock-gates and see the terror-stricken men going round from gate to gate seeking to get out with safety, and finding at every gate a mob waiting for the express purpose of half murdering them, and they would alter their opinion. On Saturday morning the rumour was spread that the strikers had the names of all those remaining at work and had appointed gangs of men to wait at every gate and settle all those who came out. In consequence of this the men at once left work, not to join the strikers but out of sheer fright. As I have myself been savagely assaulted, and still bear the marks, I speak from experience. I write this more particularly in the hope that you may be able to arrange some means whereby the men may enter and leave the docks with safety.

I am, Sir, yours respectfully,

* * *

TO THE EDITOR OF THE TIMES

Sir, – During this week I have witnessed the most open intimidation practised by the men on strike – howling crowds going from dock to dock and warehouse to warehouse, stopping business and threatening vengeance on all who did not comply with their demands, until now there are thousands who are out who had no desire to strike, but were compelled to do so, not only dock labourers, but carmen, lightermen, regular men, and many others; and what is worse still is that those who dare to honestly work for their wages are being brutally maltreated and threatened with worse if they dare attempt to work in defiance of the strikers' wishes. I saw several men severely injured today on Tower Hill (the blood being made to fly in all directions) by gangs of strikers, and the police who ought to have been there came up when the damage was done. I want to know if this is English liberty, if so I prefer a strong despotism. If this is civilization what is barbarism? What are the authorities for if not to protect peaceable citizens in earning an honest livelihood? Kindly insert this and oblige

A LOVER OF FREEDOM

August 24

The TUC Annual Congress occurred early in September, during the period of the strike. The TUC conference comprising two hundred delegates (representing less than nine hundred thousand members) gave sympathy to the strikers and had a collection which raised £10 for the strikers. It

Earning an extra bob, many dockers' wives were homeworkers – a shilling a mattress was the prize.

must be remembered that the TUC was an organisation of skilled unions whose outlook did not encompass radical ideas of social change. Indeed at the conference in the same week the delegates threw out a resolution from Keir Hardie calling for the eight-hour day. Tillett was fiercely critical of the TUC and their representatives in Parliament, saying they had got so used to being the lap dogs of society that they forgot the duty they owed to the men who made them what they were. The London Trades Council fared slightly better. They sent two delegates to help the strike committee but gave no financial or political leadership during the dispute.

Pall Mall Gazette,
Tuesday, 3 September
1889

THE TRADES UNION CONGRESS AND THE STRIKE

An Appeal to the Trades of the Kingdom:
At the opening meeting of the Trades Union Congress at Dundee yesterday, Mr. Cooper (Sugarmakers, London) proposed: 'That this Congress is of opinion that the dock labourers of London are more than justified in the position they have taken up, and consider their employers are acting in a most tyrannical and arbitrary manner in refusing the very moderate demand of the men. We therefore recommend the trades of the United Kingdom to render to the labourers their utmost financial support, believing that it will be conducive to the national interests that the position of the labourers should be improved'. (Cheers.) These men were, without doubt, the worst paid class of the whole of the labourers of the United Kingdom, and they had hitherto been looked upon as a body whom it was impossible to raise; but that was no longer the case, for they had shown that they were able to organise themselves in some manner, and to forward their demands to the companies, with a view to bettering their condition. Mr. Freak (London), in seconding the resolution, said the present was a battle between capital and labour. Let them, therefore, as Unionists, as men, do all they could to support the labourers in their struggle, not to out in sympathy with them to swell the ranks of the unemployed, but work without injuring them; work, and through their earnings give them money whereby they could fight that question with these gigantic capitalists and secure for these down-trodden people the means of subsistence for their wives and families. (Cheers.) The resolution was without discussion, unanimously adopted, and it was announced that practical effect would be given to it by a collection at the doors.

The strike leaders were becoming famous. Tom Mann recalls an amusing incident where his boots became celebrities. But there was a darker side to this notoriety – Will Thorne was assaulted at the Custom-House, but dismissed this incident as of no great import.

Tom Mann's Memoirs (1923), 67

One day I realised that my boots had become so worn out, that I must get others, or go barefoot (we always had long marches, and I invariably marched with the crowd). I slipped away from the marching column as soon as I noticed a boot shop. Hastily buying a pair of boots, I put them on and hurried to catch up with the crowd. When we reached Sayes Court, Deptford, I spoke as usual upon the general situation. A few days later, we were marching again along the thoroughfare where I had bought the boots. My eye lighted on the shop window, and to my amazement I noticed my name on a card. I approached the window, and to my still greater astonishment I saw that the card bearing my name was on the paid of old boots I had shed a few days before. The writing on the card ran: 'The boots worn by Tom Mann during the long marches in the Dock Strike.' I was positively flabbergasted, to think that importance of any kind could attach to such an articles, or to me.

Will Thorne, *My Life's Battles* (1925), 87

I got into a fight at Custom House, but suffered no great injury.

The dispute spread to the houses of the dockers themselves. With no funds to support them, the women went on rent strike.

RAISING THE NO-RENT BANNER

Evening News & Post, Monday, 26 August 1889

The weekly rents fall due today from the labourers, but it is expected there will be some difficulty in collecting them. A white banner is stretched from Hungerford Street, Commercial Road, bearing the following inscription:—

'As we are on strike landlords need not call.'

A similar banner hangs at the top of Star Street, Commercial Road, inscribed as follows:—

'Our husbands are on strike; for the wives it is not honey,
And we all think it is right not to pay the landlord's money,
Everyone is on strike, so landlords do not be offended;
The rent that's due we'll pay you when the strike is ended.

By 25 August a new section of labour had joined the strike, those whose demands had already been met by their employers. The marches themselves were now taking on a carnival atmosphere, with competition amongst the men as to who could be dressed out the best to depict their trades.

Evening News & Post, Monday, 26 August 1889

When all had assembled to join the procession the muster was estimated at between 60,000 and 70,000. There were several bands of music and banners were very numerous from the handsome and artistic productions owned by several lodges of the Sons of the Phoenix which took part to the mere sheets of calico, supported by sticks and bearing encouraging inscriptions rudely painted, which were carried by members of various trades, who joined the strikers from the docks. Some of these proclaimed

that the demands of the men had been met by their employers, but that they were taking part with the others on 'principle'. Among the trades represented, besides the dock labourers, stevedores and lightermen were coal porters, coal whippers, carpenters and joiners, ship-fitters, orange porters, the Thames Ironworks men, copper ore and phosphate and oil workers, ballast heavers, and dustmen, many of these detachments being simply participators as an expression of sympathy, as was the mission of a large contingent of the Labour Protection League. A few local friendly and political societies also took part. In a vehicle were a number of men in grotesque allegorical costumes, and some of the coal porters rode in carts on which cranes had been formed with masts, ropes and swivels, baskets of coal being constantly pulled up and down, in token of the men's calling. The dustmen also displayed emblems of their trade.

MR NORWOOD'S VIEWS ON THE STRIKE

Evening News & Post, Monday, 26 August 1889

Mr C. M. Norwood, chairman of the London and India Joint Docks Committee, in an interview with a press representative at the Dock House on Saturday afternoon [24 Aug] said there was nothing left to arbitrate upon but the question of the rate of wages, and this had now become a question affecting not only the London and India Company, but also every branch of labour connected with the port of London. There is in fact, according to Mr Norwood, a general uprising, the London and India Company being selected as the weak outworks, whereon to commence an attack for a wholesale advance of wages. The number of dock labourers actually on strike he estimates at more than 5,000 but the total number of strikers, including the dock labourers must be at least 50,000.

The masters pose while dockers look on.

130,000 MEN OUT

Evening News & Post, Tuesday, 27 August 1889

It is now estimated that the total number of men out has reached the enormous figure of 130,000

LONDON ON STRIKE

Dockmen, lightermen, bargemen, cement workers, carmen, iron-workers, and even factory girls are coming out. If it goes on a few days longer, all London will be on holiday. The great machine by which five millions of people are fed and clothed will come to a dead stop, and what is to be the end of it all? The proverbial small spark has kindled a great fire which threatens to envelop the whole metropolis.

On Tuesday 27 August negotiations began in earnest, both sides setting out their demands and appearing rigid as to how far they would concede. The strikers, to back their demands, and to show their strength, held one of their largest demonstrations, which some estimated to have had up to one hundred thousand on the streets.

THE STRIKES

The Times, Wednesday, 28 August 1889, 9

The men yesterday appeared quite steadfast in their purpose, whilst the dock proprietors expressed their determination to resist the men's demands. Mr. Benjamin Tillett, secretary of the Dock Labourers' Committee, had an interview in the afternoon with the directors of the London and India Docks Joint Committee of over an hour's duration, in order if possible to settle the dispute. It is understood that Mr. Tillett insisted on the 6*d.* an hour and employment for not less than four hours at a time, with the abolition of the contract system. The directors, the chief of whom was Mr. C. M. Norwood, gave the following written reply:— 'Sir, – I am desired to acknowledge the receipt of your communication of today's date, enclosing proposals which on acceptance of my directors will, as you state, put an end to the strike. My board desire me to say that, while much regretting the continuance of the strike, they are unable to agree to the proposal in question. – I am, Sir, your obedient servant, H. Morgan, secretary.' It is reported that Mr. Tillett, immediately after the decision, stated that there was no intention on the part of the men to yield one inch, and that the strike would proceed to the bitter end.

At midday a great procession, headed by bands, entered the City from Aldgate. There were an immense number of banners of the usual style, but some were specially inscribed. There was some talk of the procession being composed of a hundred thousand; but those accustomed to compute numbers would be more likely to fix the figures considerably lower, when it is stated that, horses and carts going at a walking pace and with many open spaces, stoppages and blocks, the procession took only an hour passing one point. The casual dock labourers, the nominal cause of the strike, were prominently to the fore. Then came ship-scrapers and coal-

whippers, most of these having model cranes in carts illustrative of their work. There were carters without number, who in most cases carried banners inscribed with the names of the firms by whom they were employed, and stating, strangely enough, that they were only out on principle.

The employers' firm line, however, was shattered by a leading wharfinger, Mr. Henry Lafone, of Butler's Wharf, who began separate negotiations with the strike committee. Champion and Mann met Lafone, who was making sympathetic statements to the press in relation to bad pay and conditions in the docks; but, despite Norwood's statement of 24 August, it still came as a surprise when on 29 August the employers issued a statement stating that they had conceded most of the demands except for the 6*d.* or 'dockers' tanner' as the hourly rate.

The Times, Wednesday, 28 August 1889, 10

Mr. H. Lafone remarked upon the great difference which had taken place in the charges made in the port since the last strike in 1872, when the wages were 4*d.* an hour. At that time the charge for working jute was 7*s.* per ton. It was now 1*s.* 9*d.* How, he asked, was it possible for an employer to pay 6*d.* or even 5*d.* an hour with such a reduction as that? Gambier was 11*s.* 3*d.* in 1872; it was now 4*s.* Shellac was £2 10*s.* 10*d.* then; now it was £1 7*s.* 6*d.* He could quote a good many other cases of a similar sort. It was decidedly not fair that the working classes should suffer from the competition between the wharfingers and the dock companies. He hoped that an arrangement would be made with all the wharfingers that the dock companies should charge a legitimate price for the work done and should pay a legitimate rate of wages to the workmen. They were all equally interested, the workmen and the masters, and they could neither earn bread and cheese unless one helped the other. (Cheers.) Mr. Champion and Mr. Mann met him on Saturday night at the West India Dock Committee Rooms and he must say they behaved in the most fair and straightforward manner. There was no Socialist principle of any description enunciated, but the causes of hardship were enumerated. The contractors were stated to be the greatest hardship, because they not only screwed the men down and made very large profits, but, as he himself knew, in many cases they gave the men pay in unloading a ship at less than half the tonnage which had been brought out, while they themselves got paid for the whole amount. That was not a fair state of things, and in 1889 would not be allowed to go on long. The proposition was that contractors should be put on piecework. The proper principle of piecework was that the foreman should be paid a certain amount for work per week, that the men should be paid so much more per hour and allowed their 'subs' until Saturday night, and that then the accounts should be made up and the surplus divided amongst the men, the foreman taking the same share as every one of the men with whom he had been working. He considered that this was

a legitimate principle, and when he enunciated it to the representatives of the men they said that if the dock companies would only do that they would be perfectly satisfied. He considered those present were all interested in seeing that the men had something to eat in this world and something to drink too, and he hoped that the next resolution to be proposed would be agreed to, and that a settlement would be brought about as early as possible. (Cheers.)

The Times, Thursday, 29 August 1889, 3

'Dock-house, 109, Leadenhall-street,
E.C.,
August 28.

'Gentlemen, – We have the honour to report to you that we have this day seen Mr. Tillett, Mr. Burns, and other gentlemen. The following was submitted as the demands on the part of Mr. Tillett and his party:—

'Outsiders called in not to be discharged with less than 2*s*. pay.

'That contract work should be abandoned and a system of piecework substituted by which the men shall receive the total gross receipts of the job direct from the companies, drawing in the meantime a *minimim* of 6*d*. per hour ordinary time, and 8*d*. per hour overtime for their work so long as the job lasts.

'The shares of the *plus* to be divided as follows, the share of each man and the foreman to be equal:—

'Pay to be 6*d*. an hour and 8*d*. per hour overtime.

'Overtime to be reckoned from 6 p.m. to 6 a.m.

'We enquired whether the demand of 6*d*. an hour was an absolute condition, as, that being withdrawn, we were of opinion that all the other points might be arranged to the satisfaction of both parties. The answer was that the rate of 6*d*. an hour was vital. Mr. Birt having stated that the companies could not consent to this, the conference was suspended.

'We are, gentlemen, your obedient servants,

'G. R. BIRT, General Manager, Millwall Dock Company.

'J. GRIFFIN General Manager, Surrey Commercial Dock Company.

'H. W. WILLIAMS,
'E. H. BAILEY, } General Managers, London and India Docks Joint Committee.

'We, the undersigned, having been present, testify to the accuracy of the above report.

'HUGH C. SMITH
'HY. LAFONE.'

The strikers were having success in getting strategic employers' labourers to join the dispute, even if this was done through weight of numbers and hard-talking negotiations. The strikers were also successful at stopping blacklegs.

The Times, Thursday, 29 August 1889, 3 (cont.)

Yesterday afternoon about 1,000 men marched, via Woolwich, Plumstead, Abbey-wood, and Belvedere, to Erith, in order to bring out the coal-porters employed at the wharves of Messrs. Beadle Brothers. They were preceded by a brass band and carried several flags and banners, the tops of the poles being decorated with sprigs of heather and fern leaves, which had been gathered as the procession crossed Bostal-heath. Some delegates had been down the previous day, and tried without effect to induce the men to go out on strike. As they would not go out, they threatened that they would come the next day in such numbers as to make them come out. As the procession entered the village the High-street and Pier-road were filled with spectators, and, without stopping, the men marched down to the coal depôt of Messrs. Beadle. A deputation of 12 men, representing the several trades and societies concerned in the strike, had an interview with Messrs. Charles and Frank Beadle, the gates being closed to the rest of the party. Messrs. Beadle's men, for the most part, express satisfaction with their rate of pay and the terms of their employment. Some of the more intemperate of the demonstrators made use of very violent language and threats, telling the men that if they did not go out on strike they would be boycotted and not allowed to work, after the dispute was settled, at any of the London wharves or coal depôts. One man went so far as to threaten to throw one of Messrs. Beadle's men into the Thames if he did not go out. It was also freely said that if the men did not consent to go out then Mr. Burns would be down on the morrow with 50,000 men and compel them to go out. After a conference of considerably over an hour, it was announced that Messrs. Beadle had given way, and ringing cheers were raised and the band struck up a lively tune. In the midst of the commotion Mr. Baker, the secretary, mounting the balustrade outside Messrs. Beadle's offices, stated that he was glad to say that they had succeeded in the object of their journey to Erith. Messrs. Beadle had agreed that no more unloading of coal should take place at their wharves until the dispute was settled, and they had given 10*s*. for the men to drink their health and £5 towards the funds. (Cheers.) He then advised the men to march away peacefully. The procession then reformed, and, preceded by the band and banner-bearers, marched out of the village in the same order that they entered it. There was a large number of metropolitan police present, but there was no necessity for their interference.

MEN BROUGHT FROM GREENOCK JOIN THE STRIKERS

Evening News & Post, Thursday, 29 August 1889

Last night about sixty dockers were brought from Greenock and secretly conveyed to one of the P. & O. boats at the Albert Docks. On this becoming known by the strike pickets this morning strong efforts were made to get the Greenock men away and they were successful.

In the closing days of August as the men were waiting for developments, their resolve stayed firm. The busy streets of docklands were quiet and

LEADER OF THE PROCESSION. THE "COALIES'" CAR. "POOR DOCKER'S BABY."

Scenes from the marches where every section tried to out-do the other with their floats and costumes.

empty, except for the unemployed men waiting in groups on the street corners to hear the latest news. It was estimated that there were 80,000 men idle and these were the poorest in London.

Burns showed no let up at ending no fewer than ten meetings. The speeches now were directed to that section, namely, the dock labourers depending on relief. Burns, Tillett and Mann made moderate speeches.

Wilson, Secretary of the Seamen and Firemen, however, in a fiery speech put forward the idea of a General Strike.

There was the customary march which was again orderly and well disciplined. The police testifying to their good behaviour, Burns pointedly told a sympathiser that he was not prepared to discuss Socialism as the strike had nothing to do with that topic.

The Times, Friday, 30 August 1889

Let me first describe the state of the docks and the surrounding neighbourhood. Those who know them under ordinary circumstances, but who have returned after a brief space of absence, hardly recognize them now. In the streets, when no meeting is going on in the immediate vicinity, a novel scene is presented. There is, practically speaking, no vehicular traffic in comparison with ordinary times. A cab progresses at a sharp trot along thoroughfares where usually the way must be picked with care, and where, when the dock labourers are not on strike, great vans and wagons laden with merchandise block the way. But of people there is an endless supply. They stand in clusters on the pavement, now listless, and now listening to the observations of a casual speaker. They sit in rows, with their backs to the street walls, patient, and without occupation. In effect some 80,000 of the poorest men in London, the

The stevedores' float, part of a procession starting from East India Dock Road.

men who can less than any others afford to be out of work, are doing nothing, and, in spite of the help which they are receiving from outside, the sight is one of the most pitiable upon which the human eye could rest.

Mr. Burns, before presiding at the meeting at Tower-hill, had attended no fewer than ten meetings.

In the afternoon, at about 2.30, came a remarkable meeting at the Custom-house. There were present, in addition to large numbers of dock labourers and stevedores, many coal whippers, ballast heavers, wharfingers' men, and others, all out on strike, but the remarks of all the speakers were addressed to the 'dockers' alone. The assemblage was large, but of one mind. To Messrs. Burns, Tillett, Mann, Wilson, and Champion it listened with the utmost earnestness. Mr. Burns made a moderate speech, and Mr. Tillett one of which, under the circumstances there was no ground to complain. Mr. Mann's oration was striking. He inspirited the men by telling them that their demands had been too moderate, that rather than yield to compromise they would be well advised to increase their claims. He was well received, but there was a certain lack of judgement in a closing sentence, to the effect that they might be called on to take more definite and decided action in more ways than one. The meaning was not quite clear, but these veiled insinuations are often ambiguous, and none the less dangerous. Then came a speech from Mr. Wilson, the secretary of the Seamen and Firemen's Union, which boasts some 60,000 members, with a speech of considerable vehemence. It was not a powerful speech, but it took the fancy of the audience, and the promises of help which he gave encouraged them not a little. One injudicious and undesirable feature in his speech was found in the fact that he did not discourage the idea of a general strike. He argued, for example, that if the strikes caused the collapse of gas-lighting arrangements, the rich men and not the poor would be the sufferers, but he omitted to say that such an event would completely alienate public sympathy, and he laid undue emphasis upon the notion of a struggle between capital and labour, whereas the remarkable thing about this strike is that capital, save in so far as it is represented by the Joint Docks Committee, is for the most part closely in sympathy with the objects which the dock labourers desire to secure.

The No-Work Manifesto

Unaware as yet of the tidal wave of support about to wash in from Australia, the strike committee felt compelled to issue a notice suspending all relief indefinitely. The coffers were empty. It seemed to them time for desperate measures; and the hints of a general strike thoughout London, thrown out in recent speeches (and deprecated by *The Times*), became concrete in the form of a 'No-Work' manifesto drafted on Thursday evening (29 August) and into the small hours of Friday – Tillett added his signature in the middle of the night, at home, at the instigation of Tom Mann, and allegedly without taking in its contents. The actual drafting was done by Mann, Llewellyn Smith and Henry Champion – as the starting date substituting Monday for the Friday that was about to dawn, a prudent measure for which Tillett and the others soon had cause to be grateful.

It very quickly became obvious that this manifesto was the quickest way to lose public sympathy, carefully cultivated thus far, and to make the strikers appear to be Socialistic or anarchist wreckers rather than responsible trade unionists – the possible disappearance of gas for lighting, plunging the whole city into nocturnal darkness, being a particularly troubling, nightmarish threat.

The counter-manifesto, withdrawing the strike call, was drawn up on Sunday morning (1 September) and endorsed by the usual Sunday afternoon mass meeting.

In the meantime, besides the news of the Australian support, the full significance of which took a few days to emerge, and the Dock House's rejection of Lafone's compromise, the other main event was the first intervention of Cardinal Manning. In fact, Tillett already regarded Manning as his mentor. Tillett later became a socialist of the Fabian rather than SDF variety.

The Times, Saturday, 31 August 1889, 5

At an early hour yesterday [Fri. 30] morning, as was briefly announced in *The Times*, at a special meeting of the general committee of the docks strikes a sub-committee was appointed to draft a manifesto addressed to all the workers in every trade in London in reply to the refusal of the

directors to meet the demands of the dock labourers. The following is the text of the manifesto: —

'Wade's Arms, Jeremiah-street, Poplar, London,
E., 29th August, 1889,

'TO THE WORKERS OF LONDON.

'On Wednesday afternoon representatives of the dock labourers, in the course of a discussion with the spokesmen of the dock companies, were informed that on one point alone of the demands of the men would there be any difficulty in arriving at a settlement – namely, on the question of raising the rate of pay from 5*d.* to 6*d.* an hour for ordinary time. This afternoon, however, the directors have definitely stated that they will only pay 5*d.* an hour for ordinary time and 6*d.* for overtime. Further, instead of the immediate and total abolition of the contract system, the directors simply pledged themselves to do away with it "as soon and as far as practicable" This phrase, in the mouths of such men as the directors have during this struggle proved themselves to be, means that the concession is to be a mere farce.

'Meanwhile the vacillation and incompetence of the dock directors is inflicting cruel suffering upon tens of thousands of dock labourers and their families. These privations have been borne with a good-tempered heroism which has excited the warm sympathy of the public, and enlisted the active support of skilled and organized labour throughout our country. In our former manifesto we urged workers of trades not directly connected with the docks to remain at work, and to avoid causing inconvenience to the general community. Our studied moderation has been mistaken by our ungenerous opponents for lack of courage or want of resources. We are therefore compelled to take a step which we could have wished had not been forced upon us, and which we are fully aware may be followed by the gravest consequences.

'We now solemnly appeal to the workers in London of all grades and of every calling to refuse to go to work on Monday next unless the directors have before noon on Saturday, 31st August, officially informed this committee that the moderate demands of the dock labourers have been fully and finally conceded. These demands, from which the men have never swerved, are:- (1) The *minimum* rate of pay to be 6*d.* an hour ordinary time and 8*d.* an hour overtime, under the company; or, under contract, 8*d.* an hour ordinary time and 1*s.* an hour overtime; (2) overtime to be counted from 6 p.m. to 8 a.m.; (3) no man to be employed for less than four hours.

'(Signed) – Benjamin Tillett, John Burns, H. H. Champion, Tom Mann, James Toomey, A. Mansfield, W. Carr, W. Booth, Geo. James Smith, A. Field, John Dowling, T. Benmore, Denis Driscoll, P. Regan, John Regan, Geo. Pearson, Michl. Tighe, John Hornback, Francis Mollison, Wm. Stone, Jonathan B. Ruark, James Nightingale, John Harrington, Chas. Allen, Cornelius Ruark, Geo. Perritt, John Walls, Chas. Campbell, Robert

Iles, W.W. Gillespie, S. Leask, James Neal, Robert Passman, James McDade, Joseph A. Clarke, G. Harvey, G.R. Bartlett, G.W. Smith, J.G. Wilson, Daniel McCarthy, A. Dawson, T.M. Williams, George Donaldson, T.H. Camp, C. Miller, Thomas McCarthy.'

The above signatures include all the representatives of the Stevedores and Sailors and Firemen's Union, with the most important of the East London trades. Every delegate present signed the manifesto.

The most important meeting which has been held in connexion with the great strike took the form of a conference, which was held yesterday afternoon at the City offices of Butler's Wharf. This arose in connexion with the meetings of wholesale tea merchants which have been held during the week, and reported in *The Times*. The committee which was appointed at one of these meetings early in the week has met twice daily, and have discussed every possible means for a resumption of trade in London. They found that the men would like to go back to the warehouses on the terms offered by the warehousekeepers were inclined to willingly offer the terms if they could get the support of the shipowners.

'36, Mark-lane, London August 30, 1889.

'Proposed agreement between dock companies, wharfingers, granary keepers, and workmen.

'Wages and conditions made with men:- Outsider called in not to be discharged with less than 2*s*. pay.

'That contract work shall be abandoned and a system of piece-work substituted, by which the men shall receive the total gross receipts of the job direct from the companies, drawing in the meantime a *minimum* of 6*d*. per hour ordinary time and 8*d*. per hour overtime for their work so long as the job lasts. The shares of the *plus* shall be divided as follows:— The share of each man and each foreman to be equal. Pay for casual work to be 6*d*. per hour for the first four hours if only working that time; if for longer, then at the rate of 4*s*. for nine hours and 6*d*. per hour from nine to 12 hours, with an allowance of half an hour for dinner.

'Overtime 8*d*. per hour. Overtime to be reckoned from 6 p.m. till 6 a.m. or 8 p.m. till 8 a.m.

'Regular men may be engaged at not less than 24*s*. per week.

'We, the undersigned representatives of dock workers and others now on strike pledge ourselves to have the following terms faithfully carried out at each dock, wharf, granary, or warehouse where the above terms are agreed:—

'1. That men shall not work at any dock or wharf on less wages or worse terms than those stated as above.

'2. That men shall immediately return to work at all docks, wharves or granaries where terms as per list herewith have been agreed.

'3. That all lightermen shall at once resume work, agreeing to submit any grievances they may have to arbitration.

'4. Coal workers to resume work at once.

'To avoid any delay in work being resumed, it is requested that each dock company, wharfinger, or granary keeper will consent to the above terms in writing. It is most important that these should be in the hands of Mr. H. Lafone, 36, Mark-lane, as early on Saturday as possible.'

Mr. Lafone at the conclusion of the conference, said the strongest efforts were being made to settle the strike that night. The proposals would be submitted to the men, and if they agreed to them, as there was very little doubt they would, the strike had absolutely reached its termination.

Yesterday Cardinal Manning called upon Alderman Sir Andrew Lusk, the acting Lord Mayor at the Mansion-house, on the subject of the strike, and, after a conversation, they proceeded together to the offices of the Dock Committee in Leadenhall-street, with the object of inducing that body, in the interests of public safety, to terminate the dispute by agreeing to the reasonable demands of the men. They were accompanied, at the request of Sir Andrew Lusk, by Colonel Henry Smith, the acting Commissioner of the City Police. Being at once accorded an interview by the committee, over whom Mr. Norwood presided, the Cardinal, who mentioned incidentally that his father, Mr. W Manning, and his late brother were successively chairmen of one of the dock companies, addressed the committee at some length, pointing out the growing gravity of the crisis and the injurious effects that the strike was having on trade generally, and urging that the sacrifice even of a problematic dividend was preferable to the continuance of a state of things which might increase in intensity and lead to far-reaching and deplorable results. ... Mr. Norwood, the chairman, thanked the Cardinal and Sir Andrew Lusk for their well-intentioned efforts to mediate between the strikers and the dock companies, and then in some detail and at length gave the committee's views of their position, and spoke of their readiness to meet every reasonable demand of their *employés*, though they could not assent to requests which they considered to be impossible, looking to the state of their finances. ... The Cardinal and Sir A. Lusk then left, and were greeted with loud cheers by the crowd of strikers outside the company's offices.

Explaining the genesis of the manifesto, Henry Champion recalled:

H. H. Champion, *The Great Dock Strike in London, August 1889* (1890), 18

'Things looked very black indeed – for though the collections made in workshops and in the streets, supplemented by contributions from the older Trade Unions and from private individuals, had reached a considerable sum, they were totally inadequate to provide even a shilling a day for a tenth of the families who were without means of subsistence.'

It was also the case that hunger was beginning to affect morale and the two major dock companies had shown no willingness to make concessions. (18–19)

It was under these circumstances that the manifesto was issued, calling upon all the workmen of London to come out on strike on the 2nd of September, unless the Dock Directors should have surrendered on the previous Saturday. This manifesto was almost universally condemned by all sorts of people except those who were on the spot and were acquainted with the strength and the weakness of the Dockers' position. The temper of those who were responsible for its publication may be estimated from the fact that the sub-Committee which drafted it (Mr. Tom Mann, Mr. Smith and myself) was originally instructed to give the Dock Directors only twenty-four hours instead of three days of grace. It was fortunate that wiser counsels prevailed, and the Monday instead of the Friday was fixed as the day for the general strike, for in the interval three things became clear: First, that the organised trades, in the great majority of cases, were not going to show such self-sacrifice as had been exhibited by the Stevedores' and the Sailors' Unions, though they were prepared, if the manifesto was withdrawn, to make very heavy levies upon their members in order to supply the Dockers with the sinews of war. Then, a division became apparent in the ranks of the enemy. It was proved that a number of the wharfingers were prepared to grant nearly everything the men asked, and it was seen that if this could be secured, the fight would practically be won – for the general public would see that the demands that could be granted by a number of the masters were not in any way unreasonable or immoderate, and the throwing-open of each wharf at which the new rates of pay were conceded would greatly relieve the Strike Committee, by making the men employed contributors to the funds instead of dependents thereon, and by releasing a number of pickets who could be used to strengthen the guard at the weaker places. The manifesto had the further effect of greatly stimulating the zeal of the various intermediaries who had been working for peace; and so it came about that when its revocation was proposed there was not a dissentient voice.

John Lovell, *Stevedores and Dockers* (1969), 109–110

The crisis of the strike was reached at the end of August. The cause was shortage of funds, and without adequate finance the strike could not be continued. Hunger was already beginning to affect morale. The joint committee of the two major dock companies had so far shown little readiness to make concessions, and the rest of the port employers had followed the committee's lead. The dominant personality on that committee was a Mr Norwood, who displayed the greatest hostility towards the men's cause. The radical *Star* newspaper, which was strong in support of the men, remarked of Norwood: 'He is in appearance and manners the very embodiment of the insolence of capitalism. He is stout, well-fed and arrogant.' [26 August] With funds running out, and with the employers apparently adamant against concessions, the strike committee at Wade's Arms felt that the position had become desperate. The only way out that it could see lay in an extension of the strike beyond the waterfront, thus provoking a really major crisis in the life of the metropolis. It was a desperate remedy for a desperate situtation. A manifesto was drawn up calling on the various trades in London to strike in support of the port workers. The committee was encouraged to believe that these trades would respond to the call by the fact that in its early days the stoppage had shown strong signs of spreading beyond the waterfront, and the Wade's Arms Committee had then been obliged to restrain this tendency, partly on the grounds that many of the potential strikers were unorganised and would, therefore, require relief. As it was, London coal porters and carmen were already out on strike. However, when it came to the point, the strike leadership was divided on the wisdom of issuing the so-called 'No-Work Manifesto'. Although there appeared to be little alternative, some feared that it would alienate public opinion and thus finally dry up the flow of outside funds. There was also the fact that some of the London unions had shown little enthusiasm for sympathetic action; this being the case, the strike call might well turn out to be a fiasco which would only expose the weakness of Wade's Arms. Thus, although the manifesto was in fact issued on 30 August, it was withdrawn almost immediately.

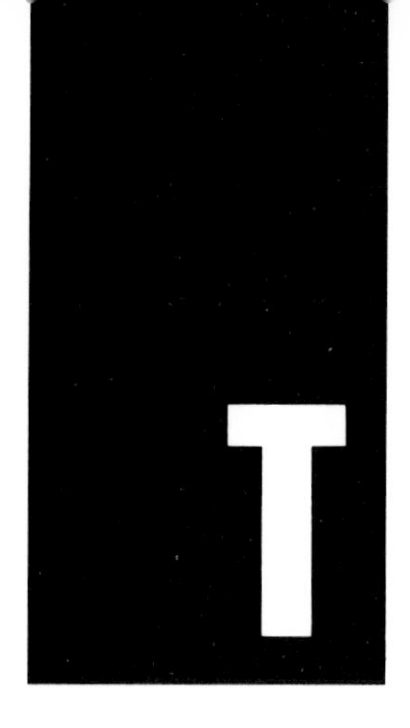

The 'General Strike' Abandoned

Tillett, in his autobiography, said that the extension of the strike was John Burns's strategy, making the point that he in no way endorsed the 'No-Work Manifesto'. This episode in the strike is the most detailed in Tillett's autobiography and he is quite scathing in his response. This is an important moment not just in the history of the strike, but in terms of the pattern of things to come. It was Tillett's view which prevailed, that it was essential that public opinion should at all times be on the side of the strikers. There is speculation whether the general strike would have been successful or not; but one has to bear in mind the number of spontaneous strikes there were and the fact that the strike leaders had previously appealed for workers *not* to join the dispute. It is evident that if the 'No-Work Manifesto' had succeeded, the nature of the strike and indeed perhaps the nature of the post-strike labour movement would have been drastically different.

Ben Tillett, *Memories and Reflections* (1931), 141–143

Failure of the peace-makers to promote an acceptable settlement, naturally caused some of us (but not myself) to think of extending the area of the Strike in order to intensify the struggle and enforce a speedier settlement. John Burns held the view that this strategy would be justifiable, and perhaps the suggestion to call on all the trades of London to stop work originated with him, but the proposal was actually formulated, through the Strike Committee, by Tom Mann; his object was to impress upon the Trade Unionists of London the importance of the struggle, then proceeding and the necessity of supporting the Dockers in their demand.

I was not present at the Strike Committee when the proposal for a general stoppage of the London trades was discussed, on the basis of a draft manifesto written by the sardonic [Henry] Champion. An incipient secession movement among the wharf labourers at Wapping had taken me there in haste that evening, and I had laboured long in persuading them not to return to work. I was tired out, and instead of going back to the Strike headquarters, that night I went home to sleep. At two o'clock in the morning, heavy with sleep and exhaustion, Tom Mann dragged me out of bed to read the manifesto, and to tell me about the

The straw hat was the symbol of a packed strike.

Committee's decision, in my absence, to call upon the London trades to cease work. I was dead beat, and having been only just rudely awakened, I did not then grasp the full import of the manifesto to which Tom Mann begged me to attach my signature, the only one lacking. I yielded and went back to bed.

This is the manifesto, and I do not repudiate the responsibilities attaching to my signature:

Text of Manifesto follows – see above, *The Times*, 31 August, 5

... The Strike Committee apparently had decided that the 'No Work' call was to become operative within twenty-four hours of the issue of this manifesto, which was drafted in the small hours of the morning of August 30. Champion and John Burns, however, in writing the manifesto, took upon themselves the responsibility of changing the date, and fixing the zero hour for Monday, September 2, as the day on which the General London Strike was to start. But the whole thing was a blunder. The manifesto had to be withdrawn. It tended to alienate public sympathy....

On the day the 'No Work' manifesto appeared, we had long and harassing discussions, but I succeeded in persuading the Strike Committee that a less menacing and minatory policy must be adopted, and at our meeting on the following day, August 31, I even secured Tom Mann as seconder on my resolution, proposing that a new manifesto should be drafted and issued to countermand the call for a General London Strike. ...

Wade's Arms,
Jeremiah Street,
Poplar, Sep. 1, 1889

Fellow countrymen – Since Thursday night we have received ample evidence that it is the dock directors alone who are responsible for delaying the settlement of the dispute. During the past forty-eight hours we have had convincing proof that public opinion amongst all classes declares that the demands of the dock labourers are just and reasonable and we have been inundated with offers of assistance, provided that our attack is confined to the few men who are willing to plunge the metropolis into anarchy rather than admit themselves to be in the wrong. We are determined to show that we are not actuated by such miserable vanity as our opponents and that the working classes are as superior to the dock directors in true nobility of character as in capacity to manage their business. We therefore hereby cancel our appeal to the workers of London to come out on strike on Monday, and invite them instead to strain every nerve and to make every sacrifice to supply us with the sinews of war; especially we ask the organised trades in the provinces, as well as in London, to send us at once the largest contributions they can afford.

Though the dock directors remain obdurate, a certain number of the wharfingers and granary keepers have offered to give terms to their men, which, though falling short of the original demands of the men, we might have advised them to consider had they been conceded by the whole of the masters. But we cannot divide our forces in the face of an enemy so unscrupulous as the dock directors. While thanking these few masters for their conciliatory attitude, we determine that the strike amongst the dock labourers and allied trades shall go on until the whole question is settled by the granting of every item of the moderate demands originally set forth by the men.

In spite of the irritation engendered by the meanness of the directors, and the terrible sufferings their obstinacy has caused, we have sufficient confidence in the courage and self-restraint of the strikers to be assured that they will maintain the demeanour which has won them the sympathy of the public. We believe that the public will respond to our call for help with a promptitude and generosity that will enable us to relieve the suffering. Meanwhile the docker starves, but does not surrender.

By order of the general committee of the dock strike—
BENJAMIN TILLETT
JOHN BURNS
TOM MANN
H. H. CHAMPION
JAS. TOOMEY
THOS. MCCARTHY
and others

Ben Tillett, *A Brief History of the Dockers' Union* (1910), 25

John Burns did wonderful things in the press-room, and they were to count as blessings to the strikers, for he had captured the vivid powers of the editors and press-writers, for the very time they disagreed with us they were compelled to believe that revolution was dawning.

But the real, live part of the fight was in the picket line; at the meetings; in the committees; in the organizing work; and Tom Mann, with panther-like agility and energy, was here, there and everywhere, restless and tireless. His powers were as overwhelming as a cataract, and his heart undaunted by whatever perils and risks had to be run. I can see Tom now, with back against the doorway of Wroot's Coffee House, keeping back a yelling, hungry mob, while Nash and Smith shivered in the pay-room.

In the afternoon [of Saturday] a meeting was held at Southwark Park, at which speeches were delivered from several platforms by Burns, Henderson, Thorne and others. Here, as elsewhere the enthusiasm and sympathy was very great. As the various bodies of men who had 'come out' in support of the Labourers were recognised hearty cheers showed the appreciation of the multitude, Spratt's biscuit men especially getting a warm reception. Many of the men, overcome with fatigue, threw themselves on the grass and slept, uninterrupted by the stream of oratory around them.

Mr McCarthy roused the first cheer – which was neither weak nor wavering – by the announcement that the Gas Stokers were in council, considering whether they should leave work, and throw London under the cloud, which as one speaker put it 'would be worse than that which plagued Pharaoh'. Good luck to the Gas Stokers.' Then he called on Ben Tillett to move a resolution: – 'That this meeting pledges itself to support to the uttermost the men on strike at the whole of the docks and wharves of the port of London and calls upon all true friends to aid the labourer in obtaining his just rights.'

The Times, which had up to now been sympathetic, mirrored the view which was almost universal in the press condemning the actions of the dockers' committee and they let it be known in no uncertain terms that they would not support men who endorsed such actions, pointing out that the men positively refused to march under the socialistic red flag, in some cases insisting that that emblem be withdrawn from the processions. They also noted that the Union Jack and the Stars and Stripes were favoured and that the lightermen's delegate had declared that he never had and never would speak under the red flag. The only light at the end of the tunnel came from Mr Lafone who was having independent, discreet negotiations with the strikers. The employers used the blunder of the no-work manifesto to take a hard line in negotiations.

The Times, Monday, 2 September 1889, 4

Throughout working London on Saturday, in trade-union and other circles, the demand made by the strike leaders in this manifesto was regarded as an enormous blunder. Some trade-unionist committees at once protested against the manifesto, and called upon their men to disregard it. ... The failure of the agitation of [February 1886], notwithstanding the desperate efforts of the same self-appointed leaders, has caused the great bulk of the most intelligent part of the London working class, the artisans, to stand aloof from the championship which has headed the dock labourers' action. Those who joined it were those who belong to the unskilled class, and even these are far from being united in views with the leaders, a fact shown by the men positively refusing to march under the Socialistic red flag. In some cases they insisted upon that emblem, of which Mr. Burns and Mr. Champion were formerly enamoured, being altogether withdrawn from the processions. The flags shown have been the Union Jack and the American in the case of the stevedores, watermen, lightermen, and carters, and the feeling of the men was emphasized by Mr. Widdington, the lightermen's delegate, who declared that he had never spoken under the red flag and he never would.

In the meantime the suggestion of the directors that Mr. Lafone was acting independently was submitted to that gentleman, who received it smilingly. He pointed out that at the great and important meeting held early in the week at the Cannon-street Hotel, he and Mr. Hugh Smith were absolutely appointed to represent the wharfingers generally. It was

true that several of the wharfingers who warehoused tea had gone over to the side of the dock companies, but these could not be said to represent the wharfingers' interests as a whole at all, and Mr. Lafone triumphantly produced a bulky parcel of papers containing the signed agreements of a large number of firms, many of them large and important ones, to the proposed terms for the settlement of the strike.

About 2 o'clock, after repeated close conferences between the representatives of the various interests, the results of which were closely withheld, Mr. Burns, with Mr. Champion, Mr. Tillett, and one or two others of their colleagues, proceeded to the Dock-house, and were soon closeted with the Board. There appeared to be some considerable difference of opinion between Mr. Burns and Mr. Tillett, one point in particular being as to who really was the head of the strikers.

'LONDON AND INDIA DOCKS JOINT COMMITTEE.
'August 31, 1889.

'During the day Mr. Burns, accompanied by Mr. Tillett, called at the Dock-house, and had an interview with the Docks Joint Committee, and submitted a proposal which, he stated, he thought would not be rejected by those he represented. This proposition is subjoined.

Their pay meant that they could never afford to eat the cargo. Frozen meat from Australia.

'The Joint Committee, having, in consultation with the representatives of the other dock companies and with the leading wharfingers and warehouse-keepers in London, given the most serious and careful consideration to this proposition, sent the following reply:–

'"Dock-house, 109, Leadenhall-street,
August 31, 1889.

'"Sir, – The Joint Committee, after consultation with the leading wharfingers and representatives of the other dock companies, regret they are not prepared to entertain the proposal submitted to them by you today. The committee feel bound to add that they have the assurance of thse wharfingers that the statement made by you that the latter had assented to the proposition is incorrect.

'"I am, Sir, your obedient servant,
'"C. M. Norwood, Chairman

'"Mr. Burns,'

'The committee take this opportunity of repeating that they are willing at all times to see any of their servants who may be selected by the general body, and, subject to the conditions of their notice of the 29th inst., to discuss any question in regard to which those in their employ may consider there is ground of complaint.

'"By order,
'Henry J. Morgan, Secretary.'
'36, Mark-lane, London, August 30, 1889.

'PROPOSITION.

'Proposed agreement between dock companies, wharfingers granary-keepers, and workmen.

'Wages and conditions made with men:—

'Outsiders called in not to be discharged with less than 2s. pay.

'That contract work shall be abandoned, and a system of piece-work be substituted by which the men shall receive the total gross receipts of the job direct from the companies, drawing in the meantime a *minimum* of 6d. per hour ordinary time, and 8d. per hour overtime, for their work as long as the job lasts.

'The shares of the *plus* to be divided as follows:—

'The share of each man and each foreman to be equal.

'The pay for casual work to be 6d. per hour for the first four hours, if only working that time; if for longer, then at the rate of 4s. for nine hours, and 6d. per hour from nine to 12 hours, with an allowance of half-an-hour for dinner.

'Overtime 8d. per hour. Overtime to be reckoned from 6 p.m. till 6 a.m., or 8 p.m. till 8 a.m.

'Regular men may be engaged at not less than 24s. per week.

'We, the undersigned, representatives of dock workers and others now on strike, pledge ourselves to have the following terms faithfully carried out at each dock, wharf, granary, or warehouse where the above terms are agreed on:—

'1st. That men shall not work at any dock or wharf on less wages or worse terms than those stated above.

'2d. That men shall immediately return to work at all docks, wharves, or granaries where terms as per list herewith have been agreed to.

'3d. That all lightermen shall at once resume work, agreeing to submit any grievance they may have to arbitration.

'4th. Coal-workers to resume work at once.

'To avoid any delay in work being resumed, it is requested that each dock company, wharfinger, or granary-keeper will consent to the above terms in writing. It is most important that these consents should be in the hands of Mr. H. Lafone, at 36, Mark-lane, as early as possible.'

This statement was received with great and evident disappointment in the City, and animated conferences at the offices of the Peninsular and Oriental Steamship Company, at offices in East India-avenue, and at the offices in Butler's Wharf were held throughout the remainder of the afternoon and late into the evening.

The strike leaders had to lift morale after the attempt to widen the strike failed. Addressing an immense meeting on Tower Hill, Tillett and Mann went on the attack. The strikers were encouraged by the fact that sympathetic action was still being taken by large sections of London's workforce, including the workers of London's drainage. It was also publicly announced that Mr Lafone of Butler's Wharf had been paying his men who were in dispute. The men were also encouraged by the news that the ship-owners were becoming increasingly frustrated by the slow progress of negotiations and wished to make their own arrangements: they formed their own committee, and addressed a letter to Mr Norwood (published in *The Times* on Monday) somewhat curtly informing him of this development and adding 'on the part of the shipowners, nothing shall be wanting to pave the way to a clear understanding on this question.'

The Times, Monday, 2 September 1889, 7

On Saturday morning an immense meeting of labourers took place on Tower-hill.

Mr Burns, who was loudly cheered on arrival, announced the receipt of a cheque for £100 from the London Society of Compositors, £250 from the Seamen's, Firemen's and Dock Labourers' Association of Australia, a cheque for £25 from Lady Ripon, and £5 from Mr. Samuel Plimsoll. Continuing, Mr. Burns said it was with lighter hearts and greater hopes that they again assembled there that morning. They were nearer to victory than ever they had been;

Mr Tom Mann said negotiations were going on between the rep-

resentatives of the dock labourers and the wharfingers, but they were only being conducted on the lines laid down in the manifesto which the Strike Committee had issued. The coal-heavers were demanding an increase of $\frac{1}{2}$d. per ton, and that if it was not granted London would in 36 hours be in darkness. The gas workers would take up the cause of the coal labourers, and even now negotiations were proceeding with the Durham and other miners to prevent coals not only being sent to the London ports, but their being taken out of the pits.

During the speeches a Socialist flag was brought on to the ground, whereupon the greater number of those present demanded that it would be taken down, saying they did not want Socialism brought into the strike.

On Saturday it became known that Mr. H. Lafone, of Butler's Wharf, who has been so conspicuous in endeavouring to bring about a satisfactory compromise, had been paying 300 of his men who are on strike 1s. each per day, and on Saturday he gave each man 2s. to tide him and his family over Sunday.

The Times announced that the shipowners were in a state of revolt against the dock companies although they also noted the hardship which was now showing on the faces of those in dispute. It was also noted that the wharfingers were divided with a strong feeling that they should concede. Although the strikers were feeling the pinch the divisions amongst the employers were working well in their favour. It was now just a matter of strength; who had the strongest will to win. Picketing was intensified. Pressure was now being put on Mr Norwood by other employers to continue with negotiations. The strikers had no illusions as to what would be their fate if they were caught overstepping the mark in picketing. One of the very rare cases of intimidation ended with a three months' hard labour sentence being meted out. Also the authorities took a very dim view of the notices being posted on the dock gates by the pickets. So serious was the strike that convict labour was now being used by the government with strategic materials for the Army. The situation of the threat of Liverpool scabs was relieved with news of a strike of dock labourers at Liverpool.

THE STRIKES

(FROM A CORRESPONDENT)

The Times, Tuesday, 3 September 1889, 3

Again, with not less regret than heretofore, it has become necessary to state that the deadlock at the docks still continues. At the same time there are not wanting signs that affairs are nearer to settlement. From two points of view, at the least, and perhaps from three, the situation is becoming more and more critical. Two strong influences are certainly at work. The shipowners are in a state of something very near akin to revolt against the dock companies, and the men, in spite of the generosity with which the public in general and the union of workmen in particular

Burns addresses dockers on Tower Hill.

have come to their assistance, are undoubtedly feeling the spur of hunger to be increasingly sharp....

Meanwhile the wharfingers are divided into two sections. At least 30 leading men among them have formally expressed by resolution the opinion that the concessions which have already been made by the companies are all that the men can reasonably require. Another section, headed by Mr. Lafone, support the dock labourers, and are of the opinion that if they could induce the lightermen to go to work again they could bid defiance to the dock companies by unloading and loading vessels in midstream and at wharves....

Yesterday news of a disquieting character came to the dock company directors. They had reported to them that Mr. Burns in a speech that morning on Tower-hill before some 6,000 or 7,000 men had urged them to go from dock to dock at once, and 'turn out every man found at work.' Mr. Burns, it was further stated, added that 'if anything serious occurred' as the result of this action the dock directors, in not yielding to the demands of the men, and no one else, would be to blame. Had the advice been given and acted on, something serious perhaps would have happened. The belief of the dock directors was that the advice had been given, and a telegram was sent to the Chief Commissioner of Police, warning him that some 6,000 or 7,000 men were on the march to the docks, taking the West India Docks first, with the object of not leaving a single man in the docks, and a letter was sent to the Home Secretary conveying the same news.

It is due to Mr Burns to say that he must have been misinterpreted in the speech he made on Tower-hill, for though very severe 'picketing' was carried out, there was no attempt to make any open attack upon men who had gone in to work.

As soon as daylight broke yesterday morning gangs of men were to be seen placing themselves in front of the various entrances of the East

A march through the City of London, led by a brass band.

and West India Docks and the London and St. Katharine Docks, and other large centres of employment. By the manner in which they took up their positions, it could be easily seen that they had been 'drilled' to properly carry out their 'picketing' duties. No person entered the docks without first being button-holed by these pickets.

An important meeting of shipowners and the directors of the amalgamated dock companies was held at the Dock-house, following a meeting of the shipowners at the offices of the P. and O. Company [at which] it was unanimously agreed—

'That this meeting of the shipowners of London consider it essential to the conduct of their business that they shall have from the dock companies the power to discharge as well as to load their vessels, and to make their own arrangements with their men.

'2d. That a deputation ... wait upon the dock authorities to request permission to allow shipowners to discharge their own vessels at the quay and into craft alongside on such terms as the shipowners may arrange with the men.'

Mr. Norwood, in reply, said that no one could be more sensible than the Dock Joint Committee of the great inconvenience caused by the strike.... he had already expressed the opinion that it would be possible to allow the shipowners, on reasonable terms and conditions, to discharge their own ships. At a fitting moment they would be prepared to enter into the whole question. (Hear, hear.) That moment would be when the great pressure now put upon the dock directors to the occupation of their whole time had passed. At the present moment, however, they felt that as business men they could not enter into a question of detail, which would have far-reaching consequences, and they thought it a little unreasonable on the part of [the] shipowners to press for a solution of the question at this period of trouble. It was a matter which demanded calmness and deliberation.

NO MORE DEALINGS WITH BURNS AND TILLETT

Pall Mall Gazette, Tuesday, 3 September 1889

The sub-committee of the Dock directors met the representatives of the press yesterday, when Mr. Lubbock said the directors had decided to have no further communication with Messrs. Burns and Tillett, but they would be quite willing to receive any of the men lately in their employ who were authorised to speak on behalf of their fellows.

STRIKE CASES IN THE COURT

Evening News & Post, Tuesday, 3 September 1889

At the Thames Police-court, Richard Groves, 22, was charged with assault and threatening two men who were working in the docks. He was sentenced to three months' hard labour.

At the same court Alfred Kreamer, 49, was charged with intimidating several persons. It appeared he issued placards to the following effect: 'Notice to all men working in the holds and on the quays. As men we beg you to clear out at once, or we must inform you the consequences

must be extremely serious.' In consequence of these placards between 40 and 50 men left work at the docks. After hearing evidence, Mr Lushington remanded the prisoner.

GENERAL STRIKE OF TAILORS

Evening News & Post, Monday 2 September 1889

The East-end tailors strike held a meeting on Clerkenwell-green this afternoon. It is estimated by the strikers that 20,000 will have joined this strike by the middle of the week.

CONVICT LABOUR

Pall Mall Gazette, Tuesday, 3 September 1889

A vessel laden with granite blocks for Chatham Dockyard is being unloaded by convict labour in default of ordinary labourers being procured, while a collier with a large freight of coals for the Royal Marine Barracks, which has been at a standstill all day, will, it is said, be discharged to-morrow by fatigue parties of Royal Marines. It was rumoured last night that some manifestations of dissatisfaction on the part of a section of the dockyard labourers had been conveyed to the dockyard authorities. The class of men likely to be affected is confined simply to the day labourers, whose pay ranges from sixteen to twenty shillings per week.

DOCKERS STRIKE AT LIVERPOOL

The men engaged to unload the ship *Methley Hall* at Liverpool from Bombay, struck yesterday for an advance of one shilling per day and 4d an hour overtime beyond the present rate, which are 5s per day and 8d per hour. The dispute was compromised by the offer of 6d per day advance, but later twenty of the men struck for the full demand.

Mr Lafone of Butler's Wharf issued his terms for settlement on behalf of several employers and their workforce. (This version, dated 2 September, was identical with the one dated 30 August (*The Times,* 2 September) and rejected by the Docks Joint Committee. These concessions went a long way in meeting the strike committee's demands. This was a major turning point in the dispute and gave heart to the strikers and their supporters, who now saw the prospect of a divide-and-conquer policy.

The Times, Tuesday, 3 September 1889, 4

The Strike Committee would again take these terms into their consideration that evening at the Wade's Arms Tavern, Poplar, and if the decision was favourable to them, work might be resumed in the warehouses and on the wharves of the assentors the next morning. If the companies did not start work and the shipping was free, they would very soon been forced to start – in fact in about a matter of 24 hours. Mr. Lafone concluded by speaking in confident terms of a speedy settlement of the strike on the basis of this agreement.

Australian Relief Funds

But the employers were not alone in having disputes amongst their own ranks. It was becoming increasingly clear that there were serious divisions in relation to the men on the south side who complained of the lack of representation on the Central Strike Committee. It took all of Mann's skills to stop a major revolt on the south side. Mann denounced the Liberal-Labour ['Lib-Lab'] Members of Parliament for their lack of support. A minor victory was, however, achieved with the announcement that the watermen and lightermen had agreed terms with their employers. It was also reported that, unusually, the streets of East London were now deserted, the public houses being empty, and the men presenting themselves at the Wade's Arms looked in a sorry state. Their spirits were lifted when a cablegram was received announcing that £1,500 had been collected from Australia and was on its way, and sympathetic messages were received with a £10 donation from Hull. It was also announced that amongst other workers taking industrial action the hands at the Bryant & May's factory had struck on principle. Strikes were also announced in other ports, and it was now being argued by Labour representatives on the London County Council that the docks should be municipalised. Such was the pressure on Mr Norwood that the directors had to assume equal responsibility in negotiations.

The Times, Tuesday, 3 September 1889, 4

Although it was agreed by the Central Strike Committee that the usual daily march into the City should be dispensed with, the prohibition did not extend to South London. Tom Mann was deputed yesterday to look after the Bermondsey and Rotherhithe districts, and after holding meetings outside the Surrey Commercial Docks at 7 a.m. and at the Plough in Plough-road at 10 a.m., a procession was formed, which marched to London-bridge, along the Borough, and away to Clapham-common, where a third meeting was held and the grievances of the different classes of employees in the Surrey Commercial Docks were ventilated, in order that Tom Mann might be able to lay before them the Strike Committee with a view to some immediate action being taken. The speakers were Messrs. Brett, Sullivan, Hassett, Lee, Ryan, Cullen,

and Donovan. In most cases it appeared that the men on strike were pieceworkers who had come out for the sake primarily of getting the dock labourers their 6d. per hour, and who had then refused to return to work unless better terms are secured to them on their own account. The men complained that both corn porters and deal porters had had their earnings reduced at a time when work was slack, and now demand a restoration of the old rates of wages.

Their lack of representation on the Central Strike Committee was also discussed with Tom Mann, and he undertook to lay their views before his colleagues last night.

It was reported in Southwark yesterday that the watermen's and lightermen's terms of 6s. for a day of 12 hours and 6s. per night, had been acceded to by the masters, to take effect as soon as the dock strike is over.

Last night the streets of the East-end presented a most dreary and desolate appearance. All the Public-houses and beershops were almost empty – a most unusual thing in this neighbourhood when the docks are in full work. Gangs of labourers could be seen congregated under arches or in any nook which afforded shelter from the heavy rain which fell almost incessantly during the evening. These passed away the time in discussing the situation and the probable result of the strike.

At the Wade's Arms, the headquarters of the Strike Committee, some 2,000 poor labourers collected about 8 o'clock, and standing there in the drenching rain they presented a most woe-begone appearance. The ravages of hunger were clearly traceable on nearly all their countenances, and they waited patiently out in the wet for tickets which would be the means of procuring them food, of which they stood in so much need. An idea of the extent of the existing distress may be gathered when it is mentioned that yesterday upwards of 16,000 relief tickets were distributed, and of this number over 2,500 were given away after 5 o'clock. About 7 o'clock last evening a van laden with tea, all of which was done up in 1/4lb. packets, arrived outside the hall in Kerby-street. This was the gift of some merchants, and will certainly bring comfort into many homes, where the luxury of tea has been missing for so many days past.

In an interview Mr Burns had with a reporter, he stated that about £1,000 had been received that day towards the strike fund. Messengers are bringing in subscriptions from all parts, in order to insure speedy delivery.

Evening News & Post,
Wednesday,
4 September 1889

A Reuter telegram from Melbourne states universal sympathy is felt there with the London dock labourers, meetings to give expression to the prevalent feeling are being organized, and numerous subscriptions have been opened in aid of the strikers.

At a meeting at Melbourne yesterday, according to a cablegram received by an evening newspaper, £1,500 was collected on behalf of the dock labourers in London, and a resolution was passed condemning the action of the directors.

STRIKE AT BRYANT & MAY

Manchester Guardian, Wednesday, 4 September 1889

The hands employed in Bryant & May's match factory are on strike. The dippers and packers demanded an addition to their wages of 3s a week. To the former, whose work is very unhealthy the concession was made, but it was refused to the latter and the dippers are out 'on principle'.

A DOCKERS' STRIKE AT OTHER PORTS:

Pall Mall Gazette, Wednesday, 4 September 1889

Some excitement was caused in Liverpool yesterday by about 100 grain porters, employed at the Southern Docks, Striking for an advance of wages from 5s to 6s per day, and 1s instead of 8d per hour overtime. The men are employed to carry sacks of grain from the holds of vessels to the dock quay, and each man is said to move five tons per day. More men soon joined the strike, and in one case at the north end of the docks the advance was granted, but it is surmised, only to secure the discharge of the vessel concerned. The owners of the ships in the Southern Docks say they will give the men a chance to resume work in the morning, but if they still stand out the vessel will be taken to Birkenhead and then discharged.

John Burns yesterday stated that if Sir Donald Currie decided to unload and load his fleet at Southampton he would go down and organise a dockers' strike there also. Already there was a strike proceeding at Liverpool, and before long there would be another at Glasgow.

The dock directors have done well to assume the full responsibility for the conduct of Mr Norwood in the struggle he is maintaining on their behalf. It was manifestly unfair that all the odium should be heaped on his head alone. Mr Norwood, too, will lose nothing by the emphatic denial he has given to the statement that he has used unfeeling language respecting the men.

Picketing was becoming the important operation, and it became increasingly clear from the reports from the pickets that they were an organised force, drilled to have the greatest possible effect. The number of pickets was now reckoned to be in the region of fifteen thousand.

The Times, Wednesday, 4 September 1889, 5–6

In the morning there was the usual inspection of pickets, and, in this connexion, the directors themselves do not now say that the pickets have been guilty, on the whole, of serious intimidation.

The organizers of the strike have some cause to congratulate themselves on the success of their tactics. During the whole of Monday men were being quietly smuggled into the docks and got to work. As soon, however, as daylight broke yesterday morning gangs of men formed into picketing parties took up positions at every entrance to the docks – both from the land and the river – as well as in front of the wharves. Men who came up with the intention of seeking work were waylaid and in persuasive terms invited to join the strikers. This they did without apparently much force of argument, probably from fear of being afterwards known as 'black-legs'. In an incredibly short time after 6 o'clock, at which hour many of those already in the docks had commenced to work, they were 'got out', and before breakfast threw up their employment, and came out of the docks amid the cheers of those on strike outside. It appears that the *modus operandi* adopted by the strikers for getting at those at work is to appoint several labourers on whom reliance can be placed as to their persuasive powers to offer themselves to the dock managers as willing to work. These, on getting inside the docks, at once set to work to induce the others to come out, and, as the event has proved, with success. the persuaders and the persuaded then leave the docks together. . . .

It was computed that the pickets on duty yesterday at the several docks and warehouses numbered nearly 15,000 men, so the difficulty of getting fresh hands to go into work will be at once aparent, many of the watermen and lightermen, who on Monday re-commenced work, again left their barges, in the face of the notice issued yesterday afternoon from Watermen's Hall. It is felt that should the Watermen's Company take proceedings against any of those on strike it would only aggravate the present crisis, besides commencing a proceeding the end of which it would be difficult to foretell. . . .

Yesterday morning the owners of Brewer's Quay were able to engage more hands than they had been able to get since the commencement of the strike, but before they had been at work many hours the pickets talked to them and they came out.

The Times,
Wednesday,
4 September 1889, 6

The strike epidemic is now spreading to the Jewish quarter of the East-end, and that was the principal reason for opening the depôt in the Whitechapel-road. it is stated that about 6,000 tailors are now out on strike, and that many more will turn out before the end of the week if their demands are not granted. In addition to the tailors, a large number of Jewish cigar-makers, cigarette-makers, and boot-finishers are out on strike. . . . In one thing they are unanimous, and that is the demand for a higher rate of wages.

The committee, too, desired to point out to the public that, while much had been said about 5d. an hour for the outside dock labour being low, it might be contrasted with the 14s. to 16s. a week paid for a day of 12 hours to the agricultural labourer, a rate which came to about 2½d. an hour, as against 5d. per hour at the docks. At the docks it was not possible to give 12 hours' labour right off, nor, as a matter of fact, was there sufficient for all applying. Under these circumstances, any increase in the rate of pay would have a tendency to drive trade from London and thus reduce the amount of employment, at the same time attracting more labour, so that if the rates were increased per hour, the amount earned by the men would be less than 5d. per hours. An increase in the rate per hour would be disadvantageous to the workers.

In the afternoon the directors stated that the position of matters was the same as it had been earlier in the day. The committee, however, wished to take that opportunity of stating to the Press that they noticed with considerable regret the violent attacks which were being made upon Mr. Norwood personally, and they desired that the public should understand that throughout the strike Mr. Norwood had acted with the unanimous approval of all his colleagues in every respect, and that every one of them wished to bear his full share of responsibility for everything that had to be done. Mr. Norwood was also anxious to state that the reports of his having made use of unfeeling language in regard to the strikers were absolutely without foundation.

An important interview between the representative shipowners and the directors of the Amalgamated London and India Dock Companies was held at the Dock-house in Leadenhall-street yesterday morning, in continuation of the conference held on the previous day. ...

The proceedings were opened by Mr. Norwood continuing the proceedings of the day before, and he spoke in a low conversational tone, which was heard only with difficulty. ... He could not see how any possible good could be obtained by carrying out the suggestions the shipowners had made. The shipowners certainly could not discharge their ships without they had lightermen perfectly ready with barges to receive the cargoes, and that was a thing which could not possibly occur – well, would not occur, at any rate, for some little time. He thought the lightermen, as a whole, did not show any disposition to resume work, and, at any rate, in unloading ships there must be lightermen ready to receive the cargo. Then, he might say with regard to this, as well as to the larger question, there were details which must be settled between the dock companies and the shipowners – namely, very practical details as to the share of the operations which the shipowners themselves proposed to take in handling the goods. It would be necessary to have that matter discussed in order that the dock companies might know what the shipowners proposed to do, where their labour would commence, where it would end, and where that of the dock companies would commence.

John Lovell, *Stevedores and Dockers* (1969), 110–111

There was another factor behind the sudden withdrawal of the 'No-Work Manifesto', a factor that quite miraculously altered the entire situation. On 29 August, the very day on which the manifesto was drawn up, news arrived from Australia that the Brisbane Wharf Labourers' Union was sending £150 to the London strike fund. In itself this was not particularly significant. The point was that the Brisbane donation marked the beginning of a steady stream of funds from Australia.... From the beginning of September onward the strike leaders had no need to worry further about the problem of relief; massive financial support from Australia banished the spectre of defeat through hunger. Taking advantage of

this situation, the strike leadership quickly switched its tactics. The processions into the City were abandoned and all efforts were now concentrated on the picket lines. If the infiltration of blacklegs could be kept down to a minimum victory was now a distinct possibility.

Although things looked black for the strikers, the announcement that £150 was being sent by the Brisbane Wharf Labourers' Union was the prelude to the largest amount of money, £30,000, ever donated to a dispute. This would ensure an adequate supply of funds for the strikers and their supporters. The other important factor was that Cardinal Manning had now entered the arena. His public esteem and support would be essential to the success of the dispute.

Ben Tillett, *Memories and Reflections* (1931), 145–147

... It was precisely at this moment that Cardinal Manning intervened. He appeared on the scene the day after our 'No Work' manifesto. He sought an interview with the dock directors and he urged them to reconsider their position. Undoubtedly the Cardinal was apprehensive of the possibilities of disorder arising from the Strike and he was, of course, aware of the menace implied in the proposal to extend the area of the dispute. About the possibility of social disorder, as far as our people were concerned, the Cardinal had no reason for anxiety. I marvel to this day at the self-restraint of the strikers. Rough elements there were amongst them under the stress of events; tempers were none too stable; angry passions would rise. I had sometimes to deal with men animated by primitive emotions, in a very primitive fashion. My hard training at fisticuffs in the Navy proved useful sometimes. Some large and lusty men had to be taught that I could not be intimidated, or my authority defied....

My respect for the Cardinal was enhanced by the feeling I entertained towards the square-jawed, hard-featured Bishop of London, Dr. Temple, who had refused to assist, and answered my appeal with a letter full of the most virulent abuse of the docker and his claim for a higher wage. Dr Temple, as Bishop of London, felt that he could not allow the Catholic Cardinal to obtain all the credit of promoting a settlement of the Strike. Accordingly he hurried back from North Wales, when he learned that the door of negotiation had been gently forced opened by the Cardinal, and joined with him in forming, with the Lord Mayor, Mr Sidney Buxton, Lord Brassey, Sir John Lambert, and others what was called the Mansion House Committee to act as mediators between the Joint Committee representing the dock companies, and the General Committee of the Strike....

From the first the Cardinal showed himself to be the dockers' friend, though he had family connections in the shipping interests, represented on the other side. Our demands were too reasonable, too moderate, to be set aside by an intelligence so fine, a spirit so lofty, as that which animated the frail, tall figure with its saintly, emaciated face, and the strangely compelling eyes.

The stevedores' banner, struck to commemorate the help given by the Australians.

The chauvinistic Britisher would look in amazement at the fact that of the £48,750 3s 1d which was raised during the dispute, over two-thirds, namely £30,423 15s 0d came from Australia. (P. F. Donovan, an Australian historian, claims the amount actually collected was over £37,000.) Australia was then seen as an outback in relation to the labour movement. In fact, the Australian labour movement, though small, had won the eight-hour day and was to the forefront of new unionism before that term had even reached this country, putting forward socialist MPs and having a very outspoken ideology. There were other reasons for this massive response. Although most of the income from Britain came from London and the home counties, Australia gave more, not just because of the issue of socialism or the dispute but because of the large numbers of Irish immigrants which there were in Australia. Their great hostility to the English state made them feel that they could help by contributing in this massive way.

Labour History [Australia], No. 23 (Nov. 1972) 19 catalogues the way in fact the monies were raised:

P. F. Donovan, in his article, 'Australia and the Great London Dock Strike: 1889'

'In each of the colonies, in the capital cities and the country towns, numerous general meetings were convened on the initiative of prominent citizens. The public meeting at the Temperance Hall in Melbourne on Tuesday, 3 September, was so well attended that many could not gain admittance, and an overflow meeting had to be organised. The programme of each meeting was similar and was begun by prominent men, speaking of the plight of the London dockers. The typical attitude was expressed by Mr W. S. Paul, M.L.A., of Brisbane, who said 'that he had always been dead against strikes, but in this instance his sympathy was entirely with the movement for the relief of the dock labourers.' A resolution affirming sympathy for the dock labourers or the support of the meeting for their cause, would then be put, after which a collection would be taken up. At the meeting at the Masonic Hall in Sydney, on 4 September, nearly £500 was collected or promised.

The principal feature of Sydney activities was the processions of trade unions and mass rallies, organised by the Trades and Labor Council. ...

Football was, of course, used to augment the funds. On Saturday, 14 September, Cooma and Nimmitabel played a ten-point draw, but raised £10, while in Melbourne the proceeds of a match between Carlton and South Melbourne swelled the funds by about £600. in both Melbourne and Adelaide, bands gave public concerts in aid of the appeal while, in Sydney, the Trades and Labor council organised a picnic for the same purpose. In fact, any expedient that could raise money was tried.

The Australian public were fully aware of what was going on. The Australian press began to report the dock strike in full. Some over-enthusiastic supporters saw the huge amount of money given to the London dockers as a way of ensuring that any future strike in Britain could be won; but although other appeals were launched in following strikes, nothing ever corresponded to the support, both practical and moral, contributed to the dock workers' strike. This, of course, enhanced the Australian labour movement itself, because they could easily boast that their money was the real source of victory.

Another blow to the employers came when the Watermen's Company issued a warning that no barge, lighter boat etc., was to be used by anybody who was not a member of their liveried society. This virtually sealed off many of the boats in the river waiting for discharge. John Burns was able to announce that they had received the £1,500 promised from Australia, and that £3,000 was expected on that day alone. The money was arriving from Australia at the right psychological and material time. A guarantee to the strikers that they could carry on and engage in a long dispute but bad news for the employers whose ranks were already divided. Burns was able to speak in brighter tones to the next major gathering of the men and their supporters. Burns was even able to joke at the fact how a battalion of Coldstream Guards were to be stationed at the Tower of London for twelve months. Burns retorted, they could remain there for twelve years if they liked. As the guards marched by Burns called out for three cheers to which the strikers responded.

The Times, Wednesday, 4 September 1889, 6

The representative wharfingers and the members of the Watermen's Company have also been in consultation. The Watermen's Company, in addition to the notice repeated to the men in *The Times*, of yesterday, have issued the following warning:—

'The attention of the freemen of the Watermen and Lightermen's Company is earnestly called to the provisions of the 66th section of the Company's act (22 and 23 Victoria, c. 133).

' "No barge, lighter, boat, or other like craft, for the carrying of goods, wares, or merchandise, shall be worked or navigated within the limits of this Act unless there be in charge of such craft a lighterman licensed in manner hereinbefore mentioned; or an apprentice qualified as hereinbefore mentioned; and if any such craft be navigated in contravention of this section, the owner thereof shall, in respect of such offence, incur a penalty not exceeding £5, subject to this proviso, that no such penalty shall be payable if the owner proves to the satisfaction of the magistrate or court before whom the case is heard, that he is unable, for the usual compensation, to obtain the services of any such lighterman or apprentice." '

Mr. Burns congratulated the men on their continued good conduct, although they had now entered upon the fourth week of the strike. That morning he had better news for them than he had on the previous day. They had received £1,500 from Australia, and before the end of that day they expected their total receipts to amount to £3,000. Each of the men on strike would have a share of this money; and he hoped they would make application for relief at the proper place as soon as possible, so that they might benefit by the generous gift which had come across the ocean from their fellow-countrymen. They would, perhaps, like to know that the shipping firms had been interviewing the dock companies, and with the wharfingers, and were now fighting like the Kilkenny cats. After these parties had weakened each other, the dock labourers would step in and 'knock the stuffing out of the three of them'. They might be sure they were going to win that strike. When it first began they were told that the men would in a few days be starved into submission; but after three weeks had elapsed they were in a firmer position than ever, and would continue so until they won.

Mr. Burns, having addressed three other meetings, proceeded to Tower-hill. Although a drenching rain was falling there were some 5,000 or 6,000 labourers present, and during the proceedings these were largely augmented.

At this stage a man in the crowd announced that a battalion of the Coldstream Guards was about to march into the Tower, where they would remain for 12 months. Mr. Burns replied they could remain 12 years if they liked, for the longer they stopped the more they would help

them. The men in Chelsea Barracks did not cheer them on Sunday for nothing. They were men of the people. When their six years were over with the colours, they would be fighting at the docks for their 'tanner'. (Cheers.)

The Guards then marched by, headed by their band. At a signal from Mr. Burns three hearty cheers were given for the soldiers. Mr. Burns then took off his straw hat, and said that, as military etiquette did not allow the Guards to cheer them, on their behalf he thanked them. (Laughter.) They had no band, and the Guards had given them one. That was a conspiracy, 'Burns in league with the Guards.' There was some picturesque copy for the Press. (Laughter.)

Immediately afterwards the relieved regiment of Guards marched out from the Tower, when these were also loudly cheered.

The relief centres were now in full swing. A hundred thousand tickets, each representing a shilling in value, were issued, sufficient to keep the families in food for twenty-four hours. Individuals, too, were also supplying relief, as was the Salvation Army which was also doing a magnificent job, nine thousand half–quartern loaves of bread being distributed daily.

The rift with the south side men was slowly healed. The Non-conformist clergy, being in support of the men, used their churches to hold vast meetings. They too complained of the neglect of the south-side men, especially in relation to relief, although they stated that this was not the fault of Burns or Tillett, and they were well pleased to see Tom Mann now in charge of operations on the south side. They also reinforced the statement that the police were not needed in this dispute. John Burns gave his word to the south-side men that they would not be neglected, and blamed the employers and especially Mr. Norwood for the continuance of the strike.

Aid was now being given both near and far, and, as on the north side of the river, the south-side shopkeepers and others were being equally generous in giving relief to the distressed. Burns also took the opportunity to answer criticisms of the call for a general strike, stating that it had effected its purpose as their relief funds has swelled by £2,500.

As if Mr. Norwood and the employers didn't have enough problems, Mr. W. Clare reminded readers of *The Times* that in a previous dock dispute the employers were taken to court in order to pay costs in relation to the loss of trade. Meanwhile, there were further calls from dividendless shareholders for a meeting to discuss the dispute.

The Times, Wednesday, 4 September 1889, 7

It is an illustration of the magnitude to which the strike has now attained, that nearly 100,000 tickets, each representing 1s. in value, were yesterday distributed. Such a distribution must of necessity dissipate a fear of the strikers or their families suffering from actual starvation for some 24 hours at least; and judging by the way in which the money still

continues to flow in a similar distribution may be expected to-day. The above has simply to do with the organizers of the strike, and is quite apart from the philanthropy which is hourly being displayed by City and other philanthropic persons to those in the East-end.

Yesterday the large Salvation Army Hall, situate at 272, Whitechapel-road, and which was formerly a drill-hall, was, at the instance of General Booth, opened as an additional depôt for the relief of those on strike, and will continue so as long as the strike continues. To-day there will be plenty of soup and other eatables for those having tickets, while others for a halfpenny will be supplied with a large piece of bread and a basin of soup. Yesterday it was computed that some 10,000 persons had used the hall. Members of the army were all last night busily engaged in erecting huge cauldrons, in which to prepare tea and coffee; and in anticipation of the rush which is expected this morning for food no less than 9,000 half-quartern loaves of bread have been stored away during the night for use.

Last night a densely crowded meeting was held in the Bermondsey Town-hall, for the purpose of obtaining 'help for the sufferers through the strike.' Mr. R. V. Barrow presided, and, in opening, said that last Friday night they held a meeting in support of the reduction of the hours of labour the lightermen and watermen have to work. They had now met on a much deeper and wider subject – viz., to obtain help for those men, worse paid, who for the last 21 days had been suffering privations and hunger to better their condition.

The Rev. J. Carlisle moved the first resolution – 'That this meeting heartily sympathizes with the dock labourers of London in their strike for the moderate and reasonable increase in their pay, and urges them to remain firm and united till their joint demands are conceded.' He rejoiced that the manifesto calling for a general strike had been cancelled and withdrawn, and he trusted that those in work would now remain in work and assist those out to the very best of their ability. It had been said that this side of the water had been greatly neglected by the strike committee, and they [had] not been able to get the relief to which they were entitled. He was quite sure that that was not the fault of either Mr. Burns or Mr. Tillett, for he had tried to see them, but he always found that there were about 100,000 men between them, and their time was fully occupied. He was glad to see that Mr. Mann had now come on the Surrey side to organize the forces here.

Mr. John Burns, who was received with most enthusiastic cheering, said that that was the sixth meeting since about half-past 4 that morning that he had held. The others were larger even than this and even more enthusiastic than this, though they were held in downpours of rain and by men with empty stomachs. Let them not think that he wanted to hold out this struggle longer than was actually necessary. Any man who would prolong this strike for personal motives, with hungry men, starving women, and famished children all around, would be a disgrace to himself

An artist's impression of dockers' children waiting for relief during the strike.

Speakers and demonstrators seek shelter as yet another unemployed march is broken up.

and would deserve to be ostracized by society. (Cheers.) With respect to what had been said about them not being able to get relief on this side, he could assure them that all connected in this movement on that committee had been working early and late till they were fairly exhausted. Now Tom Mann had undertaken to organize this side of the water all these things would be remedied. They had had some offers by persons wanting to make a speech at 3 in the afternoon, but this was no masher agitation, and if any one really wanted to help them they must be prepared to come and do anything they were wanted to do at 3 o'clock in the morning. Let them go on as they had been going on and they would soon be able to keep the oats themselves and give the sack to Norwood. (Cheers.) The men on strike now were more determined and united than ever. One thing he would like to say, and that was that, so far from having any personal interest to serve, if this strike could be brought to a termination sooner without his interference he would resign his position at once. He had been called to account for issuing Friday's manifesto for a general strike. Well, that had effected its purpose. It had added to their funds about £2,500 a day; so people who knew nothing about this great war had no right to make such observations, nor criticize them in the spirit they did. He was quite sure they were not going to tell all their secrets; that would not do. They were now nearer the Victory than ever. He knew it because the directors had sent for the police in large force. Well, they had to be on duty very late, and then very early in the mornings. Then they were yawning with their eyes shut, and if it were not for the shouts of the strikers and their brass bands he verily believed that every policeman would be dismissed for being asleep while on duty at his post. Well, they were told that the ships were going to be discharged at Southampton. He could tell them then that there would be a strike there. Why, the P. and O. Company had lost between £5,000 and £7,000 from every ship that had come in. They talked about taking their ships to Liverpool. The committee had stopped their game there, for there was a strike there now. Now they said they should take their ships to Glasgow, but he could tell them that in less than 48 hours there was going to be a strike there. (Cheers.) Some people might talk of the cold and the hunger they had to suffer through strikes, but there was no coldness that came up to the coldness of Norwood's heart, nor there was no warmth that came up to the warmth of a docker's and a stevedore's. He was sure that this strike was an epoch in the labour movement, and he was proud of the men who, with every incentive to violence and anarchy, could carry on this movement in the way they had. (Great cheering.)

The Chairman announced that the subscriptions amounted to £7 17s. 7d.

TO THE EDITOR OF THE TIMES

Sir, – I have refrained from saying anything hitherto respecting what occurred during a previous strike, as, like other owners and brokers, I do not wish to hamper the dock companies in their dealings with their men; but as day by day goes on without their permitting us to discharge our vessels ourselves, or doing themselves the work they claim the right to do, I think the following statement of facts concerning a strike which occurred in the West India Docks some 17 years ago may be found worthy of a place in your columns and interesting to shipowners and the general public.

Then, as now, I knew of a steamer whose cargo the company had agreed to discharge *en bloc* for an extra rate of 10d. per ton, when the dock labourers struck and the work was suspended. Then. as now, the brokers were willing to pay the company the extra cost of discharging which the men on strike demanded. Then, as now, the company refused to assist the owners on the ground that if they paid the labourers the extra money on that steamer they would have to raise their wages for all time, at a cost of thousands of pounds per annum to themselves.

Then, having caused the owners a very serious loss by dragging them in to fight their battle against the men (which eventually they compromised, effecting a large saving upon the advance the men required), they refused to make the owners any allowance for their heavy loss, and upon going to trial before Lord Coleridge and a jury at Guildhall the owners of the steamer ... recovered a verdict against the dock company for nearly £1,700, and, eventually, the costs of two trials, although the dock company pleaded that they had never signed a contract to discharge the steamer, and were not liable for the consequences of a strike.

Whether now, as then, they will be liable for the loss shipowners sustain by their refusal to allow them to discharge their own vessels, whilst at the same time the measures they take are inadequate for the purpose, remains to be seen....

I am, Sir, yours obediently, W. CLARE.
4, Bishopsgate-street within, Sept. 3.

Pressure was also being exerted on the employers, especially Mr Norwood, to open up negotiations with Tillet and Burns, and it was becoming obvious to everybody that the strikers were winning not just the moral victory but the victory against the employers because of the concessions that already had been made; and the prospect of the shipowners taking over the responsibility for the men was now openly being discussed.

The Times, Wednesday, 4 September 1889, 9

The strike drags along, but has lost its early vigour. The dock directors have refused to recognize the representative capacity of MR. BURNS and MR. TILLETT in any further negotiations. But the struggle will apparently be settled, not by negotiations, but by sheer endurance. All that can be said has been said. Even the powerful appeal of the shipowners to be allowed to discharge their own vessels themselves, making use of the dock accommodation, but taking upon their own shoulders the responsibility of engaging labour, has been politely declined by the dock companies for the present. MR. NORWOOD and his colleagues are ready to entertain the idea, but, as they refuse to discuss ways and means while the strike continues, the shipowners are thrown back upon their own resources. Unless they can devise any means of doing without the docks at all, which is very doubtful, their cargoes must go on rotting, and loss from demurrage will continue to accumulate. We may assume for the

A mother, old before her time, and her child with seemingly no future.

present that there is no way of setting trade in motion again short of a surrender. . . .

But, on the other hand, the strikers have immensely bettered their position. They have obtained the promise that any man who is called in shall not be dismissed without a *minimum* payment of 2s. They have been promised the abolition of the contractor. What is more, under the mixed system of piece-work and time-work which is to supplant the contract system, they are to receive 6d. an hour and 8d. overtime; so that they will obtain the wages they ask for, provided they consent to work at what is, no doubt, somewhat high pressure. They have, in fact, got everything they ever asked for – leaving aside the preposterous demand to be called in at two fixed hours of the day only, which can never have been meant seriously – except that the companies still insist upon their working by the piece instead of by the hour simply. But this is not all. There is a fair prospect that if the men return to work their relations with their present taskmasters will cease. If the negotiations between the shipowners and the dock companies are brought to a successful issue – and, strike or no strike, the shipowners appear to be bent upon attaining their object – the dock labourer will become the servant of the shipowner. Whether he will find his new masters as ready as his old ones to employ casual labour we offer no opinion. The shipowners could not be blamed if they avoided the necessity of casual labour by keeping as large a casual staff as possible. But at any rate the shipowners have committed themselves indirectly to the principle of paying a higher rate of wages for the same work that the dock labourer now performs for the dock companies.

In the meantime the watermen and lightermen were beginning to assert their independence. Although at first striking in sympathy with the dock workers, they now had their own series of demands that they would insist were to be met in full.

Lafone conceded the demands of the strike committee and went so far as to state that if the workers would go back on his terms, the dock companies would be beaten. Lafone was dealing directly at this time with Burns and Champion, Ben Tillett being conspicuous by his absence. The only obstacle in the way of settlement was the separate dispute of lightermen.

This was a major breakthrough, as Lafone and the employers he represented had conceded the dockers' tanner. A message was received from Tillett stating that he was indisposed. One can only assume that there must have been some form of disagreement amongst the strike committee following the no-work manifesto. Tillett was clearly not to be involved in these important negotiations.

The lightermen, however, were to prove strong in their resolve not to accept any terms less than their full demands, and they made these demands and the reasons behind them public.

The Times, Thursday, 5 September 1889, 4

During the day the City offices of Butler's Wharf were the centre of considerable interest in consequence of statements that the efforts of Mr. Lafone were likely to lead to a settlement of terms between wharfingers and the representatives of the strikers, which would have a very considerable effect upon the strike. Mr. Burns, Mr. Champion, and Mr. Lafone had interviews in the course of the day, and last evening, at half-past 5, Mr. Lafone stated that the following document had been drawn up, and that if the Strike Committee assented to it at their meeting at night, work would be resumed at Butler's Wharf this morning. Mr. Champion stated that Mr. Lafone had practically conceded the demands of the men, and that he was in favour of the scheme. He added that there was very little doubt that the terms would be agreed to by the Strike Committee.

The document of 4 September repeated those of 30 August and 2 September except:
"Pay for casual work to be 6d. per hour; no pay for dinner time."
This replaced: 'The pay for casual work to be 6d per hour for the first four hours, if only working for that time, if for longer, the rate of 4s for nine hours, and 6d per hour from nine to twelve hours, with an allowance of half an hour for dinner. Despite the apparent marginal improvement in terms (equivalent to 3d a day), this change later became a cause of discontent.

In reply to questions, Mr Champion said that if these proposals were accepted by the Strike Committee, the men would be allowed to work at any wharf whose owner signed them. Picketing, he observed, would prevent the men from entering other wharves. It thus appeared that Mr Lafone's efforts, if accepted, would result in maintaining the difference between employers and employed indefinitely in the cases where the employers refused to bind themselves by such a contract.

Mr Tillett was indisposed and unable to take part in the meeting. Many were the sympathetic expressions for his speedy recovery.

A meeting of the committee of the Lightermen's Association was held at the York Minster Publichouse, Philpot-street, Commercial-road. Whilst the committee were deliberating some hundreds of watermen now on strike assembled in front of the house.

Mr. Wiggington, the secretary, first spoke ... The lightermen now wished the public to know the real facts of the dispute. They also wanted the public to know that the number of hours they were obliged to work were more than those worked by any other class of men in the kingdom. They were quite prepared to admit that it was possible for a lighterman to earn over £3 a week, but to do this he must work the whole 24 hours in the seven days. This was incompatible with human physical endurance. The men did not wish to work in that way, for it told so heavily on them that their young men grew old before they reached

middle age; and most of them were at times laid up through rheumatism. It was, therefore, in the interests of the employers and men that the hours of labour of the latter should be curtailed. Even at this eleventh hour he believed it was possible for some arrangement to be made by which the question of hours might be satisfactorily settled. They wanted to have the working hours in one day curtailed to 12. Their employers argued that this could not be done, but they who did the work, and therefore knew most about it, knew that it could be. It was as easy for them to work 12 hours as to work 16. He hoped this concession would be granted, because, as it was, the lightermen hanging about Tower-street and Thames-street for employment at all hours of the night, owing to the uncertainty of their engagements, under the present system almost made themselves a street nuisance. They were not so unreasonable as not to know that at times it was necessary for the lightermen to keep on at work, which they could not leave. They had never objected to this. What they did object to was that a man should be called out of his barge and have to walk half-a-dozen miles or more to fetch up another barge. One man ought to be allowed to finish his job, and when there was a fresh one a new man should be put on. They had been told, through the medium of the Press, that they had a very nice time of it. He admitted there were moments when the lighterman could sit down in the sunshine as his barge went easily along, and this might seem to justify what had been said; but even then the lightermen had to keep their eyes open, and were, therefore, at work. Let them look at the other side of the case. Let them call to mind the work done by the man who had to carry up 100 sacks of flour or 1,000 bags of seeds or many baskets of fruit. Let them realize all this being done in the hours of the night, and then it would be seen if the lighterman's lot was an easy one. The lightermen were treated a good deal worse than the tugs, for the latter got a day's rest now and then, but the former never did. Did their employers think they were like steam engines and that there was no need to do more than turn on the steam to keep them going? They appeared to forget that the lightermen were human. The men had not complained of not making sufficient money, but, on the contrary, were satisfied with what they earned and would like to see the pay distributed over a greater area, believing this would be to the interest of all parties.

One of the delegates thought it ought to be known that if, after having been at work four or five nights, they asked for a night's rest they were in danger of being instantly discharged.

Mr. Tom Mann next spoke at a mass meeting of Bermondsey, Rotherhithe, and Deptford men assembled at Deptford Broadway. At the conclusion the men marched in procession to Southwark Park, where the third meeting took place. On the way Mr. Henry Lafone met the men, and, alighting from his cab, held a conversation with Tom Mann. They then adjourned to Wood's Coffee-house, where Mr Lafone offered to concede the full demands of the men and urged their immediate

Hearth and home.

Laid up from work through sickness or injury, their only saviour from the workhouse was the union.

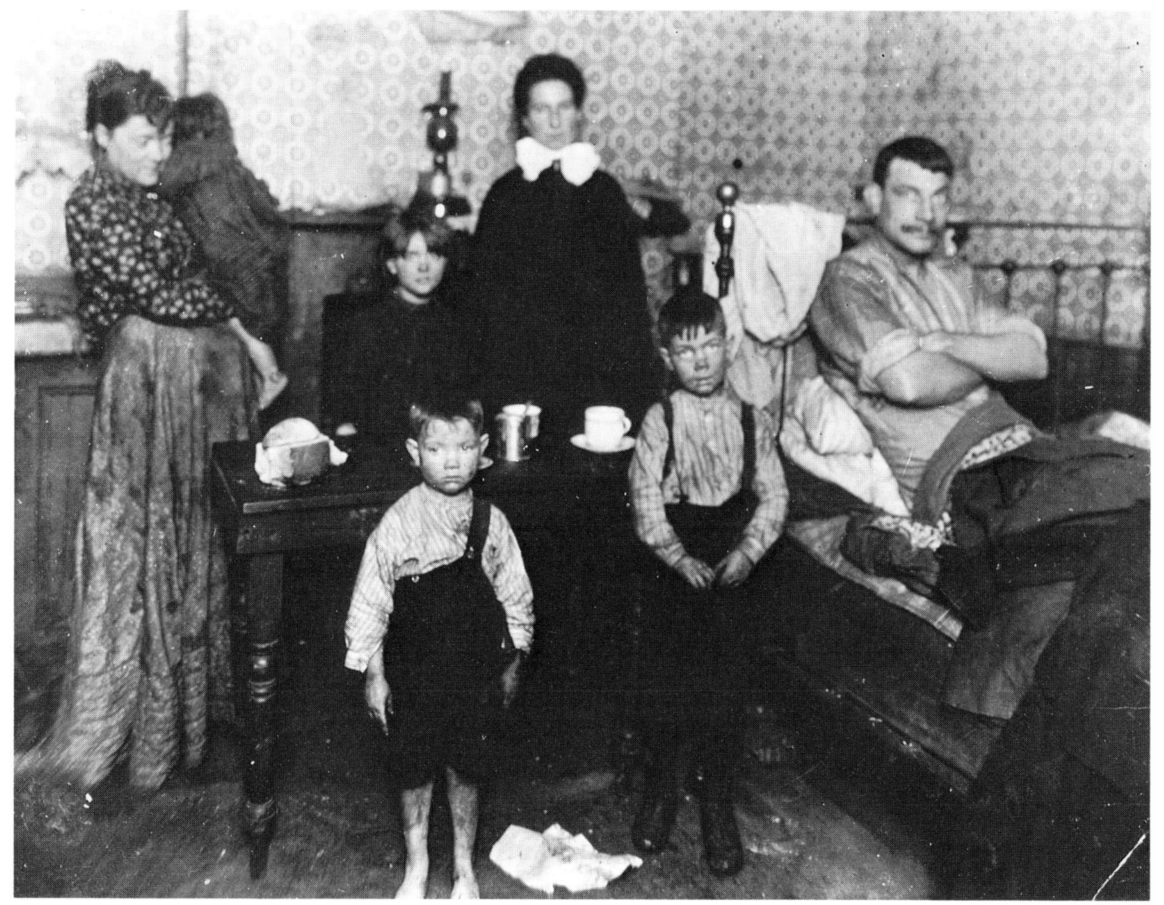

acquiescence in the arrangement, so that he might put up a notice on the gates of Butler's Wharf that work would be resumed this (Thursday) morning. Mann promised to lay the matter before the men in Southwark Park so as to ascertain their views. Mr. Lafone then left for his Mark-lane office. Upon reaching the park and recounting what had occurred, Mann took a show of hands with an unfavourable result. The question was, however, finally reserved for the decision of the general council.

At the Surrey Commercial Docks matters are just as they were so far as the men are concerned. Fresh vessels are continually arriving, and there are now 52 timber and grain ships in the docks waiting to be unloaded.

The net result may thus be summarised. On the Middlesex side the vast majority of the wharves are not idle and on the Surrey side some are at work. It can hardly be supposed that here, whatever may happen in the case of the dock labourers, the men who still remain away from work will hold out much longer.

Meanwhile, as part of the work of the late evening and the night, came the task of considering the result of the conference between Mr. Lafone and Messrs. Burns and Champion, which had occupied a great part of the day. It came out in the form of a document [which] was made nominally subject to approval by the strike committee, but since it was prepared after discussion with two at least of the leading men among them, that assent can hardly be considered doubtful. The document embodies certain terms to which dock owners, wharfingers, and granary keepers are asked to signify their agreement by signature. The terms are substantially those originally demanded on behalf of the men. It would thus seem that this is in effect a proposal on the part of Mr. Lafone, and perhaps of some other wharfingers, and that the dock companies, the wharfingers, and the granary keepers are asked to give their assent. The important people to be considered are the dock companies. Of the men employed at the wharves in ordinary times a large number have already gone back to work, and more will in all probability go soon. This fact is tolerably well known to Mr. Burns, and it is fairly well understood that, even if the men have not received his formal sanction to their taking this course, they have known very well that he would have no objection to their doing so. In effect London had to be provisioned, and if it had not been, if prices had risen, no men would have suffered more than the forces under the command of Mr. Burns. . . .

The proposal offers to those having control over the docks which are not subject to the Joint Committee an opportunity of taking an independent line, and if they did so great pressure would undoubtedly be exercised on the Joint Committee who would, as long as they held out, have to stand by and see their business transferred elsewhere. But there is very little ground, if any, for supposing that this invitation will be accepted.

Further, it assumes the assent of the lightermen who, when I saw them at the Edinburgh Castle Mission-room last evening, seemed to be full of fight, in good case physically, well provided with resources, and

determined to obtain those advantages which they demanded, if I mistake not, at the same time that they struck 'on principle', by way of supporting the dock labourers. One thing, however, is clear, and that is that Mr. Lafone at any rate must sign these terms, and so, assuming the consent of the strike committee to them, Butler's Wharf ought to be busy to-day.

SEPTEMBER 5, 2 a.m.

At an early hour this morning the terms issued by Mr. Lafone were accepted by the Strike Committee, subject to the erasure of the clause in relation to the lightermen.

The strikers' spirits were lifted by the news that £4000 had now been collected by the Australian populace, including, it was stated, Cabinet Ministers and all the members of the Queensland Parliament, and by the magnificent work of the Salvation Army.

By this time nearly six thousand tailors, mainly of Jewish origin, were on strike. The good news was received from Liverpool that the dockers there on strike had won their demands. The strain on the organisational side of the dispute was such that it was reported Mrs Burns and Mrs Aveling (as Eleanor Marx was known) were working some sixteen or seventeen hours a day. One section of employers to gain from the dispute were the bakers, who were working day and night to meet the demands of the Salvation Army and the strike committee.

MAGNIFICENT COLLECTIONS IN MELBOURNE AND BRISBANE.

Cabinet Ministers Subscribe:

Pall Mall Gazette, Thursday, 5 September 1889

A Reuter's telegram from Melbourne says nearly £4,000 have now been collected in aid of the dock labourers on strike in London. Meetings at which resolutions of sympathy with the strikers are passed are being held nightly throughout Victoria, and a similar movement is on foot in Sydney, Brisbane, Adelaide and Hobart. A further telegram from Brisbane says:— A large and important meeting of citizens was held here yesterday at which resolutions were adopted expressing sympathy with the London dock labourers on strike, and promising to support them to obtain their demands. The chairman announced that over £500 had been collected from all classes of the inhabitants, including Cabinet Ministers, and nearly all the members of the Queensland Parliament.

THE SALVATION ARMY'S NINE THOUSAND LOAVES:

The depot in connection with the Salvation Army, which has been opened in the Whitechapel road, has already been the means of relieving many thousands of those in want. The 9000 half-quartern loaves which on Tuesday night were stacked away on the premises for the consumption of those on strike were all consumed long before the hour for closing (6 o'clock) and a fresh supply had to be obtained. The other depôt in the West India Dock road is carrying on a still larger relief system, besides nightly giving shelter to some hundreds of homeless men.

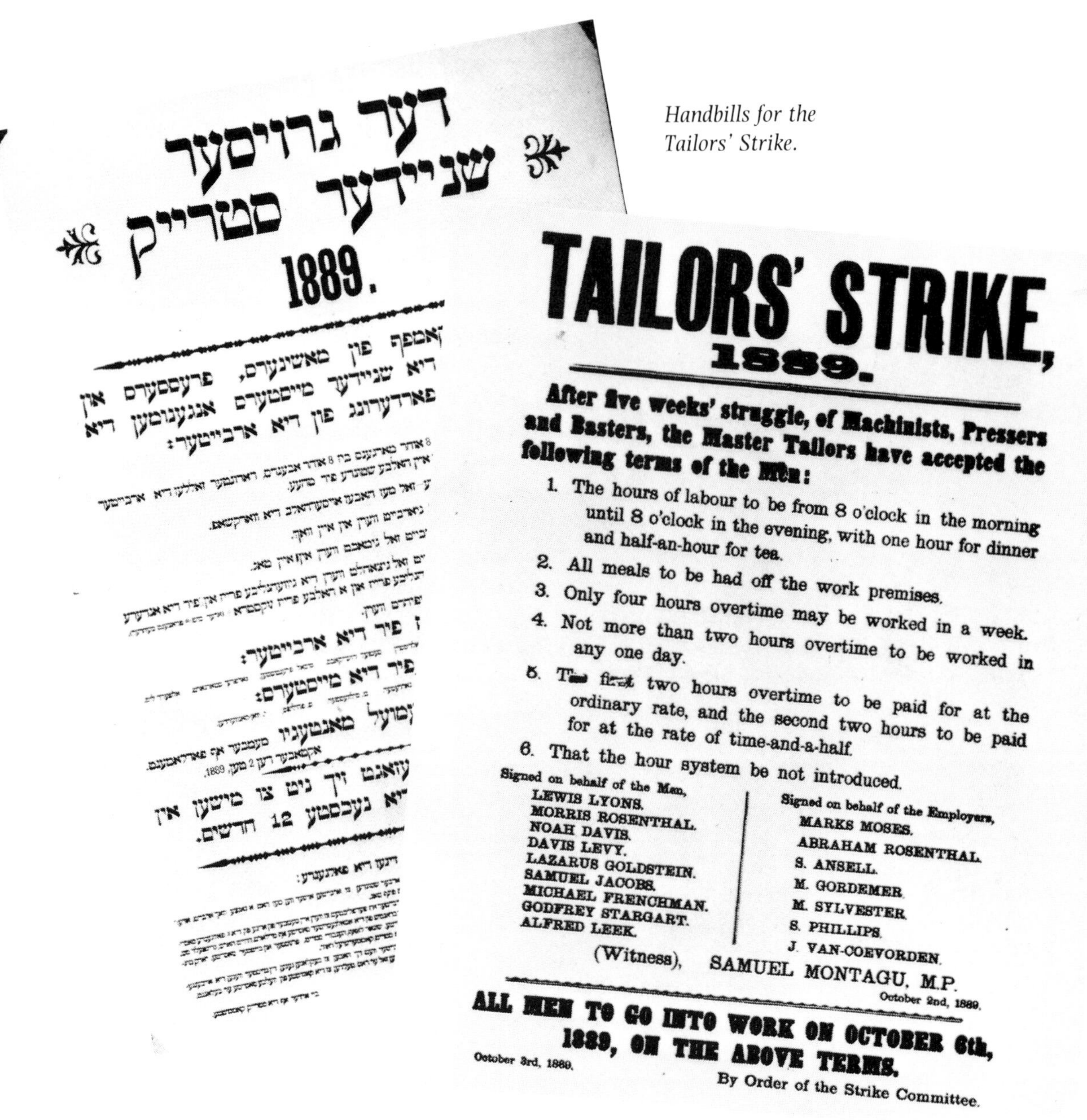

דער גרויסער
שניידער סטרייק
1889.

TAILORS' STRIKE,
1889.

After five weeks' struggle, of Machinists, Pressers and Basters, the Master Tailors have accepted the following terms of the Men:

1. The hours of labour to be from 8 o'clock in the morning until 8 o'clock in the evening, with one hour for dinner and half-an-hour for tea.
2. All meals to be had off the work premises.
3. Only four hours overtime may be worked in a week.
4. Not more than two hours overtime to be worked in any one day.
5. The first two hours overtime to be paid for at the ordinary rate, and the second two hours to be paid for at the rate of time-and-a-half.
6. That the hour system be not introduced.

Signed on behalf of the Men,
LEWIS LYONS.
MORRIS ROSENTHAL.
NOAH DAVIS.
DAVIS LEVY.
LAZARUS GOLDSTEIN.
SAMUEL JACOBS.
MICHAEL FRENCHMAN.
GODFREY STARGART.
ALFRED LEEK.

Signed on behalf of the Employers,
MARKS MOSES.
ABRAHAM ROSENTHAL.
S. ANSELL.
M. GORDEMER.
M. SYLVESTER.
S. PHILLIPS.
J. VAN-COEVORDEN.

(Witness), SAMUEL MONTAGU, M.P.
October 2nd, 1889.

ALL MEN TO GO INTO WORK ON OCTOBER 6th, 1889, ON THE ABOVE TERMS.

October 3rd, 1889.
By Order of the Strike Committee.

Handbills for the Tailors' Strike.

Pall Mall Gazette
Friday, 6 September 1889

'Upon my word, Mr. Burns, the next thing we shall hear of you is that you are in the Salvation Army!'

'Not much fear of that,' said Mr. Burns, 'but I must say, now you mention it, that the Salvation Army has indeed done magnificent service to the workmen in the crisis. I have been surprised at the practical, business-like good sense with which they have conducted the feeding of so many thousands of people from day to day. It has been quite admirable, and you cannot speak too highly of the spirit with which they have put their shoulders to the work.'

'And the Cardinal, Mr. Burns? What with the Cardinal on one side and

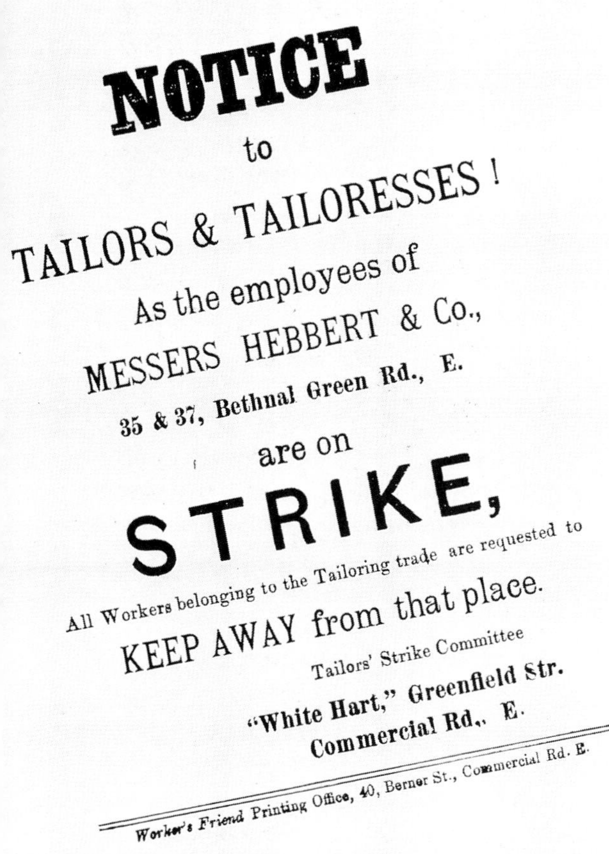

BALANCE SHEET
OF THE
GREAT STRIKE OF EAST LONDON TAILORS,
For 10½ hours per day.
EXTENDING FROM AUGUST 27th, to OCTOBER 2nd, 1889.

Introductory Note by the Secretary on behalf of the Strike Committee.

In presenting this Sheet before the attention of the public, we beg to take the opportunity of offering our heartiest thanks ...o all sympathisers who so readily and freely responded to our appeal for help, and more so to those who did not even wait for ...r appeal. And while, considering the importance of monetary assistance in such critical times to save the struggling soldiers ...m bending before the whip of starvation, we express our utmost appreciation at the way in which sympathisers of all grades, ... and poor, laborers and manufacturers, subscribed to our funds, we cannot refrain from emphasizing with great pleasure ...act that the readiness and fraternal spirit shown to us by the various Trade Organizations and other English Working Men's ...s armed us with a most effective weapon to carry the fight to victory. We only hope that our brethren all over the Globe ...t fail to take a grand lesson of solidarity from the Dock Labourers' Strike, as well as from this of the Tailors and of ... which will mark a new and splendid epoch in the history of Labour; a lesson that will lead the workers of all countries ...omplete emancipation and real happiness.

INCOME.

	£	s.	d.
...om Joint Fund of Tailors and Cabinet ... Streets	6	5	8½
...t London Shops, by West London ...r.	47	18	4¼
...lachinists' Society	44	3	10
...ssers' Society	0	10	0
...malgamated Society of Tailors	0	10	0
... Makers' Co-operative Society	25	0	0
List No. 9	0	7	2
" 5	0	5	6
" 8, 14, 29, 43 & 48	0	8	5
" 12	3	0	10
" 52	0	4	0
" 2	1	14	6
" 44	0	2	6
24 & 25	0	2	0
2	1	0	0
...	0	2	3
...	0	3	0
...	0	4	3
...	4	13	6
... Wiltshire & Co. Cigar	0	9	1
...igar Manufacturer	0	11	0
...	0	8	4
... Shoe Makers	0	12	6
...	10	0	0
...	2	0	0
...	10	0	0
...	5	0	0
...	100	0	0
...	1	0	0
...	10	0	0
...	30	10	0
...	1	1	0
...I.P.	1	1	0
...	5	0	0
...	73	0	0
...d others	5	5	0
... Club, per	4	3	0
...	1	18	8
	£398	15	5

EXPENDITURE.

	£	s.	d.
ORGANISING.			
Printing	10	2	0
Postage and Telegrams	1	17	3
Stationery	0	16	7
Banners	1	4	0
Bands	29	0	0
Vans for Demonstrations	2	3	6
Caretakers and Porters of Meeting Places	2	4	6
Fares of Deputations	2	4	11
Bill Posting	0	17	9
Pickets	1	14	4
Collection Box and Banner Bearers	2	10	2
RELIEF.			
In Cash	54	17	6
In Tickets	212	9	6
In Cash taken home to sick cases	1	19	0
Bread and Cheese to Strikers at Demonstrations	3	18	7
Refreshment to Box and Banner Bearers	2	10	10½
DEFENCE.			
Towards legal expenses of Asher Cohen...	3	0	0
Police Court Expenses to Lewis Winter	0	4	6
RENT AND DAMAGES.			
Proprietor "White Hart"...	5	0	0
GENERAL.			
Committeemen and Chairman	39	2	6
Treasurer for time lost and travelling	0	13	2
Secretary's Salary	6	10	0
Sundry Expenses, (including Collecting Boxes)	6	18	1½
Granted to Secretary in recognition of good services rendered...	5	0	0
Audit Expenses	0	15	0
	397	13	3
* Balance in hand	1	2	2
	£398	15	5

* ...l be handed over to the Silvertown Strike Fund, in accordance with the decision of the Committee.

...BE, West End Branch, Amalgamated Society of Tailors.
...'ELL, Dragon Branch, Amalgamated Society of Tailors.
...RKE, Dock, Wharf, Riverside & General Labourers' Union.
...W. PARISH, Treasurer.
...VILLIAM WESS, Secretary,
40, Berner Street, Commercial Road, London, E.

General Booth on the other, you are quite in the odour of sanctity.'

'I don't know about that,' said Mr. Burns. 'All I know is that the Cardinal has been our good friend in this business, and nothing could be better than his sympathy and support. There is no doubt about this – we have the moral support of all the best people going, and it will be a strange thing, indeed, if we cannot pull off the victory with such allies.'

The Times, Thursday, 5 September 1889, 4

The tailors' strike still continues, and the 5,000 or 6,000 men already out had their ranks barely augmented yesterday. It is believed that within the next few hours it will collapse altogether, owing to the dissensions and the necessary sinews of war, in the shape of money not being forthcoming, to help those out of employment. By far the majority of those on strike are Jews, and these, when in employment, barely earn sufficient to keep themselves decently, so it is not to be expected that those now in work can do much to assist their less fortunate comrades.

Twenty more tailors' workshops in the East-end have been affected by the strike, including that of Mr. Mark Moses, who employed some 50 men. A meeting was held at the St. James's Club, E., Mr. Louis Lyons presided, and the principal speaker was Mr. C. W. Mowbray. After a somewhat excited meeting some 200 foreign tailors paraded the streets and visited several shops, compelling the workmen to cease work. Two of the leaders were arrested.

Our Liverpool Correspondent telegraphs:— The employers having conceded the demands of the grain carriers for increased pay, the strike of labourers at the Liverpool Docks has concluded, much to the relief of the public mind, there being a dread of the strike becoming general. At the time for commencing work (7 o'clock) yesterday morning the grain carriers collected in a body at the Harrington and Toxteth Docks, and one of the master porters asked them if they were willing to resume work. They replied, 'Not under our terms.' This being the general response they were asked what terms they required, and their reply was, '6s. a day, and 1s. an hour overtime.' The master porters at once decided to concede these terms, and work was immediately resumed, the unloading of the steamers in the south end docks mentioned being proceeded with. The strike on board the steamer *Methley Hall* at the north end was similarly concluded by concession.

Mrs. Burns, Mrs. [Eleanor Marx] Aveling, and Mrs. Hickes are still busily engaged in attending to financial matters, and these ladies work, in the interests of the strikers, some 16 or 17 hours a day.

Although the relief system has now been satisfactorily brought into working order, it is evident many of the men have been put to narrow straits through the strike, and these would willingly resume work at the old terms were it not for fear of those who are still determined not to give in. A shilling ticket, while it staves off actual starvation, is not much to provide for the wants of a man with a wife and several children, and should the subscriptions cease to any noticeable extent, then the relief would have to be immediately reduced. It is also stated that many of the dishonest labourers succeed in getting hold of several tickets, which they afterwards sell at half their value and get rid of the proceeds in the neighbouring publichouses. One of those out on strike was heard to say he saw a man who had, by some means or other, obtained no fewer than 17 shilling tickets, all of which he had managed to dispose of. This, if true, is very unfair to the poor fellows who are eking out their already miserable existence on the pittance allowed them. Many of the east-end tradesmen, mostly of the Jewish persuasion, have placed large notices on their shop fronts stating that during the continuance of the strike they intend giving so much money per week towards the strike fund.

The directors' committee now tried to take the initiative in what was an obviously deteriorating position. Letters were sent to the Commissioner of Police to put pressure on the pickets, and the employers also had a series of posters printed, warning of conviction and imprisonment for intimidation and threatening. There was the usual debate as to what intimidation was, although as to what the legal situation was in regard to members of a non-registered union or their supporters was not clear; and, given the fact that the vast majority of the labourers had never been in a trade union, their knowledge of the picketing laws must have been vague in the extreme.

Meanwhile, Mr. Lafone was happy to announce that since his labourers had returned, much work had been done. The Bishop of London contacted Champion and Burns to see if they could arbitrate and set up a meeting with the employers.

The Master Lightermen and the Bargeowners met to discuss the situation in relation to the lightermen. There was obviously great confusion as to just what the lightermen were demanding, as it had been assumed that the strike was simply, as at first stated, sympathetic action for the dock labourers, but it appeared now that they were using the dispute to put forward their own demands.

Ben Tillett joined John Burns for the next big rally on Tower Hill, both speakers noting their satisfaction with the situation. Tom Mann was approached by employers from the Surrey side who stated that they would concede to the men's demands. It shows something of the strength and confidence that Mann now enjoyed when he said that he could only lay the suggestion before the committee, but could not settle if this injured any of the other men in dispute.

The Times, Friday, 6 September 1889, 4

In the afternoon, at Dock-house, Leadenhall-street, the Directors' Committee stated that during the day a great many men had gone into the wharves on the old terms. – Owing to the intimidation which prevailed, one of the directors, Sir Henry le Marchant, called upon the Chief Commissioner of Police, Mr. Monro, and stated the difficulty the companies had to encounter owing to the threats which the men had to encounter. In confirmation of what Sir Henry le Marchant said, a letter had been sent to Mr. Monro as follows:—

Dock-house,
Sept. 5. 109, Leadenhall-street, E.C.,

TO CHIEF COMMISSIONER MONRO, SCOTLAND-YARD.

'Sir, – I have the honour to state that we understand from many of our men that they would be willing to work if they were assured of protection by the police from violence on returning to their homes. I have therefore to request that you will authorize your district superintendent that if he should be of opinion that any man may reasonably apprehend

violence, to afford him whatever protection he may consider is best calculated to preserve him from injury.

'I am, Sir, your obedient servant,
H. J. MORGAN, Secretary.'

Owing to the prevailing intimidation, the directors have also decided to have the following notice printed and posted:—

'Important Notice:— Conviction and Imprisonment
'for Intimidation and Threatening.

'Whereas dock labourers and persons employed in the docks desirous of attending to their lawful employment have been intimidated and threatened and interfered with in the performance of their duties by evil-disposed persons inside and outside the dock premises, notice is hereby given that several convictions have taken place, and severe sentences of imprisonment have been passed by magistrates upon persons who have intimidated and threatened dock labourers and persons employed in the docks desirous of attending their lawful employment. And further take notice that, upon complaint being made to the London and India Docks Joint Committee of any act of intimidation or threat to any of their workmen or persons employed by them, the directors will immediately order those persons intimidating or threatening to be prosecuted according to law. By order, H. J. MORGAN, secretary, Dock-house, 109, Leadenhall-street, E.C., Sept. 5, 1889.'

In regard to the question of intimidation, the *Law Journal* says:—

'As London is suffering at the present moment from an epidemic of strikes, it is as well to recall on what terms the right to strike and lock-out, both equally illegal combinations at common law, has been conceded to workmen and employers. The offences usually known as intimidation and picketing, and punishable with a fine of £20, or, imprisonment with hard labour not exceeding three months, form a series of acts, all done with a view to compel any person to abstain from doing, or to do, any act which such other person has a legal right to do, or to abstain from doing, wrongfully and without legal authority. These acts are – using violence to, or intimidating the person, or his wife, or children, or injuring his property, persistently following him about from place to place, hiding his tools, clothes, or other property, or depriving him of, or hindering him in the use of them, watching or besetting his dwelling-house, or the place where he works, carries on business, or happens to be, or its approaches, and following him with two or more other persons in a disorderly manner in or through any street or road. The words "wrongfully and without legal authority" in what may be called the intention clause qualify all the acts which follow, and the proof of the right, or legal authority would lay on the defendant. Intimidation and picketing are offences already tolerably familiar in strikes; but a new development, which goes by the name of 'bombarding' seems to have arisen. The operation appears to be for crowds of strikers to surround the place of business of non-strikers and shout with all their might until they come out. This would, no doubt, come under the head of "besetting" in the Act of Parliament, and is the latest form of blowing down the walls of Jericho.'

In a conversation early in the day, Mr. Lafone said:—

'I am very pleased to say that we have started work again to-day with all our men and a very large number of casual labourers. The Customs have behaved most handsomely this morning to us, in order to facilitate work, and I may say that we are now virtually arranging for the provisioning of London. Butler's Wharf is the largest wharf on the river, as you may guess from the fact that it has 15 acres of floor space, and I have already been inundated with offers of work, and have had this morning offers for half-a-dozen steamers to unload at the wharf. The whole of my men have been taken on, but it must be remembered that the majority of them did not strike but were merely turned out. Work has been resumed this morning at a lot of wharves. As you pull up the river you will notice that all the buildings on this side of the river between us and London-bridge are at work with one exception. The wharves of Messrs. Beresford, Hicks, and Ash, Cotton and Bellamy, the Orchard Wharf, and numbers of others which I could name, as well as the granaries are at work and in full swing, and there [are] at least 16 of them going this morning. These are the places where the men have been allowed to go to work because they have agreed to the men's terms.

While Mr. Burns was addressing the strikers on Tower-hill he received a communication that the Bishop of London was at the clergy-house in Trinity-square, and would be pleased to confer with him on the situation. Accordingly, after the people had dispersed, he, together with Mr. Champion, went there. Mr. Burns was in conference with the Bishop and the leading clergy in the district for about half-an-hour, but it was upwards of an hour before Mr. Champion took his departure. A reporter was afterwards informed by the Bishop's chaplain that a long conference had taken place, the result of which, it was confidently hoped, would be the settlement of the question by arbitration.

An important meeting of the Association of Master Lightermen and Bargeowners was held yesterday afternoon at the Corn Exchange Tavern, Mark-lane, Mr. Samuel Williams, of Lambeth, presiding.

The Chairman said he ... wished to call their attention at the very beginning to the facts connected with this unfortunate disruption. It would be remembered that the men discontinued their employment, as they said, for the especial purpose of expressing their sympathy with the dock labourers and also for the express purpose of putting a little more pressure upon the dock authorities ... the leaders, finding that the men refused to leave their employment in so ready a manner as would have inspired them with confidence, said, 'We must make capital out of this opportunity, and unless we stir up a little strife and formulate a few grievances for these men our services will be regarded as of very trifling value.' They therefore formulated a set of grievances, which they placed before the masters, but not until some days after they had discontinued their employment. He was also sorry that the stevedores, a respectable, honest, hard-working set of fellows, should have been persuaded to discontinue their work, because when they discontinued their work and the dock labourers and the lightermen went out there was an end to the trade of the port of London, and everything and anything was brought to a standstill.

Early yesterday [Thursday] morning the leaders were at work addressing the men. Mr. Burns commenced at the Customs-house and from there went on to the Tidal Basin. At each place he announced the decision to which the committee had arrived early that morning. The announcement was well received, showing apparently that the men have had quite enough of the strike and are anxious to return to work.

The attendance on Tower-hill was again as large as it has been any morning during the present week. Some amusement was caused by a number of men against the railings of the Tower gardens having the figure of a man suspended to a pole in the act of being hanged. Underneath were the words, 'For Norwood.' The first to arrive was Mr. B. Tillett, who expressed his regret at being prevented through indisposition from being with them on the previous day. However, he was not dead yet, and there was still a lot of fight in him. He and others had been able to do a good morning's work, which proved they were not so disabled as the dock company would like them to be. They were able to get 10,000 men as pickets to watch their own case for very little remuneration, while the dock companies with all their bribes, could not get 100. That was a strong argument for the men. The men could go in to work if they liked, but he was happy to say they did not want to go in. ... If the dock companies did not give in within a very short time not only would the 'blacklegs' be got out, but all the permanent hands as well. The latter, who had stuck to the dock company, had been repaid by having two more hours added on to their day's work before overtime began. That was a specimen of the dock directors' gratitude. He had been told that while the meeting was being held the previous day a gentleman went round the outskirts of the crowd asking men to go to work. They were told that some men had been earning £6 a week, and if they liked they could draw a bit on account by going to Messrs. Tatham Brothers' office in Gracechurch-street. Where was the docker that would refuse to have a bit on account? (Laughter.) So they went and drew their bit, but did not go to work. (Renewed laughter.) They brought their tickets to him, but they kept the money. They had offered the dock directors fair terms, which they had refused, and now their hands would have to be forced.

Mr. Mann, on entering [Southwark] park, found Messrs. Wallis, Augur, Butler, Appleby, and other contractors in the deal department of the Surrey Commercial Docks waiting to inform him of their readiness

The Great Dock Strike, 1889. John Burns addressing the strikers at the gates of the East and West India Docks.

Neptune, Britannia and scores of others in these great demonstrations that were part carnival and part political.

to accede to the demands of the men, and to signify the same in writing if he would prevail upon the men to start work this morning. One of the contractors, in reply to a question, said that work could be found for 3,000 men, and added that there were so many vessels waiting to be unloaded that he felt certain the rest of the men on strike would be back at work in a very short time. Mr. Mann said he would at once lay the matter before the meeting; but though he was personally in favour of the proposal he could not say how all the sections of the men would receive it. By this time from 1,000 to 1,500 men had assembled, and upon Mr. Mann's mounting one of the park seats it was evident that they had already got wind of the proposal.

Mr. Mann said they had now reached a stage in the strike when they must keep their heads cool and take steps cautiously. The struggle had been going on for 23 days, and though there was not the slightest intention on their part to back down, but they were as determined as ever to insist on their terms, yet it had been deemed wise to close with Mr. Lafone's offer and permit the men to go to work wherever their terms were granted. (Loud cries of 'No' and cheers.) Circumstances had arisen which had necessitated a change of tactics, and for his part, he thought the sectional system was the wisest course to pursue. Originally this was a strike of the dockers, or trimmers as they were known on the south side; but though the dock companies had not conceded the terms, the wharfingers had, and he put it to those present whether the Press and the public, which had so splendidly supported them hitherto, would continue to do so if the men acted unwisely by creating unnecessary friction and unnecessarily prolonging the strike. (Hear, hear.) He urged them to oppose the enemy in front of them by splitting his ranks, and so making it easier to win. (Cheers.) It was most difficult to realize what 150,000 men on strike meant. He had only been able to realize the enormity of the business by knocking about on both sides of the river. For 23 days this strike had gone on without any mishap, and he admired the conduct of the men. He trusted they would retain the respect of the thinking portion of the world by not rejecting the offer which the contractors had made to them. If they did, what would the sympathizing public say? (Hear, hear.) It was most difficult to understand the different sections of men working under different systems in the Commercial Docks; but he thought they would all have the sense to see that if the deal-porters went to work and undertook not to do what should be done by the other bodies left out on strike, there would not only be less strain upon the strike fund, but they would be able out of their own increased wages to assist the strike funds. (Loud cheers.)

Mr. Mann's speech by this time had almost broken down the opposition, and it became clear that the men would accept the proposal.

Just when it seemed Lafone's offer, or capitulation, was to be dashed, agreement had been reached in the small hours of Thursday morning.

The strike committee, however, issued no statement of how they had persuaded the lightermen and watermen to go along with their acceptance. John Burns placed the number of men going back on the basis of the agreement at six thousand but there was some disagreement, some putting the number as low as two thousand.

This was obviously a major victory for the strikers. It was reported that there were vast numbers of the 'thriftless class' now joining in the demonstrations, the allegation being that they were 'packing' the marches.

Norwood and the employers' committee were coming under increasing pressure, especially from the shipowners, as to what was going on and when the committee was going to meet. The employers claimed that there was dissent in the strikers' ranks, since the stevedores had applied to the strike committee to be allowed to go back to work and been refused. They stated, however, that men were returning to the docks.

(FROM A CORRESPONDENT.)

The Times, Friday, 6 September 1889, 3

One result of the agreement reached on Wednesday afternoon by Mr. Lafone and some of the leaders of the strike – an agreement to which formal sanction was only given in a somewhat theatrical manner in the small hours of yesterday morning – was immediate and conspicuous. At the very wharf which, on the preceding day, had looked most desolate – namely, Butler's Wharf – work was resumed at the first moment; and without any delay, a steamer laden with fresh currants from Greece was brought up for the purpose of being unloaded. Here a large number of men, including all the old hands and a number of casuals, were taken on; and a certain number of other wharfingers are believed to have followed Mr. Lafone's example. Estimates vary remarkably with regard to the number of men who have gone to work on the new terms. Mr. Burns places the number at 6,000, Mr. Champion frankly does not know; but a foreman stevedore who happened to be at hand when I was conversing with Mr. Champion on the subject bluntly asserted that from 2,000 to 3,000 men would be nearer the mark. Be that as it may, more work is being done at the wharves on the Surrey side than has been done for many a day, and a great many wharves are more or less busily at work on the Middlesex side. These are things that can be seen with the naked eye by anybody who chooses to take a trip down the river in a penny steamboat. . . .

Yesterday the first movement in the City was a remarkable one. Mr. Burns led into the City from Aldgate a great mass procession, in which all the labourers out on strike, or kept from work by picketing, had a part. How large this was may be gathered from the fact that, going at a quick pace, it occupied half-an-hour in passing the Dock-house in Leadenhall-street, before which demonstrations were made by hooting or cheering, according to the view of the several sections. There were not only dock labourers and waterside workers in the gathering, but

men of temperance and provident societies, with their banners, and an Irish society, bearing the green banner with the golden harp which did duty in the Park on Sunday. Then, too, there were East-end tailors, mostly Hebrews now on strike, and others not connected with the carrying trade by land or water. There were as before the working derricks, illustrating the coal-whippers' trade, and one of the vans – for the procession included carried men, as well as those who marched – had an effigy of Mr. Norwood on a gibbet. A man with a pantomimic head was also made to represent the chairman of the great dock companies, and it was apparent that a strong endeavour was being made by the organizers of the procession to work the population into dislike of the chief of these companies. It was clear that an enormous effort had been put forward to enlist all who could be enlisted in this procession so as to present an apparent determination to continue the contest in face of the fact daily shown that the men are anxious to return to work, and are only prevented by intimidation. The procession contained a very large number of *bona fide* waterside workers, dock labourers, and those who came out in alleged sympathy with them; but its character was very different from the demonstration of Monday week. Then the vast majority were men who worked in ships and in connexion with ships. Yesterday there were vast numbers of the thriftless class, of whom there are always many thousands in the metropolis, composed of youths drifting into the casual class without skill in trade, or strength, and men with boys' physique. The foreign sailors were not everywhere received with sympathy.

At the adjourned meeting of shipowners a letter from Sir Donald Currie, addressed to [the chairman] Mr. T. Sutherland, M.P., was read. It was as follows:—

'Dear Sir, – Mr. Scrutton and I called upon Mr. Norwood and put the questions which the meeting of shipowners, held at 1 p.m. to-day, decided should be put by us to Mr. Norwood. The first question we asked was, When are the committee to meet? to which Mr. Norwood replied, "I think it very possible they will meet on Monday." The second question we asked was, Are you able to allow us to discharge our ships in the meantime, if we can, subject to the conditions which may be agreed to by the committee? To this Mr. Norwood replied, "No, we cannot." Then the following questions were asked:— "Do you see any way for the arrangement of the present dispute, looking to the transfer of trade from London to other ports?" to which Mr. Norwood replied, "We will not meet the men more than we have done." ' The letter was signed "Donald Currie," and confirmed by Mr. T. scrutton.

It was decided by the shipowners that, seeing the dock authorities would not meet the views of the shipowners, the meeting should be adjourned until to-day.

At the Dock-house in Leadenhall-street yesterday. . . . it was stated that the stevedores had applied to the strike committee to be allowed to go to

work, as they had come to the conclusion, in a meeting held on the previous day, that the strike should terminate. This permission was refused. At the docks it was stated that more men were coming in to work....

A timely reminder appeared in the form of a letter to the *Manchester Guardian* on the role of women in the strike. In all long industrial disputes, women play a crucial role; and in the dock strike, because of the great deprivation, their support was essential to the success of the dispute, quite apart from the women who worked long hours supporting the relief work.

The Social Democratic Federation called for municipalisation of the docks and also gave themselves credit for the strike, because of their propaganda in and around the London docks. Of course the leaders of the dock strike would nearly all have described themselves in one way or another as Socialists although they had disassociated themselves from what they saw as the extremes of the SDF. But the rank and file were not enamoured of Socialism, including that of the SDF. Perhaps Henry Champion's description of a labour demonstration gives an insight into their very English view of Socialism; but where would this leave the Socialism of the Jewish strikers, who now had 10,000 men on strike and were threatening to bring all the Jews in the East End out in support of their actions?

WOMEN AND THE STRIKE

Manchester Guardian, Saturday, 7 September 1889

To the Editor of the Manchester Guardian

Sir: Because women are not in the front in this strike, it does not mean that their hearts are less than earnestly and pathetically angry about the matter. They acknowledge it to be a time for 'deeds not words' but none the less are they taking their share of labour in the battle of wrong against right; and if I venture to break the silence as one of themselves, I only do so to remind some, so ready to condemn the strikers because of the sufferings brought upon weakly wives and innocent children, that those whom they pity rejoice to suffer. Nor is it, perhaps, too much to say that these brave-hearted women are proud to teach the innocent children at their knee that if it is only in this way that oppression and wrong can be successfully combated, it is best to meet it thus. This is a matter affecting thousands and thousands of God's poor, not only today but in days to come. Women of all people do not shrink from suffering when they are sure (as in this case) that it is a stairway leading from the pestilential atmosphere of oppression's wrongs into the open day of God's land of sunshine and right and truth....

Justice, Saturday, 7 September 1889

The third great lesson is the need to place in the hands of the London County Council the control of the London Docks, so that never again may a few individuals be able, for their own private gain, to imperil the

food supply of London. A great city should not be at the mercy of men like Norwood and the sufferings of the strikers will not be lost if they bring about the municipalisation of the Docks.

The fourth great lesson is the growth of Socialism, for they have been right who saw in this strike a revolutionary movement and not a mere trade dispute. For years past the members of the S.D.F. have gone down to the dock gates, morning after morning, preaching the rights of labour and the power of united action. The strike is the result of these years of patient, unseen endeavours, the expulsion of the mine that has been a-making these eight years past. I see that 'by desire' it is stated that Messrs Burns, Champion and Mann have 'severed their connection' with the S.D.F. but none the less are they gathering the fruits of the hard work at the dock gates in the dark of the early winter mornings by Burrows and Williams and other members of the S.D.F. ere yet public credit was to be gained in working for the then despised dockers.

Surely from such outcome we may take courage, and steadfastly pursue the policy that has led to such results. This strike will soon be over, but London Labour will never be the same as it was before it and it is for us to prepare for that great rising which will come ere long.

Labour Elector, Saturday, 7 September 1889

Unconsciously I do discern flags, green flags, red flags, blue flags. Unconsciously I see the banners of the various trades grouping themselves artistically against the green trees. What a strange love of banners, of scarves, of bands, of processions, of emblems, of badges, is implanted in the Anglo-Saxon breast. Is it the heritage bequeathed to them by their forefathers of the Trade Guilds of medieval England? Or is it only the revolt against the prosaic surroundings to which we are condemned? Again, is it an outward attempt by taking up arms against a sea of stucco to oppose and mend it?

[*H. H. Champion*]

East London Advertiser, Saturday, 7 September 1889

At an early hour on Tuesday morning, Lewis Lyons addressed the Jewish strikers, and encouraged them to hold on until their demands were conceded. There was great excitement in the Jewish quarter of the East-end, and it is computed that 10,000 men are now on strike. Tailors, cabinet makers and cigar and cigarette makers are among the number. Mr Lyons stated that if the masters do not surrender before the end of this week, all the Jewish workers in the East-end will leave work. This would mean a paralysis of the boot and shoe trade, in which many thousand Jews were engaged. The terms offered by the men are a 12-hour working day, with more wages, the better sanitation of the workshops and the discontinuance of the system under which Government tailors' contractors give out work after the men have finished at the shop.

4 THE SETTLEMENT

Ben Tillett and John Burns (left and right foreground) at the Mansion House Conference.

It was becoming increasingly apparent that the dock strike would soon be over. No matter what views the docks directors had of Lafone, his action, coupled with the massive support from Australia and the successful picketing, had ensured victory would not be too far away. The mediation committee, which soon became known as the 'Mansion House' Committee, made up of such dignitaries as the Lord Mayor (hence the title), the Bishop of London and Cardinal Manning, was bringing its voice to bear; although at first they put forward the idea that 5*d.* an hour should be accepted, their mediation was to become crucial. Their influence and authority would help to determine the result of the strike.

The ship owners too were increasingly pressuring Norwood and the dock employers for a settlement. Champion was able to announce, because of the support of the people of Australia, that they had no less than £7,000 in reserve. This gave them strength in negotiations with the employers, but the strike committee did not have everything their own way. Ship workers porters, humpers and others were now demanding that the strike should be terminated as they could get the demands from the small employers. John Burns had to use all his persuasive powers to stop literally thousands of men returning to work on the Surrey side. Such was the pressure on the Surrey side that the strike committee had to issue a new manifesto forbidding men to work on the south side. *The Times* noted 'Mr Burns does not exercise quite such undisputed control before.'

Picketing was proving a very successful weapon in the armoury of the strikers. Although there were incidents of scabs working on ships, overall because of the effectiveness of the pickets and the support coming through from other sections of the work force of the river trade, this was having no strong bearing in the dispute.

On Friday, 6 September, the Lord Mayor sent a telegram asking Burns, Champion and Mann to attend a conference at the Mansion House, thus breaking the deadlock in negotiations which had been imposed by the employers. He was able to tell the subsequent rally that 4,000 men had now gone back on acceptable terms and that other employers were conceding to the demands but he insisted that outside bodies could not negotiate settlements with employers. A further blow to the employers was a letter from the London Corn Exchange holding them responsible for the loss in trade which they were suffering. Surprisingly enough the Mayor of Birmingham presided over a rally addressed by Ben Tillett. The Methodist Church was increasingly now becoming more supportive of the dispute offering not only verbal sympathy but giving practical support in terms of relief. The fact that the Non-conformists as well as Cardinal Manning were sympathetic to the strikers was a victory for the men in the war for public support. The Mansion House Committee in a further conference conceded that 6d an hour (the dockers' tanner) was acceptable in principle. The only difference now on this last remaining obstacle was when the 6d was to be paid? The Mansion House Committee had recommended 1 January.

Burns, Tillett, Champion and Mann were asked to attend at Mansion House to be notified of the new offer. Mr Norwood had agreed on the behalf of the employers to consider their proposal. Ben Tillett shortly afterwards addressed the dock labourers, and praised the press. Such was the confidence of the strike committee that they declined to ratify the agreement between Tom Mann and the contractors on the south side, because the contractors were middlemen, not principals. Mann, like Burns, had great difficulty in persuading the men who turned up for work of the decision of the strike committee. The contractors who had offered this concession stated that they were willing to pay the men not 6d but 8d an hour and a shilling overtime. This was not the first time that individuals in the strike committee had agreed to terms only to be over-turned by the general body. Communications and perhaps a rivalry amongst the strike leaders was an obvious weak point, especially in relation to public opinion and the rank and file, who must have been more than confused by the constant changes in policy, often at very short notice.

Nonetheless it was becoming increasingly clear that the strike committee had scented victory. The success of the pickets and the Australian money had given them a new lease of life. The employers were divided and had agreed to negotiate; it was becoming apparent that the ship owners were increasingly at odds with Mr Norwood and the dock employers. A meeting of the three churches expressed their sympathy and support for the strike. The dockers' success also made other sections of the labour force in dispute to fight on and new unions were beginning to spring up all over London.

The Mansion House Conference

The Times, Saturday, 7 September 1889, 6

In all directions there appears to be increasing hope that the end of the great strike may be almost within a measurable distance ...

Yet another influence was brought to bear upon the situation yesterday. A curiously-constituted assemblage conferred in the Mansion-house in the afternoon. There were present, besides his Lordship [the Mayor of London] the Bishop of London, Cardinal Manning, Mr. Sydney Buxton, Mr. Burns, and Mr. Tillett. The opening of the conference was not hopeful, inasmuch as the Lord Mayor suggested that the men should return to work at 5d. until March, leaving arrangements to be made in the meantime. Such terms Mr. Burns was hardly likely to regard as acceptable, and with him Cardinal Manning appears to have agreed. At about 6 o'clock in the evening the Lord Mayor, the Bishop of London, and Cardinal Manning had an interview with the directors, but the directors had nothing to say save that the suggestions made by this deputation would be considered. It would be somewhat rash to expect any considerable result from the exercise of this influence.

When the shipowners met at the Peninsular and Oriental Company's office in the morning, under the presidency of Mr. Sutherland, they found a communication from Mr. Norwood inviting their committee to attend at the Dock-house in the afternoon for the purpose of discussing the vital question whether the shipowners might not be permitted to discharge their own ships. This communication appears to have surprised Mr. Sutherland.

Among the strikers generally there is a tone of considerable confidence, inspired partly, no doubt, by the remarkably successful performances of their pickets, performances which have brought about fresh communications between the dock directors and the police. There is also another cause for confidence in the fact that the Strike Committee have really abundant funds at their disposal. According to Mr. Champion, they had yesterday morning no less than £7,000 to their credit, and money was still coming in abundantly. But there have been some signs of mutiny among those whom I may call the allies of the main body of strikers, notably among those called 'ship workers.'

Hunger shows on the faces of the dockers as the strike goes on.

At the Surrey Commercial Dock gates Mr. Burns had a very narrow escape from the loss of an important section of his forces. Some thousands of men had assembled at the gates in readiness for work, and it needed the personal intervention of Mr. Burns to prevent them from entering. Subsequently a new manifesto forbidding work at the Surrey Commercial Docks without the authority of the south side central committee, was posted. In all these things there are signs that Mr. Burns does not exercise quite such undisputed control as before.

From enquiries made, the officials at the London Docks state that they are still working about the same number of hands. Very few, however, have been working at the docks further eastward. Mr. Cahill, the superintendent of the West India Dock police, is prepared to give men who wish for employment all necessary protection, but the men are not afraid of being molested or interfered with in any way inside the docks. It is after they have left their day's employment that the cause for alarm is felt. The majority of men who enter the docks are seen and known, so that there is no after difficulty in 'spotting' them as blacklegs. In spite of the efforts of the leaders of the strike a great deal of dissatisfaction exists among the men employed at the Albert and Victoria Docks, and if the dissensions are not quickly healed there is every probability of a great number of the men giving way, and resuming work. . . .

All the main line railway stations in the metropolis are now being watched to see whether men from the country are brought to work in the docks. Several small parties of men have been detected, and in each case after being spoken to by the picketers, they have refused to work. One or two ships now in the river have been loaded by men who refuse to have anything to do with the strike. These vessels are now being watched, and the crews, after being interviewed, have refused to sail. ... During the last 24 hours the number of police on duty outside the dock gates has been re-inforced, although there has so far been no need for their services. ...

The East-end last night was unusually quiet, and during the greater part of the evening not more than 20 dockers were in front of the Wade Arms. The men appear to have the impression that the strike will be concluded some time to-day.

In the City yesterday there were no indications of the continuance of the strike except when a procession passed through the streets. From early morning until evening the thoroughfares were filled with traffic, and the loaded wagons gave the City its normal appearance.

Soon after midday a strike procession entered the City from Aldgate, with bands and banners, and with such accessories as the 'Fairlop Boat,' from Epping Forest, and the effigy of Mr. Norwood. The leaders, Messrs. Burns and Tillett, were in front, and the first-named, with undiminished energy, encouraged his followers. The procession on this occasion was in greatly diminished force compared with that of the previous day, and took a little over 12 minutes to pass a given point.

Yesterday afternoon a telegram was received at the rooms of the Strike Committee, Wade's Arms, Poplar, from the Lord Mayor, asking Mr. Burns, Mr. Champion, and Mr. Mann to attend the conference at the Mansion-house. Mr. Sydney Buxton, M.P., arrived in a cab on the same mission. Meanwhile the strikers' procession was returning to the West India Dock gates. Mr. Burns briefly addressed the processionists, explaining that his words would be few as he was instantly required elsewhere for the consideration of business of a most important character. He added that at least 4,000 men started work on Thursday, and up to 10 o'clock that morning their terms had also been conceded at St. Bride's Wharf, Sharp's Wharf, and St. George's Ice Wharf. He found there was an attempt on the part of one or two persons to bring about a settlement over the heads of the men's representatives, but they were not going to submit to any such interference. The men having given three cheers for the strike, Mr. Burns left for the City.

The Rev. C. H. Kelly, president of the Wesleyan Conference was present at the ninth free breakfast given to men on strike at St. George's Wesleyan Mission, Cable-street, yesterday morning. A free breakfast is provided for 700 men, and at 1 o'clock women and children attend to receive free dinners for their families, representing a constituency of 2,600 without distinction of creed. In the afternoon 500 shilling tickets, issued by the Strike Committee, were distributed by Mr. John Jameson, the lay agent of the mission. At the breakfast the Wesleyan president congratulated the men on their good behaviour. ... He assured the strikers of the sympathy of the tens of thousands of Methodists all over the land.

The Lord Mayor (Mr. Alderman Whitehead), who late on Thursday returned from the North for the purpose of using his best efforts to effect a settlement of the strike, invited yesterday Cardinal Manning, the Bishop of London, Lord Brassey, Sir John Lubbock, M.P. (President of the London Chamber of Commerce), Alderman Sir Andrew Lusk, and Mr. Sydney Buxton, M.P., to confer with him at the Mansion-house upon the subject. All these gentlemen responded to the Lord Mayor's call, with the exception of Lord Brassey. ... Influential meetings held at the offices of the London Chamber of Commerce this week had asked the Lord Mayor and Sir John Lubbock, M.P., to confer with the dock directors and the leaders of the men, and to suggest a fair and amicable solution of the present unfortunate dispute. It was pointed out that the additional cost incident upon a rise of wages need not fall upon the dock companies, as it would be for them and the shipowners and merchants so to adjust their charges as to throw the additional expense, if any, on the consumers. But it was thought that, provided the principle of paying 6d. per hour – the only essential point at issue between the dock committee and the labourers – was conceded, it might be a reasonable and fair compromise to postpone its operation for a few months, in order to afford the dock companies and others concerned the means of readjusting their charges. It was, therefore, resolved by the Lord Mayor and his colleagues to recommend the men and the companies agreed to the 6d. per hour rate coming into operation from and after January 1 next. ... The resolution of the committee was then conveyed to Mr. Burns and Mr. Tillett, who, with Mr. Champion and Mr. Mann, were telegraphed to by the Lord Mayor to come to the Mansion-house for that purpose. They expressed their willingness to recommend the men to accept this arrangement; or, as the Bishop of London put it, to give the companies breathing time before the increased rate of wages came into operation at the docks. The Lord Mayor, Cardinal Manning, and the Bishop of London then sought an interview with the dock committee, upon whom they waited last evening, and laid before them this conciliatory suggestion. After a lengthened interview, Mr. Norwood, the chairman, intimated the willingness of himself and his colleagues to consider the proposal, and promised an answer in the course of today.

At the meeting on Tower-hill, the attendance was greater than ever. Mr. Tillett was the first to address the dock labourers. A distinguishing feature, he said, of their meetings was that their audiences represented all classes, including the pulpit, Parliament, and the Press. He desired to thank the latter for the service they had rendered the labourers during the present agitation. The Press had proved itself worthy of public confidence, and the best friend to the claims of the working men, who helped to make the wealth of the country. So long as he had any money he would buy all the papers he could as a small return for the help which the Press had given them. If he mixed up much longer with Press men he was afraid he should become as conceited as they were. They still continued their picketing, for that was a religious duty, and they were going to observe it. That morning he had good evidence that the men were in real fighting fettle. ... The dockers were tightening their grip on the enemy. They had got one class of men to give way and concede to their demands, and they would now demand from the dock companies what they were not able to give. It was a common though peculiar sight in the docks to see a superintendent and two clerks manipulating a truck. That cost more than a 'tanner' an hour. That day there would be such a demand on the dock companies that they would not be able to meet them, and they would become a byword for all that was mean and contemptible. Instead of the dockers giving way there was greater enthusiasm among them than ever. (Cheers.)

As soon as the Central Strike Committee had decided not to ratify the arrangement come to between Mr. Tom Mann and the contractors at the meeting in Southwark-park on Thursday night, Mr. Mann went to a midnight meeting of the Deptford men, which had been convened at Deptford-broadway, and informed them of what had taken place. The result was greeted with loud cheers. Mr. Mann then went to the South London Central Committee rooms at Sayes-court, and the following notice was drafted, and by 4.30 a.m. was being posted about the neighbourhood of the Surrey Commercial Docks:—'Sept. 6. – Dockers' Strike. To all concerned. No man must commence work without the authority of the South Side Central Strike Committee, Sayes-court, Deptford. By order, Tom Mann, Ben Tillett, John Burns, H. H. Champion, Hugh Brown (treasurer).' At 6.30 a.m. yesterday the contractors, who were unaware of what had transpired, met at a spot adjacent to the docks, where it has been customary to take on hands, and found Mr. Mann waiting for them. A lengthy interview took place, and then the contractors left without having started any of the men. By this time an immense number of the deal lumpers had arrived, and were greatly disappointed to find that the agreement of the previous day had been set aside. Mr. Mann addressed them and succeeded in inducing them not to go in, but to attend a mass meeting in Southwark-park later in the day. At the meeting subsequently held Mr. Hugh Brown presided, and Mr. Mann and Mr. H. H. Champion (who had been specially telegraphed for) spoke at some length, the latter especially justifying the course taken by the committee. There was a good deal of exasperation evidenced until it was made clear that the Central Strike Committee had declined to accept the contractors' written guarantee, as they were only middlemen, and the committee felt, in the interest of all the sections of men on strike, that they ought to have a guarantee from the dock directors themselves, or some one authorized on their behalf.

Last evening Mr. Mann addressed a meeting in the grounds at Sayes-court, and, alluding to what had taken place in the morning, said they

'Poor Docker's baby' was the original caption.

now knew their future position and must stand together till all sections went to work. Whether that was a wise course or not to pursue was another question. They must accept it and not waste time in jangling, but get to work afresh and stick at it till they got the 6d. and 8d. for the docker. (Cheers.) The peculiarity of the position on the Surrey side was that they were not fighting for these terms merely, but had to deal with the demands of men who were receiving higher terms than these. It was difficult to adjudicate when some sections were paid piece-work, some by measure, and some by the hour; and they had to hasten to get their demands put in a clear and definite form. He advised them to strengthen their pickets, and said, with a full sense of what he was saying, that it was their duty to let the traitors know that they had good right hands. At the same time he hoped that as they had not had to resort to violence they might have no necessity for commencing it.

At 4 o'clock yesterday afternoon a conference of representatives of the Amalgamated Watermen's and Lightermen's Society, held at the York Minster, Philpot-street, E., was attended by Mr. H. Lafone and Mr. Champion. By these gentlemen certain suggestions were made, which, in effect, were that lightermen should go to work for ships in stream, and thus give employment to a large number of stevedores, and induce wharfingers now standing out to concede the terms already accepted by certain of their fellow-wharfingers. After discussion the assembled delegates, on the motion of Mr. Iles, (chairman of the committee), seconded by Mr. Fairbairn, unanimously resolved to adhere to their circulars of August 22, under which the lightermen claim re-arrangement of their present excessive hours of labour and present scale of wages.

Work was resumed on the river yesterday morning under the terms arranged by Mr. Lafone with the Strike Committee. Great activity prevailed and many vessels were unloading at the wharves and in mid-stream.

The Mansion House 'Agreement'

The leaders of the Dock Strike suffered a public relations setback as a result of the Mansion House meeting. The Mansion House Committee was of the opinion that the leaders of the strike had accepted the proposals, notably the 6d in January and a statement to that effect had been issued.

Cardinal Manning was party to the agreement and was known to be sympathetic to labour. To contradict the Cardinal, the Bishop of London and the Lord Mayor tested their credibility.

For the first time the press turned against them with potentially serious consequences for their public support. *The Times*, which had been fairly sympathetic, now waded in against the strike leaders, who tried to defend their action by issuing a series of denials that they had accepted the proposals.

Even the *Pall Mall Gazette*, which was very sympathetic, was at a loss to understand how Burns and Tillett could have got themselves into such a situation.

The Times, Monday, 9 September 1889, 4

The tale of Saturday's [7 Sept.] negotiations may be told in a few words. On Friday, as has already been reported, the Lord Mayor, the Bishop of London, and Cardinal Manning had an interview with the directors, of which the object was to pave the way for peace and reconciliation. At the time no more was known positively than that this distinguished deputation had made to the directors, after consultation with Messrs. Burns and Tillett, certain suggestions with regard to which the directors had said, as they were bound to say, that they would consider them with the utmost care. On Saturday the actual terms of the suggestions became known. They are to be found in the opening clause of Mr. Norwood's letter to the Lord Mayor, the text of which appears below, and they amounted to a proposal that the directors should, in effect, surrender to the men, but should postpone the date of surrender until the new year. The directors, as Mr. Norwood's letter shows, accepted those terms under protest. Whether the protest was reasonable or no is not for me to say, but it was certainly just for Mr. Norwood to observe, as he did, that the departure was new. Acceptance by the directors was one step towards peace, and it was an event not otherwise than surprising. The directors

have said, over and over again, that they could not afford to pay the sixpence per hour, that surrender to the labourers would be, in effect, equivalent to a breach of trust in relation to their shareholders. It may be assumed that the concession was made because the directors saw that, during the proposed interval, they could so readjust their rates as to provide themselves with the extra funds which they say they require, or because they saw the prospect, during the interval, of making that arrangement with the shipowners in which, according to many opinions, *via prima salutis* is to be found.

Did Messrs. Burns and Tillett approve the suggested terms of compromise, or did they merely say that they would submit them to the Strike Committee? According to the Lord Mayor, the Bishop of London, and Cardinal Manning, they did signify their approbation. But they themselves deny, in the most emphatic manner, that they did anything of the sort, they declare that they would not have dared to do it, and they say – this at any rate is quite true – that they had no authority to approve or to accept before submitting the matter to the Central Committee. Meanwhile, one thing is certain – that the Strike Committee, not showing that 'sweet reasonableness' with which Cardinal Manning credits, or has credited, Mr. Burns, have, in the form of an elaborate manifesto, rejected the offer made by the dock company and have taken the course which, to speak frankly, I have always expected them to follow. The situation, therefore, is precisely the same as it was before the Lord Mayor, the Bishop, and the Cardinal took the matter in hand, as far as the prospects of argument are concerned; but the strikers have lost some strong friends. The Lord Mayor is understood to be very seriously annoyed, the Bishop can hardly be pleased, and Cardinal Manning, whose influence in the East-end of London is very strong – Mr. Champion estimates that some 40,000 of the strikers are of the Romish faith – cannot but feel that he has been slighted. Meanwhile, the negotiations between the shipowners and the directors have been delayed, since the board could hardly consider two schemes of settlement simultaneously. To-day – this cannot be too much to hope – they will, in all probability, be renewed.

Ben Tillett, *A Brief History of the Dockers' Union* (1910), 29

In the Strike Committee itself the same dry rot was setting in. Burns and Champion, not knowing the real facts of the position, favoured the compromise; meetings with the Lord Mayor favoured the assumption of surrender, making our battle all the harder. The Major indicated in haste to the press that a settlement was pending along the lines he had suggested; these he gave in great detail to the public.

We repudiated the same from Tower Hill and from that period the fight on the Strike Committee became open against the gang of stevedore foremen who manoeuvred for surrender.

Old Ruark, of Custom House, Tom Mann, Tom McCarthy and myself made an all-night fight of it to save us from disaster. We won, but the task was harder the next day.

THE SIXPENCE IN OCTOBER:

Pall Mall Gazette, Monday, 9 September 1889.

We are now at a loss to understand how Messrs Burns and Tillett can have appended their names to a manifesto which is a repudiation of what we all understood they had agreed to; and should they persist in continuing the strike we feel that they will justly forfeit the sympathy which has hitherto been shown to them and their cause.

Now, it is obvious that there has been a misunderstanding somewhere between the Mansion House magnates and Messrs BURNS and TILLETT. But surely, even if we throw all the blame of that misunderstanding upon representatives of the men, that is no reason for telling the public that they must no longer sympathise with the strike. The merits of the dispute remain exactly where they were before the Lord Mayor returned to London.

THE STORY OF THE MISUNDERSTANDING:

We print in parallel columns the story of the misunderstanding as by the Mansion House Committee and the leaders of the strike:—

THE MANSION HOUSE VERSION:

It was decided on Friday to place before the representatives of the labourers a suggestion that we should be allowed on their behalf to propose to the dock directors that they should concede the advance from 5d to 6d, but that it should not come into force until the 1st of March. Later in the day we placed our suggestion before Mr. Burns and Mr. Tillett and particularly pointed out that, owing to the great accumulation of work caused by the strike, the men could on the 5d scale earn more during the next few months than they would under ordinary circumstances be able to do on the 6d scale. Messrs Burns and Tillett demurred to the 1st of March being fixed for the increased wages to commence; they were anxious that the new conditions should be deferred for a month only. In the end, and after considerable discussion as to the wording of the proposal to be put before the directors in which Messrs Burns and Tillett took part and suggested various alterations, if it were agreed that the 1st of January should be substituted for the 1st of March. Messrs Burns and Tillett consented to these terms being placed before the directors on their behalf and promised to recommend their acceptance by the men.

The same evening the directors accorded us an interview, and after hearing us fully, promised to give their best consideration to our proposals, and especially inquired whether we could assure them that the men would assent to our suggestion. We replied that we had the best reason for believing they would.

On Saturday afternoon we received a letter from the directors, agreeing to the terms proposed and making only one or two minor stipulations. This letter was placed before Burns and Tillett, who at once acquiesced in the conditions of the directors, but they demanded that the dock authorities 'should not displace or directly or indirectly show resentment to the men who have participated in the strike'.

Messrs Burns and Tillett then left us, promising to use their best efforts to induce the whole of the men to agree to what they had accepted.

Later in the evening we received a communication from the representatives of the men asking whether 8d an hour for overtime was also conceded. To this we replied that we had 'made it clear' to the directors that this was to be so; but we added that the men should include this as one of the terms of their acceptance.

JOHN BURNS VERSION:

Speaking at Hyde Park yesterday, Mr. Burns said:—What happened? Mr. Ben Tillett and himself went to the Mansion House. The Bishop of London, Cardinal Manning (Cheers) and Mr. Sydney Buxton MP were present. They were asked by the Lord Mayor whether they would terminate the strike if the men's terms were conclude in March next. (Loud and prolonged cries of 'No'.) To that he gave an unhesitating 'No' (Loud Cheers). Mr. Ben Tillett and he said on Friday they were willing that the strike would terminate, and, if necessary, they would not object to put it to the men that the dock companies should have, in the words of the Bishop of London, 'a little breathing time to arrange their dock-rate-book'. (Hisses) But they did not pledge themselves on Friday, and after the Lord Mayor had stated what he would suggest and after telling the Lord Mayor all that they were willing to do, namely, to put to the men any conditions that might be discussed, Mr. Tillett and he went away. On Saturday he received a telegram to go to the Lord Mayor, and he went. They had another interview, at which they were asked whether the men would accept the 1st of January and not March as a means of terminating the strike. After a long discussion, the strike leaders stated that if the Docks Committee conceded this officially – as they did, for he had got it in his pocket – they would put it to the men, and if the men accepted it, it would be his duty and the duty of his colleagues to obey. Then Mr. Tillett did say that he would recommend the adoption of these terms to the men, but he understood and made it clear that whatever he might recommend in that direction would not be accepted. (Laughter and cheers) He and Mr. Tillett did consult the Executive Committee on Saturday night, and they unanimously rejected the terms. The best four months of the stevedores' and dockers' year were from August to Christmas. (Cheers) If the men waited four months until the new wage were given, though it really meant seven months' waiting, as trade did not begin to get busy until about April 1 – they would be April fools. He would not welcome a termination of the strike unless the men themselves told him straight that they were willing to have the terms which were offered to them, (Loud cries of 'No') Would they accept March? ('No') Would they accept January? ('No') He put it to them finally, did they accept the Lord Mayor's terms? (Loud cries of 'No') Were they going to

Coal porters – a tough breed and a strong element in the strike.

fight on until they win? (Loud cries of 'Yes') Were they going to surrender? (Loud cries of 'No') Was that their final No? ('Yes') Let all those in favour of the terms printed in the Sunday papers hold up their hands. (No hand was held up.) All those in favour of January or March hold up their hands. (Hisses.) Now he said he had done his duty.

Ben Tillett, *Memoirs and Reflections* (1931), 149–152

[EXTRACT FROM C. M. NORWOOD'S LETTER TO MANSION HOUSE COMMITTEE]

'The conditions under which my Committee are prepared to accede to these terms [recommended by Mansion House Committee], are:

'1. That the existing Strike shall be terminated, and that all the men connected with docks, wharves, and river return to work on Monday morning. 2. That the strikers and their leaders shall unreservedly undertake that all labourers who have been at work during the Strike shall be unmolested, and be treated in every way as fellow labourers by those who have been out on strike. 3. That we receive an acceptance of this arrangement by the leaders of the Strike through your Lordships in the course of this evening.

'In acceding to these conditions, my Committee are largely influenced by the assurance of your Lordships that shipowners and merchants and the public generally, are willing to bear an increase in rates and charges.' Mr Norwood had then the honour to be with much respect their Lordships' obedient servant.

This letter omitted as much as it contained, and even more. Its contents were bad enough, but its omissions were fatal. Our Strike Committee deliberated. From their deliberations came a manifesto declining the terms that were offered, in the following words:

[September 7, 1889]

'Fellow Countrymen,

'A statement has been published to the effect that the dock strike is over, and that the representatives of the labourers have agreed that work shall be resumed in the docks at the former rate of wages, on the condition that 6d. per hour and 8d. per hour overtime shall be granted by the companies on January 1, 1890. This is absolutely untrue. Such a proposition has been made to the dock companies by some influential persons who desire to see the strike ended. The directors are willing to accept it, but the men are not inclined to grant the dock companies, who have opposed them, terms more favourable to the masters than those which have been agreed to by the wharfingers.

The position briefly is this – that dock labourers are wiling to return to work for any dock or wharf or shipping companies, representatives of which will sign and forward to the strike committee an agreement to give the terms acceded to by the wharfingers, including a minimum wage of 6d. per hour ordinary time and 8d. per hour overtime.

The stevedores, and sailors and firemen, who have no dispute of their own to settle, and have come out 'on principle', solely to support the labourers, are willing to return to work as soon as the dock labourers are satisfied. The stevedores and sailors and firemen will work for any shipping company who will give the 6d. and 8d. overtime to the labourers, and agree to employ dock labourers only to discharge. The stevedores and sailors and firemen will also work for those shipowners who have signed the agreement and have vessels to load, only on condition that so long as the dock companies hold out against their labourers, these shipowners do not work goods from the dock company or from craft loaded by the dock companies.

The lightermen, however, have determined to stand by their circular of August 22, and if the terms therein demanded are conceded by

their masters, they will return to work provided that the labourers and stevedores and sailors and firemen are satisfied.'

As I challenged and resented the unauthorised attempt to settle, it was left to me to carry the battle to the gate on my own resources. But the Cardinal, whose silence had been ominous, now joined in. He endorsed with a sense of responsibility the two main claims of the dockers for the 6d. minimum and recognition of the Union. Other of the claims and conditions of employment, the day and night calls and regulation of things consequential, he put aside, indicating that they could be dealt with afterwards. He was now practically alone in the mediation effort. Nobody more human, more diplomatic, more skilled in dealing with the human heart and mind, could have been found: patient, persuasive, but very, very firm in handling the injured feelings of the Lord Mayor, and the harsh and unsympathetic attitude of the Bishop, no less than the thrusting aggressiveness of John Burns.

Another serious problem began to appear: the pickets were becoming frustrated with the duration of the strike, although their lieutenants had drilled them well and there had been no serious outbreaks of violence, an amazing feat when one considers there was up to 16,000 men on picket duty.

The Times, however, on 9 September, described a situation which could have turned very ugly. Fortunately John Burns was on the scene when 3,000 pickets threatened to break into the Surrey Commercial Docks. Burns was able to contain the men, no mean feat. Burns had not only a very strong moral leadership over the men but a physical one as well. *The Times* stated in other difficult situations they had seen Mr Burns place himself in a fighting attitude to preserve the peace. It noted that Mr Burns met rough threats in a like manner, threatening to break people's jaws etc.

Unfortunately it was also reported – and this indeed was an isolated incident – that quicklime had been thrown in the face of a scab, blinding the man.

The Times obviously favoured Burns over Tillett and Champion, accusing Tillett of being in an egotistic vein. But it was left to Tillett to contact the Lord Mayor stating that they would accept terms if the dockers' tanner were to be paid from October instead of January. Mr Norwood, perhaps somewhat surprisingly, given recent events, promised to lay this before his Committee. The south side still proved to be the weakest section. It was felt necessary to put a motion at a rally that all sections should stand firm. The leakage of the alleged agreement of the January date for the dockers' tanner was causing anxiety on the south side. Mann, wary of the difficulties which had been caused before in premature statements, issued a strong denial, stating that the men would not be sold out and no settlement would be agreed unless the full demands were met.

Henry Champion reminded the men that the negotiations were begun by Cardinal Manning, who was anxious to see an end to the dispute and whose interest was not just in the 40,000 Roman Catholics in the East End but in all those in dispute. The leaders were careful in their speeches to give the impression that Cardinal Manning was working for the men against Mr Norwood in the dispute.

The Times, Monday, 9 September 1889, 4

There was what is vulgarly described as a 'row' in Billiter-street [off Leadenhall Street] in the morning. Some five-and-twenty imported dock labourers were on their way to the docks, under the guidance of one of the officials of the dock companies, and under the escort of a number of detectives who were prepared to identify any persons who might be guilty of intimidation. The 'pickets' detected the body of imported men and brought every species of moral suasion to bear upon them. They were even beginning to hustle the 'foreigners', and there was every probability that, for the first time, the cause of the strikers would be defiled by a genuine outbreak of violence, when by real good fortune John Burns came on the scene. ... Nor need there be any hesitation in saying that Mr Burns met the emergency judiciously. He thoroughly understands his men. Often and often, down at the Wade's Arms, when a tendency to mutiny has been shown, when one man has grumbled because he has not had what he considers his fair share of relief, and another has complained because he has not been allowed to return to work, I have seen Mr. Burns restore quiet by placing himself in a fighting attitude. It is a curious method of preserving the peace, but it succeeds, and it shows an appreciation of the men. So, on Saturday, when the men who were making a disturbance were protesting that they were the picket and, in effect, that in trying to prevent foreigners from going down to the docks they were simply following out the instructions given to them, Mr Burns simply met rough threats with the like coin. 'I will break the jaw,' he said, 'of the first man who makes a noise,' and the men, who knew very well that he was as likely as not to be as good as his word, desisted from their disorderly behaviour at once. But this circumstance does not serve to show what 'picketing' really means. Mr Burns is not always present, but at the dock-gates, at the approaches to nearly all the main stations in London, and opposite the Dock-house the pickets may be seen at any time. ... By the open confession of some of the leaders of the agitation – I refer to Messrs Tillett and Champion in particular – a very serious incident occurred on Saturday. An individual, one of a body, was on his way into one of the docks to do what, when all is said and done, any man has a right to do if he chooses – namely, to accept work when it was offered. The pickets remonstrated and somebody in the crowd enforced the remonstrance with quicklime, which absolutely and forever destroyed the eyesight of the victim. The leaders repudiate the action; they say that it was not done by one of their men on picket duty; they say that it was done in a moment of passion, and that if they could find

Punch *thought the strike would last until Christmas.*

Gin was one escape.

The evils of the gin palace.

the offender they would hand him up to justice. For my own part I believe they could find him perfectly well if they liked, for it is obvious that the pickets must actually have seen the dastardly crime committed. ...

Mr. Tillett, who admitted that he felt his position to be difficult, was in an egotistic vein, and showed a tendency to claim for himself the credit of having originated the strike. His chief witticism consisted in a description of the directors as 'good old fat-headed old sleepies.' The words do not look humorous, but they evoked uproarious laughter. Mrs. [Eleanor Marx] Aveling, to do her justice, spoke very well and drew a striking contrast between the courtesy she had met in the East-end and the rudeness she had encountered in the City. Mr. Champion also, to a thin audience, made a good and sensible speech, emphasizing the virtue of orderly behaviour and exhorting the men to maintain it. In particular, he alluded to the probability of great social movements on the Continent, and said that in days to come Englishmen would be able to boast that here labour had been raised in position without violence, without bloodshed, and without great waste of wealth.

After the meeting in Hyde Park yesterday, Mr. Tillett, the chairman of the United Joint Strike Committee, waited upon the Lord Mayor at the Mansion-house and asked him to lay before the dock directors the proposition that the new terms should commence on October 1, instead of January 1, as conceded by them. The Lord Mayor demurred to this, on the ground that the time proposed was totally insufficient to enable the dock committees to make the necessary adjustments preparatory to the conceded rise in wages. His Lordship, however, agreed to use his good offices with Mr. Norwood and his colleagues to get from them the further concession of an earlier commencement of the increased terms than New Year's Day, and he lost no time in making a suggestion to that effect to Mr. Norwood, who promised to lay it before his committee. The prospect of a settlement is therefore again hopeful.

'Dock-house, 109, Leadenhall-street, Sept. 7

'My Lords, – My committee have deliberated very anxiously upon the proposals verbally laid before them last night by your lordships with a view to the termination of the present labour strike – viz., that in addition to the concessions already publicly notified, the payment to our casual labourers on and after January 1 next shall be raised from 5d. to 6d. per hour for the time of actual work ....

'They feel, however, that the situation has been so altered by the circumstance of your lordships' having thrown the weight of your great influence into the scale, and by the gravity of the representations which you have made to them with regard to the public peace, that they are no longer free to exercise their unfettered judgement, and must yield to a pressure from without, which they venture to regard as a very dangerous departure in disputes between employers and workmen, and one that may have very far-reaching consequences in the future.

'They have, therefore, decided, under the conditions which I now have to bring before you, to accept the terms which, as my committee understand, your lordships are prepared to recommend to the strikers, and to which you confidently expect them to agree. [*Rest of text in extract above, Tillett,* Memories, *149* (*p. 191*)]

'I have the honour to be, with much respect, your lordships' obedient servant,

'C. M. NORWOOD, chairman.

'To the Right Hon. the Lord Mayor,
'The Right Rev. the Bishop of London, and
'His Eminence the Cardinal Manning.'

This decision of the Joint Committee was received with great satisfaction by the Lord Mayor and his colleagues, and at once Messrs. Burns and Tillett, who promised that it should have their adhesion, left to communicate it to the strike committee. Before doing so, the following endorsement had been written at Mr. Burns's request on the letter of the Joint Committee:—

'Mansion-house, Sept. 7.

'We, the undersigned, accept these terms on behalf of ourselves, and also agree to recommend them to the men out on strike, subject to the condition that the dock companies do not displace or directly or indirectly show resentment to any of the men who have participated in the strike.

'F. LONDIN. 'JAMES WHITEHEAD, Lord Mayor.
'SYDNEY BUXTON.' 'HENRY E., Cardinal Archbishop.

Mr. burns said he should ask permission to retain the original document, as a souvenir of the great strike, which the Lord Mayor agreed to. Later in the evening, the Lord Mayor received the following letter:—

'United Dock Labourers' Strike Committee,
Wade's Arms, Poplar, E., Sept. 7.

'My Lord, – We have received your communication from Mr. Norwood with the statement signed by yourself and by the Bishop of London, the Cardinal Archbishop of Westminster, and Mr. Sydney Buxton, M.P. It is impossible to accept any terms without consulting the various sdtrike committees. We notice with regret that Mr. Norwood's letter contains no provision for increase in the pay for overtime to 8d. per hour. We beg to express our thanks to you for the trouble you have taken in the matter, and to assure you that we will let you know the decision of the men at the earliest possible moment.

'We are, your lordship's faithfully,

'BENJAMIN TILLETT. 'JOHN TOOMEY.
'JOSEPH BURNS. 'H. H. CHAMPION.
'TOM MANN.

'To the Right Hon. the Lord Mayor.'

To this communication the subjoined reply was at once sent to Mr. Tillett:—

'Mansion-house, Sept. 7.

'Dear Sir, – We quite understand, and we made it clear to the Dock Committee yesterday, that the 8d. per hour overtime is to stand on the same footing as the 6d. per hour for ordinary work. There can be no doubt in our minds that the reply of the Joint Committee covers this; but if, in your answer you will include this as one of the terms of acceptance, we shall be glad, as it will settle the point definitely. We are awaiting your reply, as you will see from Mr. Norwood's letter that acceptance this evening is a condition on which the committee rely.

'Yours very truly,

'JAMES WHITEHEAD, Lord Mayor.

'HENRY E., Cardinal MANNING.

'SYDNEY BUXTON.

'To Mr. Benjamin Tillett and colleagues.'

After another lengthened wait, the Lord Mayor and his colleagues received the following letter between 10 and 11 o'clock:—

'Wade's Arms, Poplar, E., Sept. 7.

'My Lord, – It is impossible for us to give you an answer to-night, as we have to see the lightermen and others concerned in the strike. Pending a definite and official answer from them, it is our opinion that they will not accept the terms of the dock company. Mr. Norwood must know that for us to accept the terms without a full consultation would be idle, and that such a consultation cannot take place at a few hours' notice, when the men concerned are spread over so large an area. As soon as their decision is known it will be communicated to you.

'We are, your lordship's faithfully,

'JOHN BURNS.

'H. H. CHAMPION.'

The Lord Mayor lost no time in conveying this intimation to the Joint Committee, who were waiting at the Dock-house, and that was the close of the correspondence and of the negotiations up to the present, for the leaders of the strike did not even forward to the Lord Mayor a copy of the manifesto which they subsequently issued as a reply to the directors' proposal, and which manifesto certainly contains statements absolutely irreconcilable with the attitude and position taken both on Friday and Saturday in the presence of the Committee of Conciliation by Mr. Burns and Mr. Tillett, presumably with the authority of the men.

Much excitement was caused in the East-end on Saturday night owing to the reported acceptance of the decision of the dock companies by the Strike Committee to concede to the dockers their full demands on the 1st of January next. Joy was universally expressed at the supposed ending of the strike, and the consequent commencement of work, followed by the increase of trade, on the Monday. Many, however, in face of the determined statements made during the morning by the leaders of the agitation, were doubtful upon the matter. The news quickly spread, and before 9 o'clock some thousands of persons were gathered in front of the Wade's Arms discussing the situation. Many of the women present loudly expressed disapproval of their husbands recommencing work unless the full terms – 6d. an hour and 8d. overtime – were at once given. Messengers were seen passing to and from the committee room, and as time wore on the excitement and number of persons outside the house greatly increased. At a quarter past 11 the following statement was handed to the reporters who were in attendance. [*Text as above, Tillett,* Memories, *151–2 (p. 191)*]

'MANIFESTO OF THE GENERAL COMMITTEE OF THE DOCK STRIKES.

Wade's Arms, Jeremiah-street, Poplar, E., Sept. 7, 1889.

By order of the General Committee of the Dock Strike, BEN TILLETT, JOHN BURNS, TOM MANN, H.H. CHAMPION, J. TOOMEY (Stevedore), J.M. WELSH (Sailors and Firemen) R. ILES (Lightermen).'

The lightermens' circular referred to demands the following:—

'Day to commence at 7 a.m. and terminate at 7 p.m.; wages 6s. A night's work to consist of one job only, the job to mean barge to dock and docking; barge to wharf and watching; delivering and steam in dock or otherwise. Sundays same as other days, 6s., and one job only as above. All reasonable railway, waterage or other expenses to be paid. Orders to be given at City offices not later than 7 p.m.'

As soon as the manifesto, a copy of which was exhibited outside the Wade's Arms, was made known those assembled appeared to agree with its contents. On the other hand, amongst the small traders the disappointment was great that the expected cessation of the struggle had not been realized. The men on strike expressed an intention of not giving in now that the dock companies had almost been forced to give what had been demanded.

On Saturday the men on strike on the south side of the Thames marched in procession through a number of the principal thoroughfares in the City, and returned to Southwark-park, where a mass meeting was held in spite of the rain which fell. The following resolution was carried unanimously:—

'That this meeting advises the urgency of all sections employed at the Surrey Commercial Docks standing firm, and whilst regarding the proverbial dockers' questions, asks that due regard shall be paid to local requirements.'

The report which got currency on Saturday night, that Messrs. Burns and Tillett had signed an arrangement by which the strike was to be ended and the higher terms to stand over till January, created intense excitement on the south side of the river, and the utmost anxiety was felt by the men as to the accuracy of the rumour. At Sayes-court, the headquarters of the South London Committee, and at the district relief stations the news was received with something like consternation and disgust, and to the relief of all concerned Mr. Tom Mann towards midnight gave the rumour an emphatic denial. Mr. Mann, in denying the report, pointed out that nothing could be final until it received the sanction not of individual leaders but of the Strike Committee itself.

The third Sunday demonstration by the strikers was held yesterday in Hyde Park. ... The people rushed to the platform where Mr. Burns was to speak; but the important statement of the day was made by Mr. Champion as to the attitude of the leaders with regard to the negotiations of the Lord Mayor, Cardinal Manning, and the Bishop of London with the dock directors, and the reported aceptance of the latest concessions of the directors.

The platform at which Mr. Champion was to speak was presided over by Mr. T. McCarthy, of the stevedores who in his opening speech said it was reported in the evening papers of the previous night that the leaders had signed a compromise; but no such action had been taken, and they meant to go on fighting until the battle was won, because they were more likely in the end to have complete victory. (Cheers.)

[Mr Champion] then proceeded to review the negotiations which had been started at the Mansion-house, and denied that Messrs. Burns and Tillett had in any way agreed to countenance the men going in on the chance of getting the 6d. an hour on the 1st of January next, or had in any way accepted the proposal. Whatever might be said by the Lord Mayor or by the Bishop of London the speaker took it that they would believe Messrs. Burns and Tillett before they would believe the Lord Mayor and the whole bench of Bishops. (Cheers.) The negotiations were commenced by Cardinal Manning, who was respected by all men (cheers) and who, after the last meeting, sent for Mr. Burns and himself, and said he was anxious to see the strike ended in the interest not only of the 40,000 Roman Catholics in the East-end work, but also in the interest of the others, for whom the Cardinal had no less regard. The Cardinal endeavoured by his own action to get from the dock directors some concession, and followed up his action by interesting other official persons when the dock directors said they would not see Messrs. Burns and Tillett again. The proposal made by the Cardinal was that the 6d. and 8d. should be conceded at once, and an inquiry instituted to see whether it was just and reasonable, and if the reverse the amounts should no longer be conceded. But these terms were refused, and then the Mansion-house proposals were substituted. Mr. Champion declared that the men could not accept less than the 6d. and 8d. for which they had fought so long and so well.

Secret Talks

Despite the setbacks the conciliation committee showed that they would not be deterred. Both sides agreed not to reveal the nature or the progress of negotiations. The situation with the south side men was eased by allowing the South London Committee to deal with their own affairs.

Meanwhile the committee of conciliation at the Mansion-House have shown remarkable forbearance. In spite of the grievous disappointment of Saturday evening they have determined to renew their efforts to promote peace, and to that end they summoned to the Mansion-House yesterday afternoon, not merely Messrs. Burns. Tillett, and Champion, but all the signatories to the manifesto of Saturday evening. Mr. Norwood also called at the Mansion-House yesterday, but only, according to the vaguely expressed belief of his brother directors, to say that the extreme limit of concession had been reached. Meanwhile, as to the course of the discussion at the Mansion-House, no certain information is to be obtained. Mr. Burns and his allies informed me that they had pledged their words not to reveal anything, and that a similar pledge had been given by the Lord Mayor. In fact, the meeting was altogether mysterious ...

THE SOUTH LONDON STRIKE A SEPARATE AFFAIR:

Pall Mall Gazette, Tuesday, 10 September 1889

A very important step was taken by the South London Committee yesterday with the concurrence of the Wade's Arms Committee. The proprietors of Coombes Granaries on the south side of the river applied to the Central Strike Committee for one of the forms of agreement to pay the men 6d and 8d. On the South London pickets hearing of what had taken place, they refused to allow the men to go in. The Wade's Arms Committee upon inquiry found that under the 6d and 8d arrangement the men would be as badly off as before and they also found that the strike on the south side was of such a complicated nature that it would be better to allow the South London Committee to deal entirely with their own affairs. This new step was accordingly taken yesterday, and under this arrangement a number of important matters were dealt with by the committee.

Meanwhile Cardinal Manning was meeting the strikers in the heart of dockland, spelling out the terms, namely a November settlement for

the 6d. The south side committee, acting as an independent unit now, issued their own manifesto, laying out their terms for settlement. All sides on the strike committee had obviously learnt the lessons of the recent past and were ensuring that their demands were made public and that sectional interests were maintained.

The Times, Wednesday, 11 September 1889, 6

The next influence to be considered is that of the Cardinal, who, undeterred by previous rebuff and failure, undismayed by the retreat of the Lord Mayor and the Bishop of London, had the courage to return to the charge anew yesterday. He was closeted with Messrs. Burns and Champion, and I believe with certain others among the leaders of the strike, for nearly four hours yesterday afternoon, in the schoolroom which lies on the opposite side of the road from the Commercial-road. Here, again, we are face to face with an almost Eleusinian mystery. I say frankly that I do not know what took place within those walls. But I have a strong impression that I can make a conjecture which will be found to come near the truth in the end. It is to the effect that the Cardinal suggested a November settlement – namely, a proposal on the part of the men that they should return to work at fivepence, *plus* the concessions already conditionally made by the directors, and that the sixpenny rate should commence in November.

The committee at Sayes Court have spent two days considering the demands of the various sections of men on strike in South London, including the men at the Surrey Commercial Docks, and late last night the following manifesto was issued:—

'South Side Central Strike Committee,
Sayes Court, Deptford, Sept. 10.

'GENERAL MANIFESTO.

'Owing to the fact that the demands of the corn porters, deal porters, granary men, General Steam Navigation men, permanent men, and general labourers on the south side have been misrepresented, the above committee have decided to issue this manifesto stating the demands of the various sections now on strike, and pledge themselves to support each section in obtaining their demands.

'Deal porters of the Surrey Commercial Docks have already placed their demands before the directors.

'Lumpers (outside) demand the following rates – viz., firstly, 10d. per standard for deals; secondly, 11d. per standard for all goods rating from 2 by 4 to $2\frac{1}{2}$ by 7, or for rough boards; thirdly, 1s. per standard for plain boards. Working day from 7 a.m. to 5 p.m., and that no man leave the Red Lion corner before 6.45 a.m. Overtime at the rate of 6d. per hour extra from 5 p.m., including meal times.

'Stevedores (inside) demand 8d. per hour from 7 a.m. to 5 p.m.; 1s. per hour overtime. Overtime to commence from 5 p.m. to 7 a.m. Pay to commence from leaving Red Lion corner. Meal times to be paid for. Holidays and meal times double pay.

Dimly lit alleyways inhabited by that submerged class which Victorian society would rather forget.

'Overside corn porters, Surrey Commercial Docks, demand 15s. 3d. per 100 quarters for oats. Heavy labour 17s. 4d. per 100 quarters manual, or with use of steam 16s. 1d. All overtime after 6 p.m. to be paid at the rate of 1s. 2d. per quarter extra.

'Quay corn porters (Surrey Commercial Docks) demand the return of standard prices previous to March, 1889, which had been in operation for 17 years.

'Trimmers and general labourers demand 6d. per hour from 7 a.m. to 6 p.m., and 8d. per hour overtime. Meal times as usual, and not to be taken on for less than four hours.

'Weighers and warehousemen demand to be reinstated in their former positions without distinction.

'Bermondsey and Rotherhithe Wall corn porters demand – firstly,

permanent men 30s. per week; secondly, casual men 5s. 10d. per day, and 8d. per hour overtime. Overtime to commence at 6 p.m. Meal times as usual.

'General Steam Navigation men demand – firstly, wharf men 6d. per hour from 6 a.m. to 6 p.m., and 8d. per hour overtime; secondly, in the stream 7d. per hour ordinary time, and 9d. per hour overtime; thirdly, in the dock 8d. per hour ordinary time, and 1s. per hour overtime.

'Maudsley's engineers' men, those receiving 21s. per week now demand 24s., and those receiving 24s. per week demand 26s.

'Ashby's (Limited) Cement Works demand 6d. per ton landing coals and chalk. General labourers 10 per cent. rise of wages all round, thus making up for a reduction made three years ago.

'General labourers Telegraph Construction demand 4s. per day, from 6 a.m. to 5 p.m., time and a quarter for first two hours overtime, and, if later, time and a half for all overtime. No work to be done in meal hours.

'Signed on behalf of the Central Committee, Wade's Arms,

'BEN TILLETT.
'JOHN BURNS.
'TOM MANN.
'H. H. CHAMPION.
'JAS. TOOMEY.

'Signed on behalf of the South Side Committee, Sayes-court.

'JAS. SULLIVAN, **Chairman.**
'CHAS. HAVELOCK, **Secretary.**
'HUGH BROWN, **Treasurer.**

Several firms visited the committee yesterday and assented to the terms demanded. As soon as the necessary agreement is signed for payment to be made on the above lines the men will be allowed to start work.

It was evident yesterday that the agreement between the Wade's Arms Committee and the Sayes Court Committee on the subject of overside unloading in mid-stream was not complete. The former committee have given permission for this to be done in certain cases, but in answer to several applications the South Side Committee came to the conclusion to prohibit the unloading.

The Nonconformist ministers of Bermondsey and Rotherhithe yesterday issued an urgent appeal for help for the wives and families of men on strike.

In the secret negotiations taking place, Cardinal Manning played a prominent role. It was noted that the relationship between the Strike Committee and the mediators were most cordial. Burns announced yet another £1,000 from Australia and subscriptions from the streets were as large as ever. Obviously every time such a large amount of money was donated to the strike fund the stronger their bargaining situation became and indeed such was the position in relation to the obvious victory that was to soon be declared that detailed discussions were being made with sectional interests amongst the work force. Meanwhile the other trades engaged in strike action were resolute in their endeavours and daily victories of one sort or another were being announced and increasingly militancy was creeping through all trades.

The Times, Wednesday 11 September 1889, 6

Yesterday afternoon [Tues 10] Cardinal Manning and Mr. Sydney Buxton proceeded to Poplar and held a conference with the Strike Committee in the Wade-street school-house. The proceedings, which lasted from 5 o'clock until 8, were strictly private, and no information as to what took place will be made public until after Cardinal Manning and his colleague have conferred with the dock companies. It is understood, however, that the relations between the Strike Committee and the mediators are of the most cordial character, and that so far the negotiations are satisfactory.

Mr. Burns said he intended to be brief, as he had important business to transact elsewhere. He had to announce that they had received another £1,000 that morning from Australia. Since Monday morning £7,000 had come from Melbourne and Adelaide alone. That did not look like losing. The subscriptions in the streets were as large as ever, and the collections from the churches and chapels were coming in very fast.

Tom Mann's Memoirs (1923), 65

I had never seen the Cardinal before, and it was a matter of no small interest to me to find myself closely identified with such a man for a colleague.

A large percentage of the men at the docks were (and are) Roman Catholics. Now that a stage had been reached when the men's representatives were of opinion that the offers of the company merited serious consideration, the Cardinal, on the suggestion of the Strike Committee chairman, agreed to go to Poplar and put the case to the men, who held him in the greatest respect and reverence.

The meeting was held [on Tuesday, 10 September] in the Kirby Street Catholic School at Poplar. The Cardinal was a very slender man; his face was most arresting, so thin, so refined, so kindly. In the whole of my life I have never seen another like unto it. He spoke of the dockers in such a quiet, firm and advising fatherly manner, that minute by minute as he was speaking one could feel the mental atmosphere changing. The result was an agreement that the conditions should be accepted, to become operative in November.

[*TILLETT DESCRIBES MANNING'S MEETING WITH THE STRIKE COMMITTEE AT A CATHOLIC SCHOOL IN POPLAR.*]

Ben Tillett, *Memories and Reflections* (1931), 152–153

By this time the Cardinal had won the hearts of the Strike Committee. He had insisted upon shaking hands with everybody and learning everybody's name before he began, by asking me to state my reasons for objecting to the settlement. I had reasons, and I stated them, emphasising particularly, perhaps with the bitterness of years of toil and hunger, with the misery which unrequited labour brings, to steel my heart and voice against any sort of compromise, the argument that our settlement should not be inferior to the standards of the stevedores. Many of my colleagues shared my view, or perhaps it is truer to say, sympathised with my feelings. I was weary, tired out in body and spirit; I could not withstand this gentle old man, who touched so tenderly the heart-strings of his hearers with solemn talk about the sufferings of wives and children, or impress him with a summary of social needs and economic complexities multiplying in the prolongation of the Strike. I never look back on that meeting without a sense of nightmare, but there was a final judgment and the Cardinal won. Our Strike Committee indicated their readiness to accept the Cardinal's suggestion for a settlement.

The Times,
Wednesday
11 September 1889, 6

The East-end Jewish tailors out on strike had a large accession to their numbers yesterday. At a meeting held in Buck's-row it was reported that other men were willing to join the movement. There was a procession of the strikers, and a rather novel feature was a cart containing three men, two at work at a sewing-machine with no coats or waistcoats on. The men marched through the City to the West-end.

The railway extension works on the London and South-Western line at Vauxhall resumed their normal state of activity yesterday morning. The men, who had been on strike since the middle of last week for a rise of wages from 5½d. to 6d. per hour, have accepted the terms offered by Mr. Butler, the representative of Messrs. Perry and Co., of Bow, the contractors. These terms are that 6d. per hour will be given on Saturday next to all labourers who are considered by their foremen to be worth the money, and the others who after that date are not satisfied with the pay must look for fresh employment. The engineers on strike in the south of London have mostly resumed work at the small advance of pay asked for, but the *employés* of Messrs. Maudsley are still standing out. All the wharves from Bridge-road, Vauxhall, to the Albert Embankment were yesterday afternoon as busy as they were a fortnight ago.

FURTHER ORGANISATION OF THE MEN:

Pall Mall Gazette,
Wednesday,
11 September 1889

A very large number of the sailing barge men are now joining the union; the tally clerks are also joining; and shipowners have been informed that the tally clerks, both import and export, will not work on any ship where the men, including the captain and mate, do not belong to the union. The Sailors' and Seamen's and Firemen's Society has decided to call out all the donkeymen upon all ships where 'scabs' are unloading. The tugmen employed on the Thames have decided to form a union of their own.

The announcement of large sums of money being put into the coffers of the strike committee was followed by demands that it be released immediately. Up to a hundred women now lay in wait for Burns and

Hard faces in a hard life.

Tillett at the Wade's Arms for further relief, not always in the most genteel manner. While there was a lull in negotiations *The Times* took stock of the leadership. Burns was the obvious favourite. Mann, they thought would in the future take south side. They did not like Tillett. Champion they judged not to have great influence among the men. All eyes were on the Cardinal who, it was generally recognised, was the key to the end of the dispute. The south side men proved to be as firm as their counterparts on the north, when it came to allowing independent agreements to be reached.

Manning in his direct talks with the strikers complimented the men on their behaviour. He also expressed the view that some concessions might have to be made. Manning was simply laying out the terms of settlement and obviously judging the response that his statements met with. The frustration was beginning to show amongst some of the men who began to grumble, obviously frustrated at the delay in settlement. Seemingly now when trouble loomed on the horizon Tillett was able to quell disquiet by announcing that the Australians had sent another thousand. There was disappointment that not one penny piece had come from America but at home every church and chapel in England seemingly was collecting funds on behalf of the strikers, their wives and children.

The Times, Thursday, 12 September 1889, 4

The strike cannot go on much longer. There is always a gathering outside the Wade's Arms, but that gathering seems to me to have altered in character. Men who had, or thought that they had, individual grievances to complain of used to go there and lie in wait for Mr. Burns or Mr. Tillett or some other member of the committee. Last night the crowd was much larger than I have ever seen it before, and consisted very largely of women who were certainly in anything but a contented frame of mind. From 50 to 100 of them were crowded round the door leading to the room where Mr. Burns commonly sits, and they were remarkably loud-voiced and querulous. By the confession of a gentleman whose name I know not [Smith?], but who is always in one or other of the committee rooms, distress is beginning to be more keenly felt, the cause undoubtedly being the difficulty of properly distributing relief.

Of Mr. Burns people may form their own judgement; I have always found him to be straightforward. Mr. Mann is very determined and will hardly like to give up the position which he has made for himself as the leader of the Surrey side. Mr. Tillett I regard as a serious obstacle to compromise in any form. His speech in the Park on Sunday shows him to be extremely anxious to claim credit for himself and to pose as a leader, and though he is, intellectually, a pygmy beside the others, his feeble jokes and assertive manner are not unpopular among the men. Mr. Champion, who is to be congratulated on having kept his main doctrines out of his speeches, is, if I have gauged him correctly, more anxious for settlement than any of the others; but his influence is not great among the men, to whom cool reason and a cultivated accent do not appeal. To bring these human factors into harmony, to prevent petty jealousies from ending a prolonged misery, will be no easy matter. Meanwhile much is to be hoped from the influence of the Cardinal, and, as I begin to think, of the wives.

Several wharfingers have already signed the conditions required in the strike manifesto, and their men yesterday commenced work in the granaries and wharves. Messrs. Coombes, of the granaries at Rotherhithe, who under an erroneous notion respecting the Lafone agreement signed that agreement at Wade's Arms, only to find that the south side pickets refused to allow men to go in at those terms, have asked the Sayes Court committee to let it be known that immediately on discovering that the Lafone agreement did not apply to their granaries, they consented to the south side terms, and their men started work on Monday. Yesterday the Sayes Court committee amended the paragraph in the manifesto relating to the Surrey Commercial Dock stevedores.

A news agency states that it is enabled to sketch the course of pro-

ceedings at the conference held on Tuesday night at the Wade-street Roman Catholic schools between Cardinal Manning and the council of the Strike Committee. Mr. Tillett, Mr. Burns, Mr. Champion, and other members of the council explained the points of difference now existing between the dock company and the men. Mr. Tillett pointed out that the strikers would not accept November 1 as the day from which the new conditions should take effect, for the reason, amongst others, that the best part of the year would then have passed. The Cardinal urged the importance of looking to both sides of the question, and commented on the difficulties which stood in the way of a rearrangement of the dock company's affairs in so short a time as that insisted on by the men. He pointed out that the dock company's business was a gigantic one, involving a multiplicity of offices. While admitting this, Mr. Tillett averred that the dock company had all the necessary machinery wherewith to bring about speedy and effective alterations. Cardinal Manning then dwelt on the necessity for some concession from the men. The principle had been conceded by the dock company, and the only question now was one of time. Answering an objection that the pledge of the dock company was not fully satisfactory, his Eminence assured the council that they need have no fear of a breach of faith on the part of the employers; neither did he believe that the wharfingers were at all likely to go back on their

Brush-making at home became a family affair.

word. It would be a lamentable thing if the dockers should lose their prize after so protracted a struggle, and if they conceded a point as to time it would involve comparatively little loss, because as work had very much accumulated a compensation would be found in the increased wages earned. After a reference to the manifesto of Sunday, the issuing of which he regretted, Cardinal Manning complimented the council upon the way in which the strike had been conducted. He had seen many trade struggles, but he had never known one in which the men had behaved with more calmness and fairness. If the dockers now repudiated concession, he feared the effect would be inimical to the best interests of labour, and that there would be spread abroad a general feeling of distrust. Mr. Sydney Buxton backed up the appeal of the Cardinal by impressing upon the men the importance of moderation now that they had won the terms for which they struck. The speakers who followed contended that it was essential to establish a basis of action that would be a security in future, and that as struggles hereafter might be very much influenced by the success or non-success of this, it was the aim of the dockers to make their position a solid one, even at the loss of one or two weeks' worth. The council passed a unanimous vote of thanks to the Cardinal for his presence and advice.

After the return of the procession from the City large numbers of men waited round the West India Dock gates in the hope of hearing the usual address from Mr. Burns. After the men had been waiting for more than an hour, Mr. Tillett arrived. He said he had heard that some of the men were beginning to grumble because the leaders could not get round to every dock-gate. Mr. Burns was now ill with overwork, and he himself was pretty knocked up. They had both done all their strength would allow them. He felt very grateful to the men for their enthusiasm, and he hoped they would all stick together and maintain their union. If they saw anything that wanted doing, let them do it without waiting for orders, for they were getting old enough now to do without nursing. He was glad to tell them that they had just received another £1,000 from the colonies. They were getting gold from the diggings, and Australia was a perfect mine. They had had yards and yards of sympathy from America, but not a single dollar. With all their boastings about the eagle and the stars and the stripes on their banner, with all their vauntings about their labour institutions, the Americans had not sent their fellow working-men anything with which to provide the ammunition of war. This week a new agency had been started, for the united trades throughout England had now taken up their cause. Then they were informed that there were going to be church and chapel collections. Then they had the season in their favour. It was a busy time coming on, for they had now to expect the new tea arrivals, the timber arrivals, and the wool also. It had been said that they were driving the trade away from the Port of London. He did not think so. If the dock directors wished to save the trade from going away, let them do as the wharfingers had done. Let

them grant the terms asked, and they would at once make large profits, as the wharfingers were now doing. He had nothing further to tell them except that Cardinal Manning was still going to use his good offices to try and bring about a settlement, and if an honourable settlement could be brought about he, like the rest of them, would be glad. (Cheers.)

The meeting then closed in the usual way with three cheers for the strike and the wives and children.

The departure of Sir H. Le Merchant from the employers' joint committee was a turning point. Merchant had been an advocate of a no-surrender policy. His resignation obviously meant that concessions had been agreed. While the strikers remained united the employers, namely the shipowners and the dock committee could not agree to discuss their differences, although sections of the wharfingers expressed their support for the docks committee. Picketing was still as efficient as ever – 150 Liverpool men were turned back at Euston. The only thing that had gone wrong was the incident of the quicklime throwing. Champion declared that if they found the man who had done this, they would give him a good thrashing before handing him over to justice. Such was the quiet which now fell over the docklands that Burns' visit to the dentist caused press speculation!

The Times, Thursday, 12 September 1889, 3

Before entering into the main subject I am desirous of correcting an error of which, by a mere slip, I was guilty yesterday. Instead of writing that Sir H. Le Marchant had resigned his seat as one of the Joint Committee because the majority were of opinion that the Lord Mayor's proposals touching the October settlement ought to be considered, I ought to have written that this gentleman resigned because his fellows were of opinion that the proposals of the committee of conciliation ought to be taken into consideration. As a matter of fact, so far as I am aware, the October settlement has not been suggested by the mediators as yet, nor do I think it likely that it will be put forward by them. Meanwhile, the error which I hasten to confess does not affect the inference which, it is suggested, may be drawn from the resignation of this member of the committee, which is that a very determined advocate of the policy of no surrender at the Dock-house has departed from the scene ...

With regard to the situation there is again ground for hope. Tuesday may fairly be regarded as having been a day wasted so far as Leadenhall-street was concerned. The shipowners would not approach the Docks Committee, the committee would not approach the shipowners. Each of the two parties were playing a waiting game, ...

Another important meeting was held at the Dock-house during the day by the important section of the wharfingers who are believed to be more or less in accordance with the directors and to regard the demands of the men on strike as they do. Twenty-one wharfingers were present, and although there are a very great number who were not present it is worthy of remembrance ...

Much enjoyed by the match-girls, hop-picking gave relief from the inner city slum life.

The strikers, on the other hand, claim a great success at Euston. Their account is that 150 men, or thereabouts, had been drafted up from Liverpool, that they were detected by the outlying pickets at Willesden, and that, having reached Euston, they went straight back to Liverpool.

Mr. Champion, in a speech made in the Park on Sunday, said that on one occasion quicklime had been thrown – in a moment of passion, which is absurd – that it had not been thrown by a picket, that if they could find the man they would first 'give him a good thrashing and then hand him over to justice.'

A considerable meeting at Tower-hill in the morning was addressed by Tillett in his habitual tone of vulgar jocularity. Mr. Burns was not present, and a rumour quickly flew about that he was ill; nay more, it went into detail. Mrs. Burns was reported to have said that her husband had fallen ill from overwork. The report was entirely incorrect, for the leader of the strike had no worse ailments than a cold and certain pains which involved a visit to the dentist, and he was at work again at the Wade's Arms yesterday evening. For the rest, there was nothing remarkable in the public events of the day, save that the procession was a greater nuisance, by some five minutes, than it had been on Tuesday. Its passage through the City now is the subject not of interest but of annoyance.

Fresh from his meeting with the strikers, Cardinal Manning was not conferring with the dock directors. A November date for the dockers' tanner was the negotiating point – but, of course, agreements had been entered into verbally before. If there was to be an agreement, it would have to be cast iron. The Mansion House Committee issued a conciliatory statement. It was obvious that through Manning's efforts the strike would soon be over.

The Times, Friday, 13 September 1889, 7

The directors held yesterday a protracted conference with the Cardinal Archbishop of Westminster. The Cardinal it is now generally recognized was holding out the olive-branch in the form of the proposed November settlement – whether the date be November the first or the fourth really matters not a particle. But the directors have been once bitten; . . . Should the men be induced to make this offer and to abide by it, and should it be accepted, Cardinal Manning will have performed an immense feat.

The Mansion-house Committee of Conciliation request us to make the following intimation:—

Yesterday Cardinal Manning and Mr. Sydney Buxton, M.P., who have been in constant communication with the Lord Mayor and Sir John Lubbock, M.P., (President of the London Chamber of Commerce), had a prolonged interview with the Joint Committee at the Dock-house, and afterwards with the representatives of the Strike Committee at the Mansion-house. On both sides a most amicable feeling was shown. It is, of course, impossible to make any definite announcement as to the

A stevedore's home, with the wife doing the best she could to be respectable.

termination of the strike until the final agreement between the Joint Committee and the dock labourers shall have been signed and published by them. We believe, however, that any delay now existing is only because the questions pending between other parties interested have not as yet been finally settled. It is, however, hoped that to-day a satisfactory solution of these points may be arrived at and the strike terminated. Apart from these extraneous questions we understand that all matters have been amicably arranged.

Manchester Guardian, Friday, 13 September 1889

Cardinal Manning's Intervention
A Settlement Expected
(From our Special Correspondent) London, Thursday night.
This is the thirtieth day of the strike, but it may be the last. Cardinal Manning, accompanied by Mr Sydney Buxton M.P., tried to persuade the magnates at the Dock House to substitute November 4th for January 1st as the date for conceding the men's demands in full. Considering that on Monday they flatly refused the Lord Mayor's proposal of December 1st, the Directors were quite gracious. They did not say 'Yea' to the emissaries but neither did they say 'nay'.

The End of the Strike

The Mansion House Committee on behalf of the employers issued a statement stating that there was practically no differences with all parties concerned in the dispute. Burns was reluctant to expand on the negotiations to the enthusiastic crowds that greeted him. Aware of past mistakes, every 't' was to be crossed and 'i' dotted before he would make a formal announcement. However, Burns conceded that there seemed to be no obstacles, but put forward the final demands issued by the lightermen. Many men began returning to work before the official announcement and the arguments in relation to working with blackleg labour began. All now seemed to be settled, although the lightermen still were not fully satisfied. However on 16 September the terms of the agreement were published. The only concession the strikers had made was to accept the dockers' tanner in November.

Conciliatory speeches were made by all sides but there was obviously going to be disquiet amongst some sections, especially in regard to working with blacklegs and indeed some 20,000 men had gathered in front of the West India dock to see if indeed the strike was over and there was a section objecting to the terms that had been agreed and they seemed to be winning the support of the assembly but after hearing speeches from Burns and Tillett explaining in detail the background to the strike and the small price that they had had to pay and the magnitude of their victory, such was the power of their oratory that those that dared heckle them were ejected.

The Times, Saturday, 14 September 1889, 9

The Mansion-house Committee of Conciliation request us to make the following intimation:—

The Lord Mayor, Cardinal Manning, and Mr. Sydney Buxton, M.P., were engaged all day yesterday in successive and prolonged conferences with the directors of the dock companies, over whom Mr. R. A. Hanley presided, the committee of the Association of Master Lightermen and Barge Owners of the Port of London, the representatives of the Lightermen's Work and Wages Committee, a deputation of shipowners, and the leaders of the dock labourers. The result of their negotiations, shortly

stated, is that there are practically no differences now existing between the joint committee of the dock companies and the various classes of men in their employ, and that as soon as settlements have been effected by mutual agreement or concession in the few other interests concerned, all classes of dock, river, and wharf labourers can go in on the understanding that such of the new terms as are deferred shall come into force on the 4th of November next, as proposed by the Mansion-house Committee. A meeting of the master lightermen will be held to-day to consider the position so far as they are affected.

The excitement round the Wade's Arms last night was very great. About 8 o'clock Mr. Burns arrived in a cab from the City, but he refused to give any answer to the many questions put to him with regard to the termination of the strike. The anxiety to know the result was very great, but for some time nothing could be learned as to what had transpired in the City. After Mr. Burns had consulted with the Strike Committee, he announced the conclusion of the strike so far as they were concerned. He said, however, that they were unable to take any steps towards issuing a manifesto until they knew that the lightermen and watermen were also willing to return to work.... The London lightermen held a meeting at the York Minster Inn, Philpot-street, last night, which was attended by Mr. Burns amongst others. At the conclusion of the meeting, Mr. Burns said that the following resolution had been unanimously arrived at by the Lightermen's Council:—

'In order to assist in terminating the strike, we are ready to accept the principle of payment of 6s. for a 12 hours day's work, and one job to constitute a night's work, all other questions to be submitted to an equal number of masters and men to be decided upon mutually, and an umpire to be nominated by the Lord Mayor. If these terms are accepted to-morrow (Saturday) by the masters we are ready to return to work on Monday morning, the arbitration to commence forthwith.'

In reply to a question, Mr. Burns said that the masters were likely to accept these terms, and that thus by Saturday there would be an end of the dispute. The Surrey Commercial Dock Company offered no obstacle.

'Resolved, that the terms proposed by the men – viz., the principle of the payment of 6s. for 12 hours' work, one job to constitute a night's work, and all other questions to be submitted to an equal number of masters and men to be decided upon mutually, and an umpire to be nominated by the Lord Mayor, be accepted, subject to the representatives of the men, Messrs. Iles, Wiginton, and others binding themselves in good faith to the Lord Mayor that business shall be resumed as if there had been no strike, the masters on their part undertaking that no resentment shall be shown towards the men who have been out on strike, but they shall be treated with the same fairness as those who have remained at work.

'Accepted on behalf of the Master Lightermen and Barge Owners' Association. 'SAMUEL WILLIAMS, Chairman.

'On behalf of the men, ROBERT ILES, FREDERICK WIGGINTON, THOMAS GRAY, C. DUNN, JAMES OWEN, T. G. HANSHAW, JOSEPH WELCH, BENJAMIN LAPHAM, FREDERICK COATES, RICHARD FAIRBAIRN, JAMES DOVE, CHARLES STILL, ALFRED WHEATLEY, CHRISTOPHER DOWMAN, ROBERT LOVE, JOHN JOHNSON, ROBERT ROBERTSON, WILLIAM MILLER, T. J. PAMPLN, GEORGE GREENLAND, WILLIAM CARRICK.

'Witnesses – JAMES WHITEHEAD, Lord Mayor; HENRY E. CARD. MANNING; SYDNEY BUXTON.'

... at the Mansion-house on behalf of the Surrey Commercial Dock Company, the men on strike, and the Lord Mayor's Committee:—

'Memorandum, – That the men go into work on Monday morning next. The company abide by the north side dock terms as to the 5d. men to be raised to 6d. That the grievances as detailed in the printed document, together with any others which the men may desire to make, will be submitted to the deputy chairman, secretary, and superintendent at the docks on Tuesday next at 11 o'clock, when they will meet representatives from the different sections of labour, and that Mr. Sydney Buxton, M.P., and Mr. John Burns be associated with the men and be present at the interview. It is understood that the deputy chairman and secretary are unable to pledge their board to any definite proposals, but that they are prepared to go fully into the demands and meet the men fairly and take the whole question into consideration with a view to a settlement. It is understood that none of the men will be placed in a worse position on resuming work in consequence of their having taken part in the strike.

'Signed on behalf of, the Surrey Commercial Dock Company,

'JOHN H. BOVILL, Deputy Chairman; J. GRIFFIN, Secretary.

'On behalf of the men, SYDNEY BUXTON, JOHN BURNS, BEN. TILLETT, JAMES SULLIVAN, CHARLES HAVELOCK, HUGH BROWN, T. W. BARRETT, E. GORHAM, P. LYNCH, J. GILHENEY, JOHN SULLIVAN, WILLIAM YOUNG.

'Witnesses. – JAMES WHITEHEAD, Lord Mayor; HENRY E. CARD. MANNING.'

'TERMS OF AGREEMENT.

'(1.) The 5d. rate per hour be raised in the case of all labour not piecework on and after November 4 next to 6d. per hour, and 8d. per hour overtime. No pay for meal times. (2.) Men called in not to be discharged with less than 2s. pay, except in regard to special short engagements in the afternoon. (3.) Present contract-work to be converted not later than November 4 into piece-work, under which the men will be paid not less than 6d. per hour, with 8d. per hour overtime, and the surplus, if any, to be equally divided between them, all payments being made to the men under the supervision of the dock officials. (4.) The hours of overtime at the docks and up-town warehouses shall be from 6 p.m. to 6 a.m. (5.) The existing strike to be terminated and all the men connected with dock, wharf, or river work to return to work forthwith. (6.) The strikers and their leaders to unreservedly undertake that all labourers who have been at work during the strike shall be unmolested and treated as fellow labourers by those who have been out on strike. (7.) In employing fresh men after the strike is ended, the directors will make no difference between those who have and those who have not taken part in it, and will not directly or indirectly show resentment to any of the men who have participated in the strike. – September 12, 1889.

This document was then signed as follows:—

'The above terms of arrangement have been fully explained by us to and discussed with the leaders of the strike and are accepted by them.

'JAMES WHITEHEAD, Lord Mayor; HENRY E. CARD. MANNING: SYDNEY BUXTON.

'On behalf of the London and India Docks Joint Committee and by their authority I accept the above terms of arrangement.

RODOLPH A. HANKEY.

'On behalf of the Millwall Company,

'G. R. BIRT.

'On behalf of the Surrey Commercial Dock Company,

'C. JOHN H. BOVILL, Deputy Chairman.

'On behalf of the men on strike and by their authority we accept the above terms of arrangement,

'BENJAMIN TILLETT,

'JOHN BURNS, TOM MANN,

'JAMES TOOMEY, T. M. WALSH,

'ROBERT ILES, JAMES SULLIVAN,

'CHARLES HAVELOCK, HUGH BROWN,

'JOHN REGAN.

'Witness to the signatures of the representatives of the men on strike,

'W. J. SOULSBY.'

Mr. Burns, addressing them, said, – On behalf of all those who had taken part in the great strike of dock labourers, he had to tender to his lordship and his colleagues their hearty thanks for bringing about a termination of the dispute. It was needless for him to dilate upon the circumstances of the strike. The great British public knew very well all the questions connected with it. The men thought they had grievances which could be removed, and they did all in their power to remove them. Their adversaries did not meet them in the same spirit, and it was left for the Lord Mayor and his colleagues to step into the breach and construct, so to speak, a golden bidge whereby the dispute could be ended. On behalf of the men he thanked them most heartily for their kind intercession, and in any future strike in the City of London they trusted they would find the Lord Mayor, Cardinal Manning, and Mr. Buxton as ready to help them as they had been in this instance.

Mr. Tillett, who said he had had the constructive building up of the strike and much of the serious and important work of conducting it, also thanked the committee for persuading the employers to meet them in a moderate manner. He concluded by thanking John Burns for the assistance he had rendered in the matter.

The Lord Mayor, in returning thanks, said, ... That mediation had only been attempted when he and his colleagues saw a reasonable opportunity for interposition, owing to the failure of the parties themselves to come to terms. Now that the strike was over he believed there would be a friendlier disposition than ever on the part of both masters and men. Equitable terms had been arrived at, and he hoped that no animosities would be shown, either by the strikers to those who had been working or by the employers to those who had been on strike. He could not conclude without saying how much he had admired the conduct of the men on strike, for never in the history of strikes had there been an example where there had been less intimidation or more commendable and peaceable conduct by those on strike.

Cardinal Manning said ... he should like to dwell upon the singular self-command and order that had been maintained during the last month. The strike had not been stained by anything which would detract from its honour, and his last words must be that he hoped the future would be equally unstained. He had simply done that which he felt incumbent on him from the position he held and what he was bound to do for the love of his dear country and the love of all men joined together in the brotherhood of their commonwealth.

It is intended to pay the men still on strike on the south side a higher rate of pay from to-day.

At the Tower-hill meeting on Saturday the attendance of labourers was again very large.

Mr. Tillett said although he had been engaged in many fights the only weapons that he used were his pen and his tongue. They were then very near the end of the strike, but he warned them not to go to sleep, and wait until he told them it was all over. They must not allow themselves to be brought into a state of inactivity. They were then waiting for the decision of the Surrey men and the lightermen, but both of these bodies of men were amenable to reason. Agencies were at work in the colonies too powerful for the snarls and despicable meanness of those who would prevent assistance being given to the strike fund. The answer to the telegram that had been sent to stop the supplies was the receipt of £2,700. (Cheers.) Up to the present they had transgressed no law, and they had shown a firmness never before equalled by a body of men. They had shown they were good agitators, and when they got back to work let them show they were good, willing workers. Let them all join the union, and after the fight was over make the 'blacklegs' join as well. Let them work hand in hand, get fair wages and hours of labour, and they would in return do their part by good labour, with the result that the companies would be none the worse off for the bargain.

The meeting then ended.

By 4 o'clock on Saturday some 20,000 men had assembled in front of the West India Dock gates to wait the arrival of their leaders, who were to announce to them whether the strike was over or not.

The men began to get very excited, and hundreds of them declared they would not go to work on Monday. At about a quarter past 7 this feeling was at its height, when suddenly there was a roar 'They are coming.' Two cabs were then seen to be driving rapidly down the West India dock-road, in the first of which was Mr. Burns, and Mr. Tillett was in the other. Both were loudly cheered. On stopping outside the dock gates both leaders got on to the top of one cab to address the assemblage.

Mr. Burns was the first to speak. He said it was nearly five weeks ago since the strike began, and it was now over. (Cheers.) They had fought this battle with a will and self-sacrifice that had secured the admiration of the whole world. They had been supported in a manner, and with pecuniary help from the middle and upper classes, and from Australia, France, Belgium, and Germany, that was something wonderful to contemplate, and which they had not conceived possible. Although the strike was over they had that day received another mark of expression of good will from Australia in the shape of £1,500. (Cheers.) The lightermen had been able to make better terms with their masters than he thought they would have been able to have done. On Tuesday the Surrey Commercial men would get three-fourths of their demands conceded. (Cheers.) He would then read the terms of agreement that had been unanimously signed by the leaders. The first condition was as to the rate per hour. (Great uproar, and shouts of 'We'll have it now.' When Mr. Burns read the condition ruling that other workmen should be unmolested the uproar rose greater than ever, men jumped about, shouting 'never.' The speaker quietly said, 'We'll see.') As soon as the disturbance had somewhat subsided Mr. Burns said the masters would save them the trouble of clearing out the blacklegs by doing it themselves, in their own interest. There was not a single blackleg in the docks worth his salt, besides his money. Did they think the masters were going to give men not worth twopence the preference? In their own selfish interests they would get these men to go quicker than they (the labourers) could. Putting the agreement into plain and simple language, what did it mean? (A voice. – 'That the directors did not care.') If they were dissatisfied with what the stevedores and lightermen had done for them – (Uproar.) If they thought they were going to bounce, bully, or intimidate him, then, by God, they had mistaken him. The attitude he had displayed to their enemies he would display towards them rather than give in. (Cheers.) In plain language, they had got all they asked. The concessions they had obtained would be regarded by every sensible man as a victory which they had won. Of course they would have liked what they had gained to come into operation on Monday morning, but there were other people besides themselves to consider. They had to first consider their starving wives and children. (Hear, hear.) It meant only £5,000 in wages by not

Doré, above all, captured the flavour of London's Dockland.

at once getting the result of their victory, but it also meant £200,000 lost in wages by not being at work. Therefore, was it not more sensible to wait to the 4th of November, than inflict on themselves such a loss as £200,000? (Cheers.) He maintained, under the circumstances, they had done the best possible thing they could do. He was not going to try and please every one, but felt sure every sensible labourer would say it was now time to stop. Let them use that victory as a means of perfecting their organization. (At this stage there was again considerable uproar, during which two men were thrown out of the crowd.) Let them see by whom this agreement had been signed. It had been signed by the lightermen, stevedores, Dock Labourers' Trade Union, Surrey Commercial Dock men, and others. They had all agreed to it, and although they would have liked better terms, they had accepted them as a termination of the strike. Had that agreement not been signed, they would have soon had to surrender. They could not fight without the sympathy of the public, or without funds. The leaders had done their best for the men. The new conditions started on the 4th of November. They were unable to get the dock companies to yield before that date. Cardinal Manning and Mr. Buxton did their best to make the company alter their decision, but could not do so. Therefore, they had been compelled to accept them. If, under the circumstances and under similar conditions, he was again asked to accept those terms, he would unhesitatingly do so in the interest of the men. Those conditions had satisfied every sensible man and had delighted the whole of London. He asked all who were in favour of accepting the terms of agreement to hold up their hands. He saw that all held up their hands. Then let them give three cheers for the dockers' victory.

Sound and hearty cheers having been given, Mr. Tillett said he laid claim and demanded their indulgence that night. He had sacrificed health and pleasure in their interests. All along they had cheered him, and when he had asked them if they would abide by what he wished them to do, even if it was to make a little sacrifice, they had replied 'Yes.' Those who were trying to create a disturbance tonight were not *bona fide* workmen. Inside the docks there was work enough to keep them employed day and night for a month; and as soon as the glut was over they would be working under a practical system, under which the profits would be equally divided, and one which would give them an interest in their labours. At this point there was another disturbance, and Mr. Tillett called out that any one who created a disturbance was not a docker, but was half-drunk. One of those who had been making a noise was dragged to the front, and being unable to produce his ticket of membership was seized hold of by a number of men and thrown heavily over a hoarding that was close by. Soon afterwards another man who admitted he was not a dock labourer was served in like fashion. Continuing, Mr. Tillett said by these incidents they had proved that the disturbers were not *bona fide* dock labourers. Mr. Burns, Mr. Mann, himself, and others had worked night and day; and they now came to them for their reward. The reward they wanted was the appreciation of the men and their thanks. He wanted to ask the men, with whom they had fought side by side, if they were satisfied. (Loud cries of 'Yes.') Were they prepared to stand by their leaders, and stand by what they had done? ('Yes.') The time had come to shake hands with the enemy, and it would soon be proved they had adopted the best policy. They had not broken the pitcher at the well. They had better accept an honourable victory than a defeat. He cautioned them all for the future not to work by the side of a man who was not a member of the union. If they had been organized before they would not have had five weeks on the stones. He wanted them to understand that the time had now come to drop all excited feelings and accept the position with a sincere desire to prove themselves worthy as workmen as they had proved themselves to be model agitators. They might rest satisfied the leaders had done their best for them, and if he asked the labourers to stand by them and not allow any addle-headed or mean-minded man to give them a black name simply because they had been unable to give them all they desired. He asked them to give three cheers for their wives, their homes, the future and the termination of the strike. (Loud cheers.)

John Lovell, *Stevedores and Dockers* (1969), 112

In the end, with the tactful assistance of Cardinal Manning, a compromise was found concerning the date upon which the new rate of 6d and 8d was to come into force. Consideration of what was to replace the plus and contract systems, which were to be abolished, was, however, postponed. This was to be the subject of a separate agreement to be negotiated at the end of October. A rough settlement having been hammered out for the north-bank dockers, it remained to deal with the lightermen and the multifarious groups represented by the Sayes Court Committee on the south bank. Both the Lightermen's Union and the Sayes Court Committee stuck rigidly to the letter of their original demands, but at last, on Saturday, 14 September, a final settlement was reached. Needless to say it was a settlement distinctly favourable to the men, although there remained many crucial details to be worked out in the aftermath of the stoppage. The resumption of work was fixed for Monday, 16 September.

OBJECTING TO THE 'BLACKLEGS':

Pall Mall Gazette, Saturday, 14 September 1889

A scene of considerable excitement was witnessed in the India Docks this morning. Two hundred of the returning strikers were escorted to the Woods wharf where they found 400 so-called 'blacklegs' (who have been employed during the strike) already busily engaged. The strikers declared that they would not lift a hand so long as the 'blacklegs' were retained. Mr. Beck, superintendant of the Docks, addressed the men, and declined to discharge those who had come to the aid of the company in the hour of need. The strikers showed a very listless feeling, but eventually one who was regarded as a leader mounted a pile of wood, and said that they intended to resume work, and advised the others to do the same. After grumbling and murmuring the men set to, and are working side by side with the 'blacklegs', though it is evident that the feeling towards the latter is very bitter.

'Ware Traitors *Justice*, Saturday, 14 September 1889

We have one word of advice to offer the dock labourers now on strike, that is to be careful of the men whom they trust. Above all distrust any man whose means of livelihood are unknown to you, on no account place any confidence in men about whose sources of income there is a mystery. The enemies of labour are always ready to bribe men to betray the cause. We have seen several organisations of waterside labourers started which if they had been properly managed, would have become powerful combinations, and might have rendered the present strike unnecessary. But it has been their misfortune to get into bad hands; the hands of men who, having made a little reputation in some popular movement, seek to turn this reputation to their own personal advantage, even if this can only be done by selling themselves to the enemy. The Kellys, the Peterses, the Lemons are by no means an extinct class, and we hope for the sake of the Dockers that all such will be carefully avoided.

Celebrations

On the last great Sunday demonstration to be held in Hyde Park, the dock leaders – including Tom McCarthy of the Stevedores –spoke under the flag of Australia and quite rightly gave special thanks to Australia.

The strikers were in joyful mood as they paraded through the East End en route to Hyde Park, with rousing choruses of the 'Marseillaise' and 'Rule Britannia'. The only dissenting cries from the crowd concerned what was going to happen to the blacklegs. The leaders played down this problem, though it kept cropping up as soon as the men returned to work. (Looking back on these events forty years later, Ben Tillett paid due tribute to the women who had given such support during the strike, especially his own wife.)

The Times, Monday, 16 September 1889, 7

The fourth and last of the strike demonstrations in Hyde Park was held yesterday. A very large number of people attended, and perfect order prevailed.

At the first platform Mr. T. McCarthy, of the stevedores, presided, and the flag of the Australian colonies waved above and was surrounded by flowers. The flag and its decorations were much cheered, as also was Mr. John Burns when he climbed into the crowded wagon with his wife. The chairman said that they were there to celebrate the dockers' victory in the great battle they had had for right and justice, and also to thank those who from the outside had given them the assistance which had made the victory secure. He thanked Mr. John Burns and Mr. Benjamin Tillett, and also the Lord Mayor, Cardinal Manning, and Mr. Sydney Buxton M.P., who had come in as mediators, and then urged that they should form a federation of labour, in which should be joined all workers of all races and creeds.

Mr. John Burns, who was received with great cheering, proposed the resolution of the meeting which commenced by giving thanks to those who had assisted in the strike. Special mention was made of Australia, and the resolution pledged the workers to organize a federation of labour. This victory was but the precursor of still greater victories they hoped to secure in the near future. (Cheers.) It was true that the strike had been

helped by benefactors in all parts of Great Britain, France and Belgium, and other places, and the New World – Australia – had given of its bounty to redress the grievances of the Old World. It was strange that the most help should have come from across the seas. The fact showed that the internationalization of labour was no longer the myth it was once supposed to be, but was becoming more absolutely a reality from sea to sea and from continent to continent. (Cheers.) The strike had had great moral effects. It had struck a blow at the selfishness of the rich man and had put straightly the plain fact that a man had a right to live. In conclusion Mr. Burns said that would be his last speech for a month, and he made a warm appeal to them to organize to meet any other battle to which the late strike would be as only a skirmish. (Loud cheers.)

Mr. Tillett seconded the motion, and said that the dockers must go into work, but they must not touch the men they found at work, and that all must unite.

The resolution was carried amid cheers.

Ben Tillett, *Memories and Reflections* (1931), 153–155

Three times had John Burns [on the Saturday] to read out the terms of settlement before the meeting was willing to treat them as anything but the announcement of a surrender. It became necessary for me again to intervene, which I did by pointing out that a vociferous element in the crowd opposing the settlement, were not really dockers at all, but 'lazy loafers, who foisted themselves on the funds, sponging on subscriptions.' Opposition was quelled; the terms were endorsed; and the crowd broke up to seize our cab, unharness our horse, and draw us through the streets to the 'Wade Arms', where our Strike Committee had its headquarters.

[*Tillett then quotes*]

Smith and Nash Dockers' Strike *(1889) 154–156*

All along the Commercial Road [on Sunday morning], the women turned out in thousands to see their husbands and their sons pass in triumph. The sun seemed brighter, the music more inspiriting, the banners more in number than ever before; and never in any one Sunday procession had so many actual dockers walked together. There was a holiday look about them, and all seemed fresher and tidier than was their wont. Benjamin Tillet and John Burns took the lead as usual, in a space jealously cleared by the marshals. Tillett, in his Sunday best, was devouring the newspapers, while Burns seemed to be making notes for his final speech, and now and then roused himself to eject an intruder from the sacred space, or to burst through the crowd and buy a few pennyworth of plums at a costermonger's stall. All the usual emblems were there. Neptune and his suite, Britannia wrapped in her Union Jack, the 'coalie' on the ladder – scarcely one of the old familiar features of the five weeks' processions was missing from the great triumphal march. On went the procession with a good swinging step to the sound of the 'Marseillaise' and 'Rule Britannia' – the latter with a big drum accompaniment, that left no doubt of the intention of the marching Britons, never, never to be slaves again. The stirring marching music gave place to the more rollicking strains of 'He's a jolly good fellow,' as the processionists halted before the Mansion House and dipped their flags and cheered the Lord Mayor and Lady Mayoress, who were espied on the balcony.

On they went, through Queen Victoria Street to the Thames Embankment. But the sun was shining fiercely now, and the men were getting fagged, so 'halt!' was cried as Westminster Palace, with its fairy skyline, came in sight. Banners were laid on the hard-baked ground, or propped against the parapet of the embankment, and the wearied crowd found seats on the low granite wall, or loafed about, eating such lunch as they had brought. The luckier patronised the ginger-beer and plums of enterprising costermongers. The police had been prepared for the halt, and producing their lunch ate it in all good fellowship with the processionists. Father Neptune and his suite dismounted from their trolley, and trailed off, regardless of dignity, to the nearest eating-house.

At two o'clock the order was given to fall in again, and the procession wound on, with its accompanying fringe of open-eyed boys and curious spectators, through Victoria Street and Hyde Park Corner, to the spot which had seen the beginning of so many labour movements, and had celebrated the triumph of so few. Four platforms were erected in the park, but none attached so much attention as the first, from which Burns and Tillett were to speak. Fiery Tom McCarthy presided, but there were no fiery words today: only mutual congratulations on the victory that had been won. It was a picnic rather than a fighting demonstration.

Alongside the poverty London was developing apace.

John Burns spoke from three platforms. The tone of all three speeches were the same – gratitude to friends, moderation in the hour of triumph, forgetfulness of bygones, hope for the future. Ben Tillett's speech was one of the best he had made throughout the strike. The note he struck was the value of union to the men, and the absolute necessity of keeping the word they had pledged. Some men had been hesitating about returning to work, but they must all go in on Monday morning. A voice was heard, 'How about the blacklegs?' 'Never mind the blacklegs,' he replied; 'everyone who has been on strike must return to work in the morning, if' – and here his words became slower and more emphatic – 'you have any respect for your leaders or for yourselves.'

[*Tillett continues:*]

. . . I pay my tribute to the women who helped us, not forgetting my own wife who made our little home, otherwise a centre of great activity throughout the whole dispute, a haven of rest for me, whilst giving herself the very best in watch and work whilst I was prowling around pickets and giving late hours, which did not distinguish night from day, to the duties of leadership in the Strike; and James Toomey's wife, in her house in a quiet side street, not five minutes' walk from the Strike headquarters, where she ministered to our needs, providing meals at all hours for those of us living at a greater distance from the centre of events as I did, and watching over us to see that we did not kill ourselves by overwork.

BURNS ON THE SCENE:

Pall Mall Gazette, Tuesday, 17 September 1889

Early in the [Monday] afternoon Mr. John Burns drove up in a hansom cab to the West India Docks, and a great crowd rushed to meet him, and attempted to put all sorts of grievances before him. Not a few were inclined to grumble as having been 'sold', but after a few words from Mr. Burns they were ready to listen to reason. Their grievances briefly stated were these: That the blacklegs were being kept on by the company, and that consequently only a few extra hands had been engaged, that special favour had been shown to the blacklegs by making their situations permanent, and that the dock officials had tried to break their arrangement to give not less than four hours' work by not offering to employ men until ten o'clock, the agreement which terminated the strike permitting less than four hours pay to be given for special jobs at a late hour. The men, who were excited, were once or twice inclined to be somewhat disorderly, and Mr. Burns threatened that he should have to give some of them a 'good hiding'. He then assured the meeting that he would not retire from the agitation until all the grievances of the men had been removed. He had been speaking to some master stevedores, who had told him that, whether the Dock Company liked it or not, they were not going to be troubled with employing blacklegs who could not do the work of a genuine docker. No doubt not employing men until 10

o'clock was an attempt to break through the fours hours' agreement. If the Dock Company thought they were going to violate the terms of the settlement, he would have another strike and clear every man out. (Cheers.) He would paralyze the trade of the port of London until the company acted up to the agreement. If the men asked him whether they should work beside those who refused to join the Union, he emphatically replied 'No'. He advised his hearers, however, to have patience. If they would have confidence in him, he would heal the few wounds that remained. (Cheers.)

The *Evening News & Post* pointedly asked the question, 'How could the dockers forgive the blacklegs?' This was a problem that the leaders now had to face.

Evening News & Post, Tuesday, 17 September 1889

The dockers were asked to forgive everybody, and to be friends again all round. This they readily did up to a certain point, but they drew the line at 'blacklegs'. They could forgive the dock directors and the few newspapers which had been hostile to them, but they had a grudge not to be overcome against their own mates who had been untrue to the cause. Friction was an inevitable result; and when it became aggravated by what seemed to the men to be favouritism towards the 'blacklegs', explosions followed.

There were many celebratory sermons issued following the dockers' victory. Typical of these was the one held in Abbey Street Baptist Church, attended by some two thousand persons, noting pointedly that the strike was 'not a Socialist or political movement ... it was a labour struggle.'

Southwark Recorder and Bermondsey & Rotherhithe Advertiser, Saturday, 5 October 1889

On Sunday afternoon [29 September] the respected minister of Abbey Street Baptist Chapel gave an address entitled 'The Story of the Strike', to a crowded audience, about 2,000 persons being within reach of his voice. The Rev J. Farren of Jamaica Row Congregational Chapel opened the proceedings with prayer. It would seem the meat of the audience were frequent attendants at places of worship, but some became more enthusiastic as the address proceeded and cheered most heartily.

Rev J. C. Carlisle said the strikers on the Surrey side had through the representatives asked him to tell the story of the strike to that splendid audience of Christian men. It was very desirable to clear away some popular mistakes. The strike was not sprung upon the Dock Companies; the whole question had been before them in some form or other for over two years. The Directors might have prevented the strike by meeting the men in a reasonable spirit. The strike was not a Socialist or political movement. Men of all opinions had joined them, they had no politics, it was a labour struggle.

5 THE AFTERMATH

The Foundation of New Unionism

For Ben Tillett, the end of the strike was just a chapter. The real battle of organisation now began. A meeting was immediately called and the union was renamed the Dock, Wharf, Riverside, and General Workers' Union of Great Britain and Ireland. Tom Mann threw in his lot with Tillett, although this was to be shortlived. Harry Orbell became an organiser, as did Tom MacCarthy of the Stevedores (who, in recognition of his sterling support for the dockers, had virtually been dismissed from his post at the Amalgamated Stevedores' Union by the master stevedores who dominated the Executive), and the grand organising tour of the provinces was organised.

Jonathan Schneer, *Ben Tillett* (1982), 48

The London dispute had hardly finished when Tillett undertook an organising tour of the provinces. He travelled to Hull, Gloucester, Bristol, Sharpness, Southampton, Ipswich, Liverpool Harwich and 'many other ports'. McCarthy and Orbell covered the towns he missed. 'We scoured the country and added to our ranks port after port,' Tillett recorded. Some 63 new branches were formed in the first three months of 1890 alone. Recalling the way the Tilbury strike had been defeated, Tillett advocated the formation of union branches for agricultural labourers too. Mann successfully organised some of them in Lincolnshire and Oxfordshire.

Ben Tillett, *A Brief History of the Dockers' Union* (1910), 35

[After the strike]
Mann, Orbell and McCarthy worked like Trojans, but there was a deal of work to be done, and the men did not see the practical and the necessary work which we felt we were entitled to expect.

Hull and Bristol called for attention, the Bristol men making a very good fight of it.

The men of Bristol were in the hands of the most rapacious set of sub-contractors one could imagine even for dock-work, where the very worst type of thief and bully had free play. Men were being robbed wholesale of both money, time and quantity on day and piece-rates.

Then the bully was employed for a few pots of ale to do the dirty work

of brutality and violence. But here, as in London, the men had risen to the sense of right and justice, and so the return meant that at least the worst-treated of the men received as much as 100 per cent increase, varying down to the lowest rate of 25 per cent wage uplift, together with conditions of meal hours, overtime, and regulations as to times of calling-on and the places of same.

Organising for the Future

However, Will Thorne was not pleased with the outcome of the strike in terms of the organisation that developed. His idea of one great union encompassing all sections of labour was rejected by Tillett, who chose to develop the dockers' union on the model of the stevedores', and other exclusive unions. Thorne accused Tillett and Mann of putting a ring fence around the docks, and said that this caused much bitterness.

In the aftermath, controversy about the future pattern of union organisation seemed inevitable given pre-existing debates. Tillett was set on consolidating the dockers' strength and also set about organising other sections of workers in different trades and industries, often well-removed from the dock side. Will Thorne's idea of one great union encompassing all sections of labour regardless of their trade was the subject of fierce debate. A further pattern of labour federation emerged amongst south side dockers.

Cardinal Manning's assessment remains invaluable:

Will Thorne, *My Life's Battles* (1925), 90–91

The formation of the Dockers' Union led to certain complications, and a little friction between their union and ours. Our principle was contained in our motto: 'One Man, one Ticket, and Every Man with a Ticket.'

This in short meant that as long as a man or a woman had a trade union ticket they should be allowed to work side by side, in factories, workships, at the docks, or anywhere else without any interference from any other trade union. Our object was to secure the consolidation of the trade union and Labour forces; we wanted to eradicate quarrels between the workers because they belonged to different organisations, and realise the unity and oneness of the working class.

To this ideal, opposition immediately came from both Tom Mann and Ben Tillett. They wanted to put a 'ring fence' around the docks and allow only the employment in the docks of members of the Dockers' Union, in a similar way to which the stevedores protected their preserves. I was strongly opposed to this policy, because years before either my union or the Docker's Union had been formed, it was the custom and practice of many of the dockers to work in the gas works during the winter when dock work was slack, and for the gas workers to work in the docks in the summer time when work was not so plentiful in the gas works.

If the formation of trade unions was going to enforce the hardship of unemployment on the workers, unless they belonged to more than one

union, I knew that that cause of trade unionism would suffer. I was certain that the Docker's Union policy would fail, because of so many general labourers being unemployed from time to time, and because such a system would intensify the inhuman competition for employment.

A great deal of friction was caused by the enforcement of this policy of the Dockers; several times it almost led to strikes at the Beckton, Poplar, Wapping, Stepney and Rotherhithe gas works, because our members took the view that if the Dockers' Union would not recognise our ticket, they would not recognise theirs. This policy was finally abandoned by the Dockers. I remember Tom Mann addressing a big mass meeting at the Canning Town Public Hall on his return from Australia. He said that 'the time is now ripe to enforce the policy advocated by Thorne, that trade unions all over the country should recognise each other's tickets; men should work side by side and create real solidarity and comradeship.' This started the abolition of the practice of poaching men away from different organisations. The workers were getting sick and tired of having to transfer from one union to another and then back again, paying fresh entrance fees each time, and in some cases after paying for benevolent benefit into one union the benefit would be lost on the transfer. Many of our best and most enthusiastic members had to join the Dockers' Union whereas we had a rule that exempted members from other unions joining us.

And the differences of the north and south side when the south side men set up their own union, the South Side Labour Protection League, further sectionalised the organised dock labour on the waterfront.

John Lovell, *Stevedores and Dockers* (1969), 112–113

The 1889 strike resulted in an expansion of trade unionism throughout the port of London. The chief beneficiary of the process was undoubtedly the Tea Operatives' Union, whose membership grew from a few hundred at the start of the strike to nearly 18,000 at its close.

The position at the end of the stoppage was, however, not regarded as entirely satisfactory by the leaders of this society. They had naturally hoped that, in so far as unorganised workers could be enrolled as trade unionists, they would be enrolled as members of the Tea Operatives' Union. So far as workers on the north side of the river were concerned, this hope was to a considerable extent realised. On the south side, however, events had taken a different turn. During the course of the strike the Surrey men had gone beyond the establishment of a separate strike committee, and had in fact begun to evolve their own union, independent of the Tea Operatives. Thus at an early date they eliminated the possibility that all unorganised workers might be brought within the one dockers' union.

In the latter part of August 1889 branches had begun to spring up in the districts south of the river. It was here that the strength of the old Labour Protection League had been concentrated, so that there existed

SOUTH SIDE
CENTRAL STRIKE COMMITTEE,
SAYES COURT, DEPTFORD.

SEPTEMBER 10, 1889.

GENERAL MANIFESTO.

Owing to the fact that the demands of the Corn Porters, Deal Porters, Granary Men, General Steam Navigation Men, Permanent Men and General Labourers on the South Side have been misrepresented, the above Committee have decided to issue this Manifesto, stating the demands of the various sections now on Strike, and pledge themselves to support each section in obtaining their demands.

DEAL PORTERS of the Surrey Commercial Docks have already placed their demands before the Directors.

LUMPERS (Outside) demand the following Rates, viz:—1. 10d. per standard for Deals. 2. 11d. per stand. for all Goods rating from 2 x 4 to 2¼ x 7, or for rough boards. 3. 1s. per std. for plain boards. Working day from 7 a.m. to 5 p.m., and that no man leave the "Red Lion" corner before 6.45 a.m. Overtime at the rate of 6d. per hour extra from 5 p.m. including meal times.

STEVEDORES (Inside) demand 8d. per hour from 7 a.m. to 5 p.m. 1s. per hour overtime. Overtime to commence from 5 p.m. to 7 a.m. Pay to commence from leaving "Red Lion" corner. Meal times to be paid for. Holidays & Meal times double pay, and that the Rules of the United Stevedores Protection League be acceded to in every particular. *conceded*

OVERSIDE CORN PORTERS (S.C.D.) demand 15s.3d. per 100 qrs. for Oats. Heavy labour 17s.4d. per 100 qrs. manual, or with use of Steam 16s.1d. All overtime after 6 p.m. to be paid at the rate of ½d. per qr. extra.

QUAY CORN PORTERS (S. C. D.) demand the return of Standard prices previous to March 1889, which had been in operation for 17 years.

TRIMMERS AND GENERAL LABOURERS demand 6d. per hour from 7 a.m. to 6 p.m. and 8d. per hour Overtime; Meal times as usual; and not to be taken on for less than 4 hours.

WEIGHERS & WAREHOUSEMEN demand to be reinstated in their former positions without distinction.

BERMONDSEY AND ROTHERHITHE WALL CORN PORTERS demand:
1. Permanent Men 30s. per week. 2. Casual Men 5s.10d. per day and 8d. per hour Overtime; Overtime to commence at 6 p.m. Meal times as usual.

GENERAL STEAM NAVIGATION MEN demand:—1. Wharf Men, 6d. per hour from 6 a.m. to 6 p.m. and 8d. per hour Overtime. 2. In the Stream, 7d. per hour ordinary time, 9d. per hour Overtime. 3. In the Dock, 8d. per hour ordinary time, 1s. per hour Overtime.

MAUDSLEY'S ENGINEER'S MEN. Those receiving 21s. per week now demand 24s., and those receiving 24s. per week demand 26s.

ASHBY'S, LTD., CEMENT WORKS demand 6d. per ton landing Coals and Chalk. General Labourers 10% rise of wages all round, this making up for a reduction made 3 years ago.

GENERAL LABOURERS, TELEGRAPH CONSTRUCTION demand 4s. per day from 6 a.m. to 5 p.m., time and a quarter for first 2 hours Overtime, and if later, time and a half for all Overtime. No work to be done in Meal Hours.

Signed on behalf of the Central Committee, Wade Arms,
BEN. TILLETT,
JOHN BURNS,
TOM MANN,
H. H. CHAMPION,
JAS. TOOMEY.

Signed on behalf of the South side Committee,
JAS. SULL
CHAS. H
HUGH

side to be sent to Mr. HUGH BRO Central Strike Committee, Sayes Court,

South Side Committee handbill.

a tradition of organisation among the lower grades of workers which was not present on the north bank. The pockets of organisation which sprang up south of the river in 1889 were deliberately modelled upon the 1872 union. They called themselves 'Lodges of the Labour League', and, in the manner of 1872, the men were organised in autonomous branches based upon occupational groupings. These branches were represented upon the Sayes Court Committee, and, after the strike had ended, they turned that committee into the executive council of a separate south-side union. The continuity with 1872 was reflected in the title of the new organisation – the South Side Labour Protection League (S.S.L.P.L.) – and a further connection with the movement of 1872 is to be seen in the linking to the new organisation of the overside corn porters' branch, the sole survivor of the old union on the south side.

Southwark Recorder and Bermondsey & Rotherhithe Advertiser, Saturday, 5 October 1889

On Wednesday se'nnight [25 September] an important meeting, convened by the South Side Strike Committee and composed of several hundred delegates from all the labour organisations on the south side of the Thames was held at Sayes Court, Deptford. On the motion of Mr Brett, seconded by Mr Garlick and supported by Mr Quelch and others, it was resolved to form a central committee of delegates of all south side labour organisations to be known as the central council of the 'South Side Labour Protection League.'

The object of this council is not to destroy any existing organisations but bring them all into line, so as to secure united action and fraternal co-operation with the unions on the North side.

As evidence of this, a further resolution was unanimously adopted, declaring that henceforth that any man holding a card of membership of any labour organisation will be regarded as a good union man, and will be allowed to work with the men of any other organisation, in any department of riverside labour; always provided, of course, that he does not work for less than the standard rate of pay in that particular department.

This is an important step in the direction of labour federation and will get rid of the friction that has hitherto existed between the members of different sectional organisations.

Cardinal Manning's View

Cardinal Manning, in a foreword to John Burns' article on the dock strike, said that not since the cotton famine of the North had there been a more noble example of self-command by the dockers. He also hoped that the strike would bring about organisation of labour in the docks. Burns pays tribute to the sacrifice of the men and women in the face of hunger and hardship. He also pays special tribute to the Australian people for their donations. He goes into detail about what had been gained apart from the dockers' tanner, which was a total change in which labour was used and employed in the docks, which in essence was far more important than the tanner. He also pointedly states that the dock employers did not seem to know their own business. He rejoices as a socialist that labour has shown how fully it can meet the forces of capitalism.

John Burns, *'The Great Strike'*, *New Review*, vol I no 5 (Oct 1889), 411, 418, 420–422

... What we may hope will come from this strike is a registration of labourers and an organisation of labour. This will clear the dock gates and the East of London of thousands who year by year flow in from the country without knowledge or skill. They become a floating population of disappointed men; indolent because unemployed, living from hand to mouth, and dangerous because they have nothing to lose: starving in the midst of wealth and prosperity from which they are excluded.

Nevertheless without any blind self-praise, I believe we may say that since the Cotton Famine of the North there has been no nobler example of self-command than we have seen in the last month.

I am bound to bear witness not only to the self-command of the men, but also to the measured language and calm courtesy of the employers ...

FOREWORD BY CARDINAL MANNING

[*Burns gives his view of the strike.*]

But the very willingness of the men and their women to make nothing of the nip of hunger (perhaps the final test of endurance) pricked us to use our best to keep them in daily bread. We sent out our appeals, none too confidently at the first, but with increasing confidence as the days went on. I myself was astonished at the inpouring of public money. No appeal of strikers ever drew such continuous solid help before. Literally, we asked and we received. It seemed that we had only to say in the baldest terms that we were the dockers' treasurers, and the moneys that we asked for were forthcoming. Had ours been a Mansion House appeal on behalf of the sufferers by some sudden great disaster at home or abroad, it could not have been responded to with more extravagant generosity. Australia's subscription of £25,000 is known. In England, union after union pelted us with cheques; and every cheque was accompanied by an assurance that contributions would not be lacking, whether the strike lasted for weeks or for months. The Compositiors sent us £500, the Engineers £700....

[*He concludes:*]

I must now turn for a moment to generalities. I am asked, What is the net result of the Strike? I can answer in a word. The strikers have gained 1d. per hour for ordinary time; 3d. per hour from 6 to 8 pm; 2d. per hour after 8; whilst the four hours' call for 2s. pay gives a permanency that has only now been secured. Contract has been abolished. By the abolition of contract the men cease to be sweated by the gangers, as they have been hitherto. The contract system has been a material injury to the men throughout. We have given that system its quietus, and by so doing have

removed a hundred causes of discontent and anxiety from the dock labourers. What other result has the Strike accomplished? It has destroyed now and for all time the system of sweating under which the docker found himself compelled to labour at starvation wages for the profit of his employer. It has abolished, or done much to abolish, jealousy and bad feeling of every sort amongst the dockers as a body. The brutal relations (I can give them no other name) that have existed between foremen and men have disappeared, or are bound to disappear in the immediate future. And, touching the relations of the men with their employers, those also will of necessity be bettered, inasmuch as the employers, dreading another strike, will have a substantial motive for keeping on the best possible terms with their men. Hitherto the relations of employers and men all through the docks have been degrading to the men. It will not be so in the future.

Must I say a word as to the relations of the leaders in the Strike with the representatives of the dock companies? Now that the victory has gained I am as anxious to say as little as possible. But, as an old agitator, I am bound to express my own personal feeling that in this strike I have had to deal with men who, from first to last, seemed to me to have a very imperfect appreciation of their own best interests, and very little regard for the feelings of others. More than this, I might say that the representatives of the dock companies never seemed to me to know their own business. It is not the first time that I have had to deal with employers as antagonists to the claims of labour; but in my dozen years of agitation I do not remember to have had relations with men more completely imbued with the spirit of pure 'cussedness'.

What then is our immediate position on the issue of the Strike?

The gain in wages I have already touched on. That is not the most important result to be considered. We have to note, above all, that labour throughout the whole East End of London has, by the outcome of the Strike, been placed upon a higher and more substantial footing with regard to capital than it has ever stood upon before. Still more important, perhaps, is the fact that labour of the humbler kind has shown its capacity to organise itself; its solidarity; its ability; its readiness to endure much for little gain. Then, the labourer in the East has acquired hope. He has learned that combination can lead him to anything and everything. He has tasted success as the immediate fruit of combination, and he knows that the harvest he has just reaped is not the utmost he can look to gain. He has learned the value of self-sacrifice in a large movement for the benefit of his class. Conquering himself, he has learned that he can conquer the world of capital, whose generals have been the most ruthless of his oppressors.

I have ceased to wonder all through the Strike at the moderation and the honesty of the strikers. I have been in the thick of starving men, with hundreds of pounds about me (they knowing it), and not a penny have I lost. I have sent men whom I did not know, for change of a gold piece,

and have never been cheated of a penny. Not a man through all the weeks of that desperate Strike ever asked me for drink money. I have learned by things like these that the educational value of the strike has not been inconsiderable. I saw no drunken striker in any procession; I heard no one cadging for charity. One instance of the high spirit of these dockers occurs to me. A friend came from the West to search for me. He fell in with a striker, who walked with him two miles to the committee-rooms, and refused to accept a shilling for his services as guide. We had to deal throughout with men who were capable of this sort of self-repression, and it was because we had such stuff at our backs that we were able in the end to bring our opponents to terms.

A hundred things escape me that I might set down as showing the sympathy of the community; but I remember how generously all classes have acted towards us – the East End shopkeepers, and the pawnbrokers who refused to charge interest on goods pledged with them during the Strike; the landlords and lodging-house keepers who refused rent during the same period. I remember the subscriptions of sailors, soldiers, policemen, fishermen, and the blind men of Southwark. I remember the letters (with cheques enclosed) of noblemen, Club-men and clergymen. I remember the half-sovereign which an officer of the Guards gave me in the Park, with a half-uttered suggestion that if he were called upon to act against the strikers he would give them 'blank cartridge'. I remember that out of the thousands of letters I received from every part of the kingdom, there were two abusive ones, and two only.

As a Trade Unionist, my own notion as to the practical outcome of the Strike is that all sections of labour must organise themselves into trade unions; that all trades must federate themselves, and that in the future, prompt and concerted action must take the place of the spasmodic and isolated action in the past.

As a Socialist, I rejoice that organised labour has shown how fully it can meet the forces of Capitalism, and how small a chance the oppressor of labour has against the resolute combination of men who, having found their ideal, are determined to realise it.

Champion in his contemporary account as to the reasons for the victory states 'We were extraordinarily fortunate in matters of the weather.' Another major factor was that the dockers were able to prevent their places being taken by other workmen. Champion adds that the workers who went back early loyally contributed their earnings. He also comments that from the day the men returned to work on the wharves, the tide of battle had turned. He acknowledges the extraordinary generosity of the Australians. Finally, he points out an aspect which he claims to be unique in industrial conflicts; namely, that Mr Henry Lafone actually paid to each of his men on strike a larger amount than the strike committee were giving as strike pay to other men.

H. H. Champion, *The Great Dock Strike in London, August 1889* (1890), 24, 21

And this brings me to the explanation of what it was that really won the Strike. There were many minor matters that contributed to our success. To mention one which, so far as I know, has been entirely overlooked, we were extraordinarily fortunate in the matter of the weather. It is not often that we get five weeks of uninterrupted dry and fine weather in autumn in London; but during the strike we were so favoured, and this made an enormous amount of difference in the spirits and good temper of the men, while it deprived the Dock Companies of an ally almost as powerful as hunger– *i.e.*, cold. A bitter east wind, or a drenching downpour, will take the courage out of a crowd in a way that the most fervid oratory can do little to counteract. Some of the other minor factors which made up the labourers' victory I have recounted above; but they might all have been present, and the Dockers yet have been defeated, but for the one solid fact that they were able to prevent their places being taken by other workmen. Burns might have shouted, Mann might have organised, Cardinal Manning might have pleaded and the public at home and a broad might have subscribed ten times the amount they did; but if the Companies could, by hook or by crook, have got vessels loaded and discharged, the Dockers would never have got their 'tanner' an hour. The importance of this point dwarfs every other into comparative insignificance.

Then occurred one of the most encouraging incidents of the campaign. The men who went back loyally contributed from their earnings to the fund for the support of the rest, and it is remarkable that their employers sympathised so heartily with them that more than one suggested to me personally that he should have the contributions stopped out of each man's daily wages, and remit the total to the treasurer. But it was a nice legal point on which I did not feel competent to advise, whether such deductions from wages would not render the employer liable to punishment under the Truck Act, which is popularly supposed to forbid any deductions from wages, though it seems never to be enforced against firms which fine their employees.

From the day that the men returned to work at the wharves, the tide of battle turned. The only remaining difficulty was to persuade the Dock Directors that their dignity would suffer no fresh damage by their open acknowledgment of a defeat which was patent to the whole world. Luckily, the Dockers were by this time in a position to hold out. The fact that the wharf-labourers were now earning wages greatly relieved the funds, which were largely increased by the extraordinary generosity of the subscribers in Australia. The first cheques from our kin beyond the sea arrived in the very nick of time. Their amount was £750, which represented a day's relief to fifteen thousand families. As every one knows, this first instalment was rapidly followed by much larger contributions from Australia, but the subsequent tens of thousands were not really anything like so useful in putting heart into the men as those first few hundreds. I am at a loss to discover how we over here can adequately

Docklands high warehouses showing a prospering Britain.

express our gratitude to the men who gave such timely aid.

In this connection I must point out one circumstance which seems to me to be unique in the history of industrial conflicts. It is a fact that when the men at Butler's Wharf joined the Strikers, the Manager, Mr. Henry Lafone, actually paid to each man a larger amount that the Strike Committee were giving as 'strike pay' to the other men! If there be another instance in which an employer has subsidised a strike against himself, I have never heard of it.

The SDF's Dissenting View

The Social Democratic Federation, through its paper *Justice*, condemned the strike settlement and the leaders, noting the 'interference' of Cardinal Manning and the Lord Mayor. It also talked of the men 'who now have to work with the scandals and traitors (i.e. blacklegs) who have been fighting against them,' and attacked Henry Champion, the editor of the *Labour Elector* and member of the strike committee, as being 'a political trickster and intriguer.' Hyndman, the probable author of this polemical piece, concluded that only in the ranks of social democracy under the red flag a new Labour Party could be formed.

***Justice*, Saturday, 21 September 1889**

Then came the ill-advised manifesto. Immediately on the withdrawal of the manifesto came the interference of Cardinal Manning and the Lord Mayor.

From this time forward it was easy to see a marked change, not only in the attitude of the leaders, but in the disposition of the men themselves. One of the worst things that can possibly happen in a Movement of this description is to let the men feel they have no voice in the settlement of their own affairs. The idea that 'someone' is interceding for them and ready to make terms on their behalf destroys the idea that they are fighting their own battle, and the answers to questions at the mass meetings on Tower Hill have been mere 'automatic utterances' the men simply thinking 'I suppose it's all right'.

That it is a compromise no one can deny. The men had left off work because their rates of wages were not high enough, and had declared their intention of not returning until they got their 6d an hour. Had they stuck to this it would have been all right, but as it is they have consented to go back without getting the advance, trusting to the promises of the Norwood fraternity to receive it on the 4th of November. This concession – trifling though it may seem to the ordinary observer, and supported as it undoubtedly is by the pandering capitalist press – is a most serious sign of weakness on the part of the leaders, whether from having got tired of the struggle or (as we firmly believe from our personal knowledge of at least one who has been counselling the strike committee) from some hidden and ulterior motive of personal interest, doesn't matter. The men through their leaders went back on their word. All this excitement, all

this hardship, all this privation, and only one solid advantage – and that advantage not to be enjoyed until November. In the meantime, which is the worst thing of all, the men who have been struggling and fighting for the last five weeks have been pledged to behave well to the scoundrels and traitors who have been fighting against them. Why this compromise above all others? Do the leaders think that the dockers are without all sense of right and without any conception of treachery? But such things are worthy a political trickster and intriguer. A man who is villain enough to suggest leading the unemployed to Trafalgar Square, camping them there for three days, and then leaving them to the mercy of police and soldiery is bad enough for this, and his confederates seem bound to obey. Even the iron will of John Burns is completely softened by the oily tongue of the 'boss' of the Labour Electoral Association.

Justice, Saturday September 28th 1889.

At the same time our comrades who are devoting so much time and energy to the formation of these unions of unskilled labour must never lose sight of the fact that the complete emancipation of labour from the thraldom of capital is the end to work for. This end can never be achieved by mere trade unionism. With the progress of organisation among the workers there is all sorts of talk of a 'new Labour Party'. It is only in the ranks of Social-Democracy, under the Red Flag, that such a party is possible. Outside of this any labour party will be a sham.

Conclusion

Given the appalling conditions which prevailed in the London docks, why did it take so long for the dock labourers to organise themselves? The answer lies in the success that the employers and the establishment were able to achieve in imposing a particular view of the individual's recognised place in society. The ideology of the Poor Law of 1834 had done its work. The poor in many respects accepted that they were an inferior class, poor and deprived through some moral fault. The United Kingdom was a totally class-ridden society. Social mobility was only possible for a narrow section of society, and then only if they accepted the respectable values presented to them by Victorian society; thrift, sobriety and chastity. These virtues were not actually practised by the middle and upper classes themselves, as the figures for child prostitution (both male and female) and the wide spread of venereal disease clearly show.

Since the demise of Chartism in the late 1840s, the moral argument had won the day over direct agitation as the means to bring about social change. The New Model Unions of the 1850s and 1860s could point to some success through these methods with the extension of the franchise to their skilled members and a rise in their living standards. Indeed, the establishment seemed to almost welcome the Trade Union Congress when it was formed in 1868, recognising the necessity for organised labour among the respectable working classes and perhaps seeing this as a measure of their compliance and 'respectability' in distancing them from the urban poor.

From 1850 the majority of people in England lived in urban areas with totally uncontrolled laissez-faire development; reform in sanitation and public health only came about when the respectable classes were threatened with disease. The politics of the skilled unions were at best liberal; they were concerned with their sectional interests, keeping apart from the urban poor and the unskilled, especially if they happened to be of Irish or foreign descent.

While the urban poor in East London had organised themselves into great demonstrations in the 1870s and 1880s, their rioting was met

Excise men test the cargo.

with harsh repression from the authorities and the idea of change through violent protest withered away. Indeed, the establishment used this in propaganda to prove the uncivilised nature of the urban poor, and their unsuitability for responsible public support.

Nevertheless, throughout the 1870s and 1880s much public research was done into the nature of poverty, culminating in the publication (1889–1903) of the social reports by Charles Booth. The Salvation Army was also publicising the social iniquities prevalent in the East End and similar areas. The *Pall Mall Gazette* and other papers regularly ran public campaigns on poverty and exploitation, exposing the severe social conditions and especially child prostitution and the widespread prostitution forced on women by poverty. It also exposed the depths of the poverty and the incredible numbers that were involved, though it was not in any way disguised or locked away in ghettos. One thing the Booth colour-coded survey maps show is that poverty was not a hidden condition. The major streets in East London were populated by middle and in some cases upper-class families. What the publication of these reports did was to put the whole question of poverty and immorality on the public agenda.

The match-girls' strike of 1888 clearly demonstrates this movement towards social investigation. The match-girls had been on strike previously without any public attention being drawn to their disputes. But when Annie Besant exposed the plight of the girls, she widely did it under the banner of 'white slavery', and the great propaganda battle which won the girls their strike was over the moral dangers caused by the physical conditions rather than just their industrial grievances. Ironically, because of the low esteem that the girls suffered in the East End, their victory acted as a catalyst to the male members of society. It was a group such as the match-girls (and the fact that they were girls was of vital importance) could achieve national publicity as well as a great victory, then surely it would be easy for the men to do the same. Will Thorne, a barely literate labourer, then organised the gas workers in a successful strike at the Beckton gas works, winning for the men the eight-hour day, something which the TUC still regarded as an impossible aim. And all the time trades union organisers like Ben Tillett and Tom Mann and other socialist leaders had been working away at establishing elementary organisation around these areas of trade and employment.

Thus it was with this background of social awareness and industrial militancy that the dock strike began. What we do know is that the initial localised strike was called by a tugman named Harris, who then disappears from history. Tillett was close at hand with his existing involvement with dock labour and an established position through having worked with and been known by many of the leading labour people of the time. He quickly found himself a named leader in the dispute. His organisational skills and his powers as an orator were the essential ingredient in the formation of the Dockers' Union and he was a powerful figure inside the emerging new trade union movement and later Labour Party.

John Burns was also a leading figure in the dispute but much of the credit, I feel, has been taken away from him because of the fact that a few years after the dispute, he became a Liberal – destined to serve as a Liberal Cabinet Minister. Nevertheless, the contemporary descriptions of the strike show him to be an essential figure, whose physical presence was often needed to save the strike spiralling into violence.

Tom Mann also played a key role, perhaps being given the hardest task of all, taking charge of the south side, where there were obvious difficulties and rivalries with the north side men. Henry Champion's role has perhaps also been underestimated. Much good propaganda work with the press obviously derived from Champion's skill as a journalist and one cannot doubt his integrity in publicly acknowledging that the socialist convictions of the leaders were not an asset in the eyes of the men.

I can find little evidence that socialism in general or that brand of

The original Dockers' Union banner.

socialism which came from the Social Democratic Federation, played any major direct part in the strike. It was obvious from the men's attitude to socialist rhetoric and banners that, if anything, this was anathema to them, despite the claims of the SDF that it was their propaganda that had raised the class consciousness of the dock labourers. But it had to be recognised that Mann and Tillett and Eleanor Marx and Champion were deeply socialist by formation.

There is a bigger question here. If anything, the dock strike brought into being a new kind of socialism, a popular and practical type of socialism which, like the strike, needed support from a larger section of the population than just that of the labour force if it was to flourish. Indeed, I have included material from the SDF to illustrate this vital difference between a narrow sectarianism and the new politics of socialism which emerged from the strike.

Although the ILP was not formed until 1893, much of the ideology which emerged from the success of the strike was to be implicit in its policy. The TUC was virtually transformed by the New Unionism. Its membership more than doubled in the next two years, and the influence of the newly organised labour had a profound effect on its policies, allowing it to move away from liberalism to socialism, even if this was marked with a gradualist approach.

The very fact that the unskilled now chose to enter the TUC was important. In other European countries which went through a similar experience, the unskilled – with their leanings to more radical or socialist ideas – chose to form their own organisations. The new unions' principles in relation to social policy might have been at odds with the old TUC but their desire to be respectable and recognised was as strong as that of the old tradition.

Not the least of the outcomes of 1889 was the formation of the Labour Representation Committee or Labour Party in 1900. Its success had deep roots in the New Unionism. The LRC was made up of trade unions, the ILP, the Fabians, and the SDF. It was a motion condemning the SDF for wanting to insert class politics in the 1901 manifesto which led to the SDF's leaving the LRC. Ironically, that motion was put forward ty the Dockers' Union, which in turn went from strength to strength. This process culminated in 1921 when the Transport and General Workers' Union was formed when many of the smaller unions formed in 1889 joined forces with the Dockers' Union. Sympathetic action shown by stevedores, lightermen and other skilled groups was essential to the success of the strike. The breaking down of sectional interests was crucial. Without this, the strike could not have succeeded. The determination of the men, and especially their wives, was another major factor.

One can argue whether the dispute made the leaders or the leaders made the dispute, but one thing is sure; Tillett, Burns and Mann became giants in the Labour movement. Their skills as orators and organisers had never been surpassed, but the strikers also appear to have luck on their side. They found a group of employers totally divided amongst themselves. The dock companies were an obvious disgrace: their inefficient methods of dealing with hordes of middlemen had ensured the paradox that the biggest port in the world was unable to pay a dividend to its shareholders. The low regard and distrust which other captains of capital felt for the dock directors became obvious to all concerned. And then there is the case of Henry Lafone. One can only conjecture at the reasons why he paid his men during the strike, or why he did his level best, with great success, to destroy the thin veneer of solidarity among the employers. Putting speculation aside about all sorts of machiavellian reasons for his action, perhaps history had provided what all workpeople have always sought for in vain, a good and honest employer!

Another factor was the role of Cardinal Manning, and indeed the Non-Conformist churches. Manning might be thought a strange bedfellow for the strike leaders, but his pedigree in terms of standing up for the oppressed and organised labour was unquestioned. His moral support for the men and women, not just the Catholics, was a major uplifting factor in their morale. Given his previous involvement with radical politics, Manning was clearly in no sense a neutral mediator; his sympathy lay with the strikers.

Credit must also be given to the Salvation Army for their support. The fact that the press, including *The Times*, were generally on the side of the strikers throughout was crucial. Some papers, however, were not wholly sympathetic to the dispute. Ironically the chief amongst these was *Justice*, the paper of the Social Democratic Federation.

The support of the papers was no doubt one major reason why the strikers enjoyed such wide-ranging public support. This support allowed the fifteen thousand or so pickets, with their marshals and lieutenants, to have almost free rein. The police's good relationship, especially with John Burns, enabled the docks to be sealed off. Even the Home Secretary

THE DOCK LABOURERS' STRIKE FUND, 1889.

"CENTRAL COMMITTEE."

INCOME AND EXPENDITURE ACCOUNT,

14th August, to 16th November, 1889.

Dr. — Expenditure.

To Sundry Expenditure, viz.:—	£	s.	d.	£	s.	d.
RELIEF.						
Cash paid to Tradesmen in exchange for Tickets for Food supplied	21,396	1	11			
Payments to sundry persons for Relief and by way of Compensation for losses sustained during Strike	600	12	7			
Per Salvation Army	153	5	6			
Grant to Mr. Charrington for Relief purposes	150	0	0			
Ditto Chadburn ditto	100	0	0			
Ditto Tailors' Strike Fund	100	0	0			
Ditto Silvertown ditto	250	0	0			
Ditto Poplar Hospital	50	0	0			
Ditto Bristol Strike Fund	60	0	0			
Cash to Sayes Court Branch Committee	175	0	0			
Ditto Tilbury ditto	15	0	0			
Ditto Alderman Phillips' Fund	200	0	0			
				23,250	0	0
PAYMENTS to various Trade Unions during Strike towards the Support of their Members, and also in settlement of Final Claims made by them for re-imbursement of Expenditure, viz.:—						
Amalgamated Seamen and Firemen's Union, Green's Home Branch	1,023	11	6			
Ditto Tidal Basin ditto	903	13	0			
Ditto Union Branch, Tower Hill	397	18	6			
Ditto Tilbury	311	8	6			
United Stevedores' Protection League, No. 1	651	15	0			
Ditto No. 2	815	13	0			
Grays and Tilbury Stevedores	40	3	4			
Amalgamated Stevedores' Protection League, No. 1	524	14	0			
Ditto No. 3	1,861	16	0			
Ditto No. 4	1,121	4	0			
Ditto No. 9	403	13	0			
Ditto No. 35	445	5	0			
Ditto No. 33	250	0	0			
London Ships' Clerks	6	15	0			
East London Painters	194	13	1			
Amalgamated Society Watermen and Lightermen	639	0	0			
Amalgamated Coal Porters	72	4	6			
Carried forward	9,663	7	5	23,250	0	0

Income. — Cr.

By Sundry Income, viz.:—	£	s.	d.	£	s.	d.
Contributions from the public generally, remittances by letter and otherwise	10,661	1	10			
Ditto. per Street-Box Collections	1,039	13	3			
Per Benefit at "Queen's Palace of Varieties"	31	17	4			
				11,732	12	5
CONTRIBUTIONS FROM BRITISH TRADES:—Councils, Unions, and Societies generally; including Amalgamated Society of Engineers, £670; London Society of Compositors, £301 1s. 0d.; the Co-operative Wholesale Society, £213 6s. 6d.; the Shipwrights' Provident Union of the Port of London, £100; Machine Managers' Trade Society, £100; Amalgamated Society of Railway Servants, £104 17s. 2d.; Birmingham Typographical Society, £50.; Butler's Wharf, £70 5s. 2½d.; Friendly Society of Ironfounders, £30—(£20 to South side); East London Painters' Trade Union, £50; Philanthropic Society of Coopers, £60 5s.; Amalgamated Society of Carpenters and Joiners, £50; and the several Branches of the Gas Workers' Association, and others too numerous to admit of their being specially mentioned, in all amounting to				4,234	10	2
CONTRIBUTIONS from France	6	18	11			
,, ,, Belgium	21	10	4			
,, ,, Berlin	51	5	0			
,, ,, America	29	0	4			
				108	14	7
				*16,075	17	2
Carried forward				16,075	17	2

*Included in this amount of £16,075 17s. 2d. are the collections per "Star," £6,723 19s. 5d.; "Pall Mall Gazette," £696 4s. 2d.; "Reynolds," "Evening News and Post," "The Labour Elector," and other papers, as also the remittances sent direct to the credit of the Fund Account at the London and South Western Bank.

The balance sheet of the 1889 Strike.

declined to intervene at the employers; request, despite the 1871 Labour Act, like most acts, being very open to a variety of interpretations.

No doubt the police could have interpreted it in a totally different way, detrimental to the strikers' interest. What seems to have taken place was a tacit agreement between Burns and his lieutenants to keep law and order in return for the police not intervening. So in that sense the policy of peaceful picketing, orderly marches, and a respectable image was effective. It provided a lesson about future politics for some sections of the labour movement.

The strength of public opinion veiled press attention to the many communications problems between the leaders and the men. Indeed such was the support for the men on the south side, that bad organisation and communication were allowed to pass without serious trouble, although this came very near.

But perhaps the most significant factor of all was the £30,423.15s. sent from the Australian people through their trade union movement. Never in the annals of labour history has such a large sum of money been donated to an industrial dispute. Ironically enough, on the strike fund balance sheet Australia was not directly mentioned – it was referred to as 'the Colonies', possibly because the Australian Colonies were not as yet federated. P.F. Donovan even questions what 'Australian' flag they could have flown in Hyde Park.

So a mixture of socialists, Non-Conformists, the Salvation Army, a Catholic cardinal, a good wharfinger, and, of course, the Australian working class helped the great mass of the poor in East and South London to change labour history. For it was this great mass of people, disregarded by Victorian society, and beyond the pale of the skilled unions, which through its own courage and fortitude and against incredible odds, changed the course of social and political history in this country. The victory of the dock workers ushered in a new era of enlightenment to the English labour and political scene.

The dock strike was a catalyst for the vast unskilled sectors of the working class. The New Unionism born from the dock strike gave birth in its turn to the vast majority of the unions that we know today. And although there were defeats amongst the ranks of the unskilled when the employers launched their counter-offensive, this was only short term. It took some unions many years to get official recognition, but they succeeded in the end. The employers and government, in their turn, had become acutely aware of the effectiveness of the disciplined picketing, which had been demonstrated during the dispute, so it was not long before laws to curtail the power of pickets were passed.

But a historic turning point had been reached, and progress could not now be halted.

The measure of this achievement can only be taken by recalling the nature of British society and the place of the dock workers before the strike. They had to fight not just against their employers but also against a total system of beliefs which identified them as a worthless underclass. Against such odds, they proved to the world that their fighting spirit and determination were on a par with any other group of workers in the world. Truly, they became workers of the world, liberating themselves and their class from wretchedness and social isolation and building a new basis for trade unionism and socialism in Britain.

Bibliography

After consulting the autobiographies and biographies of those involved in the dock strike and consulting the only book, (by H. L. Smith and V. Nash,) which was published in 1889, it became obvious that to get a fair assessment of the dock strike I would have to consult contemporary newspapers, as there was no concise and accurate record kept by the strike committee on the dispute. Books relating to the dispute which I have read give a picture of a strike caused by socialism and socialist propaganda. This is a most simplistic and inaccurate view of a very complicated dispute. *The Times* is obviously the paper from which most of the media derived their information. The unique way in which they were able to relate and inform the development of the strike is truly remarkable. The strike leaders themselves paid special tribute to the reporting of the media, especially *The Times*. I have used other contemporary newspapers and journals in order to place *The Times*' reporting in context. Only two short pieces were issued at the time, which in any way chronicled the events. These are an article by John Burns and a pamphlet by Henry Champion. Ben Tillett's pamphlet which appeared some time after the dispute (1910) is full of generalities, but is useful. The autobiographies of Mann, Tillett, and Thorne were written some thirty to forty odd years after the event and owe much to their development as leaders of the labour movement in terms of being economical with those truths which might have caused friction so many years after the event. Thorne, however, does lay bare the differences between Tillett and himself following the strike. This book is designed for a general readership; therefore I have tried to give a readable but accurate account of the dispute, laying the evidence before the reader, leaving him or her, wherever possible to come to their own conclusions about the strike, although obviously my own interpretation has influenced the linking editorial text.

BOOKS, PAMPHLETS AND ARTICLES

Charles Booth, *Life and Labour of the People in London*, First Series: *Poverty*, Vol. I (1903 ed. in 17 vols. Originally published 1889)
John Burns, 'The Great Strike' *New Review*, Vol. I, no 5 (October 1889), with foreword by Cardinal Manning (410–) 412–422
H.H. Champion, *The Great Dock Strike in London, August 1889* (1890, pamphlet)
H.A. Clegg, A. Fox and A.F. Thompson, *A History of British Trade Unions since 1889*, Vol. I *1889–1910* (1964)
William Collison, *The Apostle of Free Labour* (1913)
Concise Dictionary of National Biography Vol. II, ed. Helen Palmer (1950) Revised ed. 1962
Dictionary of Labour Biography, ed. Joyce M. Bellamy and John Saville (7 vols. 1972–1984)
P.F. Donovan, 'Australia and the Great London Dock Strike: 1889', *Labour History (Journal of The Australian Society for the Study of Labour History)*, no 23 (Nov. 1972), 17–26
William J. Fishman, *East End Jewish Radicals, 1875–1914* (1975)
William J. Fishman, *The Streets of East London* (1979)
Robert Gray, *Cardinal Manning: A Biography* (1985)
E.J. Hobsbawm, *Labouring Men* (1964)
Eric Hopkins, *A Social History of the English Working Class, 1815–1945* (1979)
William R.G. Kent, *John Burns: Labour's Lost Leader* (1950)
London Trades Council 1860–1950: A History (1951) rev. ed. of 1935 publ.
John Lovell, *Stevedores and Dockers: A Study of Trade Unionism in the Port of London, 1870–1914* (1969)
Tom Mann's Memoirs (1923) Reissued 1967
Cardinal Manning, 'The Dignity and Rights of Labour', (1874) in *Miscellanies*, Vol. II (1877)
Karl Marx and Friedrich Engels, *Correspondence, 1846–1895: A Selection* (1934)
Henry Mayhew, *London Labour and the London Poor* (1851) 4 vols.
V.A. McClelland, *Cardinal Manning: His Public Life and Influence 1865–92* (1962)
Political World Yearbook 1889
John Pudney, *London's Docks* (1975)
Giles and Lisanne Radice, *Will Thorne, Constructive Militant: A Study in New Unionism and New Politics* (1974)
Millicent Rose, *The East End of London* (1951) Reissued 1973
Jonathan Schneer, *Ben Tillett: Portrait of a Labour Leader* (1982)
H. Llewellyn Smith and Vaughan Nash, *The Story of the Dockers' Strike, Told by Two East-Londoners* (1889) Reissued n.d.
Ann Stafford, *A Match to Fire the Thames* (1961)
Ralph Stern, *Dock Strike 1889*

Walter Thornbury, *Old and New London* (1873–8) Vol. 2 (of 6)
Will Thorne, *My Life's Battles* (1925)
Ben Tillett, [*Dock, Wharf, Riverside, and General Workers' Union:*] *A Brief History of the Dockers' Union, Commemorating the 1889 Dockers' Strike* (1910, pamphlet)
Ben Tillett, *Memories and Reflections* (1931)
Dona Torr, *Tom Mann and His Times*, Vol. I, (*1856–1890*) (1956) No further volumes published
David Wasp and Alan Davis, *The Great Dock Strike 1889* (1974)
Sidney and Beatrice Webb, *The History of Trade Unionism* (1894) Revised and reissued 1896, 1907, 1911, 1920
J. H. Wilson, *My Stormy Passage Through Life* (1925)

NEWSPAPERS AND JOURNALS

East London Advertiser & Tower Hamlets Independent
Enquirer
Evening News & Post
Financial Times
Justice
Labour Elector
Manchester Guardian
Pall Mall Gazette
South London Press
Southwark Recorder and Bermondsey & Rotherhithe Advertiser
Sunday People
The Times

Law Journal 1889 and various documents in the National Museum of Labour History

Index